EDGAR
REMEMI
PAS

A powerful

Other books in this series:

EDGAR CAYCE ON DREAMS
Dr Harmon H Bro

EDGAR CAYCE ON ESP
Doris Agee

EDGAR CAYCE ON HEALING
Mary Ellen Carter and William A. McGarey

EDGAR CAYCE ON MYSTERIES OF THE MIND
Henry Reed

EDGAR CAYCE ON PROPHECY
Mary Ellen Carter

EDGAR CAYCE ON REINCARNATION
Noel Langley

EDGAR CAYCE ON SECRETS OF THE UNIVERSE
Lin Cochran

EDGAR CAYCE ON REMEMBERING YOUR PAST LIVES

ROBERT C SMITH

Edited by CHARLES THOMAS CAYCE

Aquarian/Thorsons
An Imprint of HarperCollins*Publishers*

The Aquarian Press
An Imprint of HarperCollins*Publishers*
77–85 Fulham Palace Road,
Hammersmith, London W6 8JB

First UK edition published by The Aquarian Press 1990
This edition published by arrangement with Warner Books, Inc.,
New York
3 5 7 9 10 8 6 4 2

© The Association for Research and Enlightenment 1989

A catalogue record for this book
is available from the British Library

ISBN 0 85030 862 3

Printed in Great Britain by
HarperCollinsManufacturing Glasgow

All rights reserved. No part of this publication may be
reproduced, stored in a retrieval system, or transmitted,
in any form or by any means, electronic, mechanical,
photocopying, recording or otherwise, without the prior
permission of the publishers.

Acknowledgment

I would like to express my great appreciation to those who developed the original A.R.E. program, *How to Discover Your Past Lives:* Lynn Sparrow, Phyllis Embleton, Karen Fili, Marilyn Peterson, Nancy C. Pohle, and Delores Sloan. Part III of the present book is an adaptation of their work, and Parts I and II have derived much of their structure and approach from it.

Table of Contents

Part I: Background from the Edgar Cayce Readings

Chapter 1: Reincarnation   3
Chapter 2: Karma   28
Chapter 3: Psychic Ability and Past-Life Investigation   49
Chapter 4: Purposes and Ideals in Past-Life
            Study   66

Part II: Practices for Use Throughout the Course

Chapter 5: Dreams and Journal Writing   85
Chapter 6: Meditation   101

Part III: How to Discover Your Past Lives

Introduction   121
Session 1: Awakening Memories   129
Session 2: Wardrobe Fantasy   139
Session 3: Tracing the Laws of
            Reincarnation   150
Session 4: You and Your Surroundings   159

Session 5: A Trip Around the World   183
Session 6: Hereditary and Environmental
           Influences   192
Session 7: Analyzing Your Emotional
           Reactions   202
Session 8: Constructing Past-Life Theories
           from Present-Life Clues   209
Session 9: Exploring Your Talents, Hobbies, and
           Interests   217
Session 10: Discovering Past-Life Clues Through
            Dreams, Meditation, and Your Religious
            Feelings and Experiences   233
Session 11: Identifying Patterns in Your Life   243
Session 12: Past-Life Reverie   250
Session 13: Forming Your Own Past-Life Theories   255
Session 14: Your Future Life   266
Conclusion   270
Further Reading   273
The A.R.E. Today   275

PART I

Background from the Edgar Cayce Readings

CHAPTER 1
Reincarnation

Introduction

During his lifetime, Edgar Cayce gave thousands of psychic discourses, or readings, on a wide variety of topics. Over 14,000 of these discourses were stenographically recorded and have been preserved to the present. Of this number, approximately 2,500 were of the type that has come to be called "life readings," records of the previous incarnations of the individuals for whom they were given. The people who received these readings obtained from them a picture of their souls' progress through their former experiences in the earth. This information enabled them to reach a greater understanding of the reasons behind the circumstances they were meeting in their current lifetimes and the ways in which they could derive the greatest benefit from the situations they were encountering.

Though these life readings portray the past history of other individuals, they undoubtedly can be of use to us as well. The specific pieces of information they present may apply only to others, but the broad picture of reincarnation these pieces form applies to every one of us. Viewing the reasons for one person's successive lifetimes can help us grasp the reason for reincarnation in general. And seeing

3

how one incarnation affects the next for one soul can enhance our ability to recognize and use the past-life influences in our own lives.

Helpful as the life readings can be, they are not the only source of understanding about reincarnation available to us in the Cayce material. Edgar Cayce also delivered many readings for individuals requesting mental and spiritual guidance, and a number of discourses for groups seeking knowledge about various aspects of human existence. Each of these bodies of work contains a great deal of information about the purpose, meaning, and operation of life—and therefore of reincarnation.

Of course, it is quite possible to believe in reincarnation without agreeing with the way it is portrayed in the Edgar Cayce readings. And it would not be necessary to accept the philosophy described in the first part of this book in order to derive insight and benefit from the course on discovering your past lives presented in Part III. But the picture of reincarnation given in the Cayce material is consistent, hopeful, and potentially helpful to us in dealing with the conditions of our current lifetimes. Familiarity with this perspective can do much to help us understand the reason for reincarnation, how it operates, and how we can make the best possible use of our opportunities in the present.

It would be a good idea to clear up one possible source of misunderstanding at the very outset. To some people new to the idea of reincarnation, this concept suggests a series of lifetimes including experiences both as animals and as humans. While some schools of thought do teach that we develop through animal and human incarnations, this is by no means the general view. Many sources, including the Edgar Cayce material, hold that human beings reincarnate only as humans, never as animals. The readings clearly indicate that animals and humans are two different orders of creation, and that animals lack a human soul. So as you read this book, put aside any thought that you might have had a past life as some sort of animal. We'll be dealing entirely with your history as a human soul, experiencing human incarnations only.

Our Creation

In order to grasp the reason for reincarnation and how we came to be involved in it, we must first understand why we were given existence in the first place. Each one of us was created by God as a soul long before the earth or the material universe itself came into being. The Cayce readings state very clearly that the reason for our creation was "God's desire for companionship and expression" (5749–14).

The idea that we were created to be companions with God can help us greatly in our effort to understand our own nature. It implies that there is something of Divinity within each one of us. Like many Christian denominations, the readings tell us that the human soul was made in the image of God. A great number of people were reminded in their readings that God is within and that we can commune with Him there. From this we can conclude that the awareness of the Father's everlasting presence within us and the personal relationship with Him that is the heritage of each soul is among the most important concepts we can bear in mind.

Let's look for a moment at the second reason given for our creation, God's desire for expression. We might see some of the implications of this statement more clearly if we stop and ask just what our creation is an expression of. If we were given our existence as a result of divine self-expression, then our very beings are a manifestation of God. But what is God? Once again, the Cayce material is in agreement with widespread religious tradition of both East and West. Simply stated, "God is love" (1942–3, among many similar references). Thus our lives were in the beginning and are ever meant to be an expression of love.

What does this tell us about ourselves? For one thing, if God is infinite and eternal, each of us is the object of unbounded, everlasting love. It also tells us that in the beginning each of us was a divinely perfect manifestation of that love. And it leads to the conclusion that according to the Creator's plan, the purpose of our being is to express His love in all that we do throughout our existence. Our intended role, the readings frequently inform us, is to be "in companionship with Creative Forces [a phrase the readings often use to denote God]. For the purpose is that each soul should be a co-creator with God" (4047–2).

Our Rebellion as Souls

So what went wrong? If we were perfect at our creation, how did we come to be imperfect at present? If our existence was in the beginning completely an expression of divine love, why is there so much that is unloving in our lives today? If God is truly within us, if each of us has a deep, personal relationship with Him, why does He at times seem to be so totally absent from our day-to-day experiences?

The answer lies in man's free will, with which each of us was imbued by God at our creation. God does not force Himself upon us. If He were to do so, we would become mere automatons, unable to be the companions and co-creators with Him that we were meant to be. We all have the freedom to make choices of our own. Through the exercise of our will, we have the potential to act in accord with divine plan, expressing only love, or to express that which is unloving, ungodly. In the words of the readings, "The *will* may be made one *with* HIM, or for self alone . . ." (262–81).

Having been given these alternatives, some of us chose to act in a way that was outside God's plan. This original act of rebellion occurred not in the earth, for it happened before the material universe had been brought into being. Rather, it was an act of spiritual rebellion, of choosing to express in spirit things that were not compatible with divine love.

What form, exactly, did our rebellion take? The Cayce material tells us quite plainly, "Self is the only sin; that is, selfishness—and all the others are just a modification of that expression of the ego" (1362–1). We turned away from the loving oneness we had been created to experience with all other souls and chose instead a course of self-gratification and self-aggrandizement. Our free will and our power as co-creators with God gave us the ability to partake in universal love for all, or to build our own personal egos. Those of us in rebellion chose to follow the second path.

One aspect of free will that must be borne in mind is the law of cause and effect. Each choice we make, whether it involves following the way our Creator has planned for us or moving off in some other direction, is a cause and has its effect. This is law, not in the sense of an arbitrarily imposed ordinance, but simply in that it is part of the way choice works.

In trying to understand the result of our choice to rebel, we should keep in mind another universal law: Like begets like. A loving decision will not produce inharmonious results, nor will a selfish one produce good results. This concept is expressed in the Bible, in both the Old Testament and the New: "To him that soweth righteousness shall be a sure reward. As righteousness tendeth to life: so he that pursueth evil pursueth it to his own death" (Prov. 11:18–19; all biblical quotations in this book are from the King James version); "God is not mocked: for whatsoever a man soweth, that shall he also reap" (Gal. 6:7).

In the spirit of rebellion, we chose self. The result was that we lost sight of the loving union our Creator had planned for us. We chose separation. The effect was that we experienced a sense of separation from our God, the source of unlimited wisdom, power, and love. For any other result to have occurred would be a violation of our free will.

It was thus that evil entered into our experience. Evil is both the act and the result of choosing to follow the spirit of rebellion against God's wishes. We chose to act in this way, and since at our creation we had been given power as co-creators with God, what we chose to express came into being. Thus there arose conditions and experiences that were out of harmony with the universal love we were meant to enjoy as companions of the Creator.

Our Involvement in the Earth

Our rebellion and the sense of separation from God that
resulted from it were at first on the spiritual level, for we
had not yet become involved in materiality. It was not until
later that the earth and the rest of the material universe came
into being as a manifestation of divine creative power.
Originally the earth and its environs were not necessarily
intended for habitation by man. It was simply the three-
dimensional realm that had resulted from the creative activity of the spirit of God. As such, it was perfect in its own
way.

As souls, some of us came upon this developing earth and
were attracted to it. Being co-creators with God, we pos-
sessed the ability to create with our minds. That is, our
thoughts had a reality and a force to them, and we could use
them to modify our physical surroundings. Through the
power of our mental images and their physical manifestations, termed "thought-forms" in the Cayce readings, some
of us projected ourselves into the developing earth and
influenced its evolution in ways that were not in accordance
with God's plan. It is not that involvement in the earth was
in itself evil. But in choosing to experience and use the
earth in ways that furthered the aims of self rather than those
of God, we continued our rebellion and brought it into
material manifestation.

In time, some of us became so attached to our activities
in the flesh that we began to forget our true nature as
spiritual beings and children of God. We chose to make the
experiences of the earth and our limited selves more important to us than our companionship with the Father. As a
result, we lost our awareness of the divine spirit within and
became entangled in materiality to the extent that we could
no longer withdraw from it.

Not all the souls that had been created by God chose the
way of rebellion. There remained some, perhaps the great
majority, who had continued to act only in the way their
Creator had intended. They had retained their awareness of

themselves as spiritual beings, companions and co-creators with the Father. And in their experiences throughout the universe they manifested only the love they were created to express.

Some of these souls were drawn to the earth, where they discovered that many of their fellow beings had forgotten their spiritual heritage and become entrapped in materiality. Among these souls who had not rebelled were some who chose to enter the earth in order to help the wayward ones, to remind them of their oneness with God and show them how they might overcome their entanglement in the earth.

One of these rescuing souls was the being who is known to us as Adam. The biblical story of his creation out of the dust of the earth portrays the formation of the body his soul would inhabit in the three-dimensional world. Unlike the distorted bodies created by the souls who had gone astray, the bodies of Adam and those who accompanied him were created in harmony with divine plan. They were fit instruments for the physical perfection of the human race and proper vehicles for our return to the Father.

In time, however, this second group of souls too went astray. Once again, involvement in things of the flesh began to become more important than the spirit of God within. Choices were again made that caused us to lose sight of our companionship with God and gave us a sense of separation from Him. And once again, souls who had been created to express the love of God and maintain a continuous awareness of His spirit became encased in materiality.

It was not until much later, in the person of Jesus of Nazareth, that we would be shown how a human life could be a perfect expression of divine love. According to the Cayce readings, the same soul who had incarnated as Adam was the one who, after many ages and many intervening incarnations, reachieved perfection as Jesus. Thus this soul showed us the way of return to the Father, fulfilling the original purpose for which he had first entered the earth so many years before.

Up to a point, the story of our creation and fall given in the Cayce readings parallels that portrayed in the biblical book of Genesis. Both sources tell of man's original creation as a perfect soul, made "in our [God's] image, after our likeness . . ." (Gen. 1:26). Both tell of the soul's coming to inhabit the earth in a physical body, and of the earth's being given to man to exercise dominion over. And both describe how man eventually turned away from God, used his powers in selfish ways, and thus introduced pain and suffering into the earth.

There is, however, one crucial difference between the creation story set forth in the Cayce readings and the literal interpretation many people give Genesis. The Cayce material makes it very clear that we are not being punished for a transgression committed by one of our ancestors thousands of generations ago. Each of us in the earth today is here because we, *as individual souls,* chose to be here. Each soul that feels cut off from God is in this situation because of its own choice to forsake its original awareness of the divine presence. And each soul that finds itself subject to the sometimes unpleasant conditions of life on this planet has chosen to submerge itself in materiality. We are experiencing the consequences of our own misuses of free will—not someone else's.

The Father's Abiding Love

The story of our creation and fall, if it were the sum total of our history as a race and as individual souls, would be a dismal one, indeed. But throughout the Cayce readings there is evident a message of hope, the assurance that each of us has the potential to regain that which we have lost. We have the ability to reawaken our awareness of the divine spirit within, to make choices that will bring our lives back into alignment with the Creator's plan, and to become once again companions and co-creators with God.

The unchanging and eternal nature of the Father's love makes this possibility available to us. Throughout the misguided decisions we made in our original fall, and throughout every ungodly choice we have made since, that love for us has remained constant. The Cayce readings assure us that "God is in His heavens and . . . His love endureth even to those who harden their hearts . . ." (262–44). With our free will we can refuse to let His love flow through us, preferring instead to live for self-indulgence. We can so fill our minds with concerns of the earth that we even forget that divine love for us exists. But we can never destroy it or change it into something else, for it is of God and therefore is eternal.

Like the Creator's love for us, His presence within us is everlasting. The activity of His spirit brought us into being, and the presence of that spirit has sustained us since our creation. As He was with us and within us in the beginning, He has continued to be within us and will continue to be so throughout eternity.

In speaking of our turning away from God and our *sense* of separation from Him, we are not referring to an actual absence of the spirit of God. It is merely our awareness of His presence that is lacking. By continually choosing to ignore His voice so that we can follow in the ways of self, we can impair our ability to detect His presence. The natural result of this is that eventually we reach the point where we feel separated from Him. But His spirit still abides with us, no matter how unaware of it we may become.

Regardless of how far astray we may have gone, we can turn within ourselves and find God there. Our personal relationship with our Creator cannot be destroyed. His infinite love for us will never fail, if only we will seek it and live our lives in ways that are compatible with it. Many passages in the Cayce material offer us the Father's comforting assurance that, " 'though you be afar off, if you will call I will hear—and will answer speedily' " (1326–1).

Reincarnation, Our Way of Return

God, with His unending love for us, never abandons us. The readings echo the Bible in assuring us that for every soul there is provided a way of return to the Father: "What has been given as the most meaning[ful] of all that [was] written? *He* has not willed that any soul should perish, but from the beginning has prepared a way of escape!'' (262–56; cf. II Pet. 3:9).

What can we know of this way of return that is open to us? If the universe is to remain as the purposeful expression of divine love that brought it into being, our experiences in it through which we make our return to God must be in accord with the universal laws that our souls have always been subject to. Thus our return must be in accord with the law of cause and effect, it must come about through the exercise of our free will, and it must involve our becoming once again perfect expressions of the Father's love. Having once chosen to turn away from God to experience the ways of self, we must now learn to make choices that will bring our lives back into alignment with the will of our Creator.

Our need for a way of return to God is the basic reason for our incarnation in the earth. Here in materiality we can see the consequences of the choices we make. We can learn through the unpleasant results of those choices which build only our limited selves, thus accentuating our sense of separation from God, that this is not the way to attain true happiness.

It is not that God is punishing us for our misdeeds by forcing us to undergo painful experiences in the flesh. Rather, in His love for us He is giving us the chance to see what the undesirable effects of our unloving decisions are. In this way, we have an opportunity to learn to make better decisions, to become more aware of the spirit of God within us and more responsive to its promptings, and to regain our former state as companions with the Father.

Each of us who is in the earth chose at some point to become involved in materiality and to use it in ways that were contrary to God's purpose in creating us. We chose materiality as a medium for our rebellion. Having done so, it is necessary that we now learn to use this same medium in ways that are compatible with divine love. Only by doing so can we overcome our former misuse of free will and retrace our steps back to a fully realized oneness with the Father.

Incarnation in the earth is the means by which we can learn to express love in materiality.

But why is *re*incarnation necessary? Why must we return again and again, rather than learning our lesson in just one lifetime? Here again we can see the Father's abiding love for us. The Cayce readings point out that, "as He gave, '. . . ye shall give *account* for every *deed* done in the body!'" (69–4). Few if any of us lost our awareness of our oneness with God as the result of a single misuse of free will. Our rebellion involved making many selfish decisions over a very long period of time. It would not be reasonable to expect that we could meet and overcome the effects of all these decisions within the span of just one lifetime. Instead we are given many lifetimes to find our way back to God, many opportunities to learn the lessons we need to learn, and as much time as we need to develop spiritually, to grow in strength and in our ability to express love. Our Creator's patience with us is truly infinite.

Even if a single lifetime could be sufficiently prolonged to enable us to learn all our needed lessons, reincarnation would still be a superior process for our attainment of reunion with God. There are several reasons for this. One of the most important things we need to rediscover is our true spiritual nature. We have to become aware that in essence we are of God, not of the earth, and that our true identity is not enclosed within the single body and personality that are ours during a lifetime on earth. Our full spiritual development could require ages. If throughout this entire time we were to inhabit just one body and experience only physical life on earth, it would be easy for us to overidentify with that one body and this one planet. We might well lose sight of the fact that our true nature is not to be confined to either one.

Reincarnation, on the other hand, allows us to experience life in a succession of different physical vehicles. Through it we are shown that who and what we are extend far beyond the limitations of any material body. The very experience of physical death itself, when combined with the survival of the soul, is a powerful, repeated demonstration that the body is not the entirety of our being.

Reincarnation is also an effective antidote to our tendency to regard the earth as our true home. We do not reincarnate immediately into another physical body at the moment of death. We are given an interlude in which we are not involved in materiality, a time in which we experience other realms of being. Thus instead of a single long span on earth, during which we might become so involved with life here that we forget our true nonmaterial nature, reincarnation provides us with constant reminders that these other realms exist and that our habitation of this material world is only temporary.

Reincarnation also counteracts any tendency we might have to identify with the actions of any single personality. There is much evidence of divine love at work in this process of death and rebirth, through which we periodically take on a new earthly identity. The following passage from the readings brings this out: "Life as indicated in the eyes, the countenance and the expressions of a babe, gives one the consciousness of opportunity, and of the mercy of the Lord—in that He has not willed that any soul should perish, but has allowed each—even as the Christ-Child—to be born as a babe, and to thus have a new opportunity" (1152–9).

With each new incarnation, we receive, in a sense, a fresh start, loosening the ties of guilt that would bind us to our past mistakes. It is true, of course, that we still have to meet the consequences of those mistakes. But we don't have to do so while burdened by troubling conscious memories of what we had done. Reincarnation helps us maintain an attitude of hope and self-respect as we go about learning the lessons we need that will guide us back to our Creator.

We should also consider not just the number of mistakes we're likely to have made in turning away from God, but the probable diversity of those mistakes as well. Selfishness can have many forms, and unloving choices can be made under many different sets of conditions. The various ways in which we might misuse our free will are likely to give rise to a great variety of results. For any of us who have made ungodly choices in a number of different phases of life—and this is undoubtedly the case for the overwhelming majority of us—there will be many diverse conditions that we must meet as a result of those choices. Reincarnation gives us the opportunity to experience life in a wide variety of situations, as we are born and live in a different set of circumstances during each successive lifetime. Thus we have a chance to meet and overcome the effects of all the sundry forms of selfishness in which we as individual souls have indulged and to learn all the varied lessons we need to assimilate.

The Cayce material assures us that the total process of reincarnation is necessary for our spiritual development. But the readings go beyond this. They state that *every individual incarnation* we experience has a purpose behind it, a part to play in God's plan for us and for the earth. "No soul enters by chance, but that it may fill [what] it has sought and does seek as its ideal" (3051–2). Every lifetime we live is an opportunity for us to bring ourselves into closer alignment with God's will. Each new birth will be into a set of conditions which we can use as a step in our quest to become once again the perfect expressions of divine love we were created to be.

Jesus as the Pattern for Our Return

Evidently, most of us have quite a bit of work to do in order to overcome all the flaws we have built into ourselves and reattain our perfect oneness with the Father. But in His great love for us, God has not left us on our own to achieve this monumental goal. He has provided us with a pattern of what each of us can become, a model of how our lives can be lived. This pattern was manifested for us in the human life of Jesus, who made his will one with the Father's and thus became the perfect expression of divine love on earth.

The pattern that Jesus brought into manifestation on the earth is one that is within each and every one of us. It is the imprint of our Creator, the image of God in which each soul was made at the beginning, and it endures throughout eternity. With our free will we can refuse to express it, we can incorporate so many ungodly characteristics into our makeup that for a time it may become hidden and lie dormant. But we can never erase it. The Cayce material terms this imprint of the Creator the Christ Pattern and our awareness of it the Christ Consciousness. The Christ Consciousness is succinctly described in the readings as "the awareness within each soul, imprinted in pattern on the mind and waiting to be awakened by the will, of the soul's oneness with God . . ." (5749–14).

A couple of problems might arise when we speak of Jesus manifesting the quality of life we are all meant to attain. One of these involves an understandable reluctance on the part of some people to adopt a belief they consider to be exclusively a principle of a religion not their own. Such a person might say, "I'm not a Christian and I'm not about to become one, so this system of thought is not for me."

But it is not membership in a certain religious sect that counts. The truth that was exemplified by Jesus is not the sole property of Christian denominations. The soul that incarnated as Jesus "influenced either directly or indirectly all those forms of philosophy or religious thought that taught that God was One" (364–9). If God is One, the truth of His relationship with man is the same regardless of which formal religious body it is professed by. One passage from the readings clearly combines the concept of Jesus' demonstration of the divine pattern for all men with the idea that this pattern can be followed regardless of an individual's religious affiliation: " '*His* love made manifest among men, as shown in the carpenter of Nazareth, is *alone* the way, the truth, the light.' And as same is expressed or manifested in other words, even though the teachings may have come from Siam [?], Said [?], or Brahma, they are one; so long as they are for *Him* and not for self" (2067–1). Accepting the pattern of divine love that was shown in the life of Jesus is what matters, whether or not we belong to a denomination that considers itself Christian.

Some of us might have another difficulty with the idea that we are to show forth in our lives the same spirit of divine love that Jesus manifested in his. We might feel that he was so special that what he did is completely beyond the potential of the rest of us. There is indeed something special about this soul who became the full manifestation of divine love in human form. The Cayce readings indicate something of this specialness of Jesus by frequently referring to him as the "Elder Brother" of us all.

And yet this same source informs us that this soul incarnated many times before taking on the life as Jesus and that he underwent the same temptations as the rest of us. In short, he was subject to the same universal laws that all of us are. Most important is the assurance that the Christ Pattern that he manifested is the image of God in which each of us was made. This pattern is not something foreign to us. It has been part of our nature from the moment of our creation.

In living his life completely in accord with the will of God, Jesus demonstrated the love, wisdom, and power of the Christ Pattern in action. He brought this pattern into manifestation in the earth, thus showing forth for all of us the way of return to the Father. But his role in our salvation goes beyond providing in his life a model on which we can base our own. The readings tell us that, "as He, thy Master, thy Lord, thy Christ fulfilled the law by compliance with same, He became the law and thus thy Savior, thy Brother, thy Christ!" (1662-1). That is, in so living that his entire existence and being expressed only the law of divine love, Jesus made himself one with that law. In doing so, he achieved oneness with the infinite and eternal love of God. Like the Father's love for us, his is boundless and constant.

As a being of limitless love for us, Jesus stands ever ready to help us in our spiritual journey back to God. The comfort and aid that is offered to us through him is always available to us, always sufficient to meet our needs. This truth is powerfully stated in a passage from one reading, in which a spiritual seeker was told, "Know that in all such [problems], while ye may not be able to meet them alone, there is a friend, a brother, who knows the sorrow, who knows all such disturbances. Having promised to be ever

present in time of trouble, in time of sorrow, in time of trial
of any nature, He is able to fulfill and to keep that promise''
(1467–10). In Jesus we have not only a friend who showed
us how to attain our full potential as children of God, but
one who continues to give us whatever help we need in
reaching this goal, if only we will call on him.

Human Makeup and Our Levels of Consciousness

What do the foregoing material and related information
from the Cayce readings tell us about our present condition?
Primarily, this source underscores our essential nonmaterial
nature. We do not have souls; we *are* souls, distinct beings
created in the image of God. It is the soul that carries our
individuality on from one experience to the next, on the
earth and in other realms.

As souls, we have certain attributes, components that
determine who we are, both as individuals and as members
of the human race. One of these we've already discussed at
some length. This quality of the soul is will, the ability to
make choices that have an effect. Through these decisions
the will has a central part in making each of us different
from one another. It is thus an important ingredient in each
soul's individuality.

A second attribute of the soul is spirit. Spirit is the spark
of the divine within that gives us life. It is the source of our
power to create. While souls are many and individual, spirit
is something we have in common with every other living
being, whether human or not. In reality there is but one
spirit, the spirit of God.

An additional facet of our beings is referred to in the
Cayce readings as mind. Though mind includes what is
commonly called the intellect, its scope extends far beyond
the ability for logical thought. Mind encompasses all the
attitudes and thought-forms we have built up during all our
experiences throughout our existence. It includes those mental elements we are not consciously aware of, as well as the
ones we do recognize. Mind is the aspect of ourselves that

determines the form that the spiritual energy which flows through us in our creative efforts will take. It is what gives the pattern to the physical results of our creativity. Thus it partakes of both the spiritual and the physical aspects of our nature.

Along with the above components, each of us who is manifesting in materiality has, of course, a physical body. Despite our tendency to identify ourselves with the physical body, the body is best seen as merely the vehicle that the soul is using on its journey back to God. It is the part of us that wears out and is replaced for each of our successive incarnations. The readings frequently give the following formulation of the relationship between spirit, mind, and body: "The spirit is life; the mind is the builder; the physical is the result" (349-4).

In order to comprehend our nature more fully, let us now consider the levels of consciousness, or awareness, that each of us possesses. These are the superconscious, the subconscious, and the conscious levels of mind. Perhaps the relationship between these aspects of ourselves will become most clear if we approach the subject by noting how each of them arose.

The superconscious awareness is that which recognizes our oneness with the Father. It has been a part of us from our very beginning, for it felt the presence of God at the moment of our creation, and the imprint of that presence can never be erased. The superconsciousness is thus immortal. And, since it is the awareness of our contact with God, it gives us access to the source of all love, wisdom, and power. Information received through this channel is therefore infallible. We may, of course, choose not to pay heed to the messages that come from this level. We may so fill our minds with concerns that are not of godly origin that we are unable to hear this transmitter of the voice of God within. But if we do become sensitive and responsive to material from the superconscious mind, we can be sure that any information we receive will be true and helpful to us, for it speaks to us with the voice of divine wisdom and love.

As we as individual souls each began to have our own

experiences, we began to collect impressions of those events. Everything we did and everything that was done to us was added to this storehouse of information. Also included here was every thought-form we constructed with our minds, every mental image we ever created. This vast array of experiences, impressions, and thoughts was recorded in what has come to be the subconscious. In our normal waking life, the subconscious is submerged beneath the conscious mind. But in times when the conscious mind is laid aside—in sleep and at physical death, for instance—the subconscious comes to the fore.

The subconscious level of awareness has a number of subdivisions, some comparatively accessible to the conscious mind, some much deeper. At the deeper levels, the subconscious minds of all souls are in contact with one another. Thus it is possible for each of us to derive information from the minds of others.

The third level of awareness, and the one with which we are most familiar, is the conscious mind. This portion of our awareness arose as we began to have experiences on the earth. Its function is directly related to receiving, processing, and responding to the information that reaches us through the physical senses regarding conditions surrounding us in the three-dimensional, material world. The working of the conscious mind is tied to the physical brain, the physical senses, and the rest of the central nervous system. This is the level of awareness at which we generally operate during the waking hours of our day-to-day lives.

Since its function involves the regulation of a physical body during physical life on earth, the conscious mind is not present in beings between earth lives or those who have never incarnated in this realm. It is laid aside when we die, at which time the subconscious takes over much of the role filled by the conscious during earthly incarnations. Being concerned primarily with actions in materiality during a single lifetime, the conscious mind is generally not aware of memories from previous lives.

Mechanics of Incarnation

As has been noted, reincarnation is of the soul. The soul is that part of us which exists throughout time, both during periods when it is inhabiting a physical body in the earth and during the interval between earth lives. Whether the soul is involved in an earth life or not, it is undergoing experiences that it can use in its development, its return to an awareness of its loving oneness with God.

According to the reincarnation concept, new souls are not created at the moment of conception or at birth. Souls that are about to enter a new body have been here before and have inhabited other bodies during previous lifetimes. During their former incarnations these souls have undergone a wide variety of experiences and made a vast number of decisions. Those decisions, whether in accord with the will of God or not, have produced definite effects and have determined the present stage of each individual soul's development. Because of each soul's choices, that particular individual has reached a state where it has certain definite lessons to learn if it is to progress along its spiritual path. Each one also has certain abilities it has already developed in its earlier lifetimes. There are consequences of previous actions to be met, weaknesses to overcome, and strengths with which to overcome them.

For every one of us, each incarnation is a God-given opportunity to learn what we need to know and fulfill the portion of the divine plan that our current development has best suited us to accomplish. In answer to one person's question as to whether there was anything specific she could do to fulfill the purpose of her present incarnation, one reading emphatically stated, "If there hadn't been you wouldn't be allowed to be in the earth in the present!" (3051–7).

Certain conditions in life are more conducive to learning certain lessons and achieving specific goals than other life situations would be. At the time of each incarnation, the soul draws to itself the set of circumstances of birth that is most appropriate for accomplishing its individual purpose during that particular lifetime. Thus the physical body, family, environment, culture, and other conditions into which we are born reflect the developmental needs of our soul that have been built through our choices during previous incarnations.

The conditions into which we are born are not the only ones that arise because of the specific needs of our individual soul development, however. The law of cause and effect is active throughout our lifetimes. We are continually confronting situations built by our past decisions, ones that give us a chance to learn needed lessons, to overcome our weaknesses, to build upon and use our strengths. Wherever we find ourselves, we can be sure that our circumstances contain within them a chance to learn and to grow. In the words of one reading, "In whatsoever state you find yourself, it is by the grace of God; and there is an opportunity, there is a lesson to be gained from same . . ." (3161-1).

Soul Development Between Earth Lives

Not all of our souls' development occurs during our earthly lifetimes. We do not move directly from the death of one physical body to birth in another. There is an interval between earth lives, during which our souls experience other phases of their journey back to the Father. Part of this period between incarnations is typically spent in the environs of the earth, and part is spent elsewhere.

Immediately following physical death, the soul may go through a period of disorientation. Some newly discarnate souls evidently do not comprehend what has happened to them. It may take quite awhile for the realization that the physical life has come to an end to sink in: "Many an individual has remained in that called death for what ye call *years* without realizing it was dead!" (1472-2). Others, presumably ones who have not identified with the body so completely and so are more readily able to accept continued existence without it, may not experience this period of confusion or may pass through it more quickly.

Another phase of our development between earthly incarnations involves the evaluation of the use we have made of the opportunities given us during our recently concluded lifetime. We receive here a chance to review the choices we made, so that we can come to recognize the times we used our will to move closer to God and the instances in which we used it selfishly, rebelliously. In this way we can identify the types of decisions that we can constructively continue in and build upon, and the ones we might wish to move away from as being hindrances to our spiritual quest.

This period of post-incarnation evaluation is not the condemnatory judging of the soul pictured in some religious traditions, for "there is no condemnation in the Father; rather love—that they each may find their way" (1173-11). It is a stage of our spiritual education, one that can help us to see the positive and negative aspects of the life we just finished leading, so that perhaps we can do better during our next chance at physical life on earth. This life-evaluation period is thus a very useful part of the divine scheme through which we can each work out our own salvation.

Much of the period between earth lives is spent on other planes of existence. The earth is that plane in which we learn to express God's love in the flesh, in materiality. But our separation from the Father involved rebellion in other dimensions of consciousness besides the physical, and so our return must involve development on the nonmaterial planes as well. These other planes are represented in the material universe by the planets of our solar system. Each of these realms evidently provides us with an opportunity to develop in a specific aspect of our being, such as the mind, our perspective on love and beauty, and our psychic and mystic qualities. Like the earth, each nonphysical plane has its own part to play in the growth of our souls back to reunion with God.

All our experiences, whether they take place on the earth or in these other dimensions between earthly incarnations, leave their imprint upon our souls. The soul never forgets. Every decision we have ever made, everything we have ever done, and everything that has ever been done to us is carried as a memory of the soul, within the deeper layers of the unconscious mind. All we have experienced throughout our existence as individual souls is part of us now and has a role in shaping the person each of us is during the current earth life. The events of our former physical incarnations are important in determining our emotions and feelings in the present, while our experiences on other planes of existence have their main effect on our mental attitudes.

Ending the Need for Reincarnation

Let's conclude our overview of reincarnation by considering where this cycle of return to life on the earth will lead us. We can get a clearer picture of the culmination of our series of earth lives if we focus for a moment on the purpose for reincarnation. This process, remember, is a means by which we can overcome the separation we initiated through the rebellious use of our will and return to the state of loving oneness with God. It teaches us the physical consequences of our selfish choices and gives us the chance to learn how to express divine love in materiality. Once we have learned this lesson and have overcome the flaws that our misuses of will have produced in us, reincarnation in the physical will have fulfilled its purpose. At this point, the individual will no longer be subject to the need for rebirth in a physical body.

It might seem that this goal is far beyond the reach of most of us. If the Cayce readings are any indication, it is indeed rare for a person to reach the stage of not needing to return for additional lives in the earth. Of the many people who received life readings from Cayce, only a very few were told that their current incarnations might be the last ones they would have to undergo. But the fact remains that *some* people were told that they had overcome the need for reincarnation, and in this we can all find hope.

On the whole, these people were not doers of great deeds, at least in the common sense of that phrase. They were simply individuals who lived lives of attunement to the spirit of God within and loving service to the people around them. In doing so, they demonstrated that reincarnation does fulfill its purpose, that even today souls who had been in rebellion are learning to use their physical lives to express God's love. Thus these people are completing the material phase of their journey back to the Father. This is something to which each of us can aspire.

This leads us to the question of how we can reach this state. What measures can we as individuals take to grow beyond our need for reincarnation in the earth? The philosophy of reincarnation presented in the Cayce readings makes it clear that each soul is responsible for its own salvation. It was our own choices that led to our separation from God and involvement in the earth. It must be through our own choices that we overcome our entanglement in materiality. Our thoughts and mental attitudes, our actions, and our willingness to manifest the spirit of God in our dealings with one another are the tools that will enable us to rise above our need for physical reincarnation.

Since it is through the use of will that each of us can make his return to God, the primary prerequisite for achieving this goal is the sincere desire to do so. Having chosen the way of rebellion, we have to choose to return to the way of God. The temptations toward selfishness are all around us. Most of us find it very difficult consistently to think, speak, and act in ways that foster the good of others rather than our own self-interest. If we do not truly desire to live our entire lives in accordance with the will of God rather than our own limited self-will, our chances of finding the strength to manifest divine love, and thus to overcome the ties that bind us to the earth, are slim indeed.

While we must make this spiritual journey ourselves, it does not follow that we have to do so on our own. God hasn't abandoned us to our own devices. His love for us is infinite and abiding. He will provide us with all the help we need and are willing to accept. This love was manifested most perfectly in this world in the life of Jesus, who showed us the way back to the Father and stands ready to help us on our own quest for reunion with God.

In order to avail ourselves of this divine aid, we need to open ourselves to it, accept and use it in our daily lives, and believe that it will be forthcoming. This points up our need for faith. If we refuse to call on God for help, or if we do so merely as a matter of form without believing that His aid is in fact available to us, we close ourselves off to the spirit of God and limit the extent to which it can be active in our lives.

When we think of obtaining God's help, many of us picture Him intervening through external means, changing the circumstances in which we live so that they become more to our liking. But miraculous external events are not necessary for us to perceive the presence of God. We do not need a thunderbolt from the sky to bring divine power into our lives, for each of us has within himself the imprint of the Father, present from the moment of our creation. We have as part of our very nature the ability to call on God in prayer and listen to His response in meditation. In this way, we can receive as much divine guidance as we are willing and able to use in our lives.

The desire to express love, the willingness to call on God and to seek His guidance from within, and the faith that this help and direction can be effective in our lives are all necessary internal elements of our spiritual growth. But what of our external lives? How will these inner characteristics influence the way we live in the physical world and our relationships with others?

With the great number of decisions each of us faces each day, there is no way the specific choices that will lead us back to God can be enumerated. We can, however, discern certain characteristics that these positive choices will have in common. In each of them, the good of others will be put before the good of the self; the will of God will be considered before self-will. Our separation from God came about because we rebelled against His love and chose to travel the way of self. To achieve reunion with Him, we must retrace these steps, leaving off our self-centered actions and replacing them with ones that reflect divine universal love.

Expressing the will of God rather than that of self is not a matter of adhering to a lengthy list of dos and don'ts. There are just too many different types of decisions confronting us, in too many different sets of circumstances, for any of us to live creatively if we try to formulate a set of rules to cover each of these possibilities. A better way is to establish a single criterion, an ideal, by which we can measure each of the alternative choices we are faced with in life. Specific suggestions on how to go about setting such a standard will be given in Chapter 4 of this book. For now, the important points to note are: for each of us the ideal should be an expression of the best motivation we can conceive of; we should each have a very clear understanding of what the ideal for us is; and we should strive to make all our thoughts and actions be in harmony with our ideal. If we consistently make choices that are in accord with the best we know, we can be sure that at least we are moving in the right direction.

Another attribute that will prove invaluable in our endeavor to regain our birthright as children of God is patience—patience with ourselves, patience with others, and patience with life. Many of us, however, do not have a complete understanding of what this virtue entails. The quality of patience that is prescribed in the Cayce readings is not a helpless submission to what we might erroneously perceive as predetermined circumstances in our lives. It is, rather, an active force: "persistent patience, active patience—not merely passive" (1968–5). Active patience is the drive that enables us to keep doing our best to relate to others lovingly, no matter how long it may take them to respond in kind. It gives us the resiliency to persist in our efforts to live the best life we can, regardless of how often we may falter.

If we are to achieve oneness with a perfect God, we must ourselves eventually grow into perfection. But we shouldn't get discouraged if we can't do it all in one day. What is required of us is sincere, consistent, persistent effort. We have the assurance that "it is the continuous and continued 'try' that is counted—as in the soul development—for spiritual righteousness'' (1391–1).

We might feel that we have a long way to go before we accomplish our reunion with the Father. But we have available everything we need to reach this goal. We have the will, with which we can choose thoughts and actions that manifest selflessness, faith, patience, and sincerity in our desire to return to God; we have the ability to formulate and apply our ideals; we have the promise of divine help and guidance, which we can receive through prayer and meditation; and we have physical life, the opportunity to show forth the love of God in the material universe.

Reincarnation is not only the process into which our separation from the Creator has led us. It is also the means by which we can make our return. We may indeed have a long way to go, but we have forever to complete the journey. The infinite love and patience of the Father provides us with as many chances at life in the physical as we need, for as long as it takes us to learn to get it right.

CHAPTER 2
Karma

Definition

Karma can be defined most simply as the action of the law of cause and effect. As we noted in the preceding chapter, every use of our free will, every choice we make, is a cause and has its effect. We were made in God's image, to be co-creators with Him, and as such we have creative power. With each purpose and action of the soul we build something, and what we build is manifested in our physical world through the action of mind. The spirit is the life, mind is the builder, and the physical is the result.

Our loving thoughts and actions build good, both in the external universe and within ourselves. That is, through them we not only bring something of the love of God into manifestation in the world around us, we also build within ourselves the habit pattern of acting lovingly. Thus we make of ourselves beings who can more readily express divine love. Similarly, our rebellious choices build evil both within and outside ourselves, bringing disharmony into the world and increasing our own sense of separation from the Father.

What we build determines our experience in the physical world, for one of the immutable laws of the universe is: like attracts like. What we've built within ourselves through the decisions we've made in the past draws to us similar manifestations from our surroundings. In this way, our external circumstances—in other words, our karma—come to reflect the inner beings that we have made of ourselves. The following excerpt is quite typical of the Edgar Cayce readings' frequent references to karma as the process by which we meet what we have created: "For it is self that one has to meet. And what ye sow—mentally, spiritually, physically—that ye *will* eventually reap" (257–249).

Perhaps a couple of hypothetical examples will make it easier to see how this works. Suppose a person makes a habit of sharing his material resources with others. By doing so he builds a pattern of generosity within himself, and he also creates in the world around him a feeling of abundance. Because like attracts like, the generosity within will draw to him expressions of generosity from without. Though it might not always seem so over a short term, in the long run the generous person will be treated more generously by others than the miser will be.

Or suppose a person consistently adopts an attitude of distrust of others in financial matters. He makes of himself a suspicious person, and through the actions that arise from this attitude he creates distrust in the outside world. The suspicion which he displays toward others is likely to evoke similar reactions toward himself, and in time he may come to find that his own honesty is repeatedly being questioned by his associates.

The reason that life sometimes doesn't seem to work this way, with each of us drawing back to ourselves what we create in the world, is that there is generally a time lag between cause and effect. The choices we make today might not manifest their complete results until the distant future. We may not meet the consequences of our decisions in this incarnation at all. It might take until our next lifetime, or the one after that, for us to feel the full impact of our present choices.

From the perspective of one lifetime it may seem that there is injustice in the world, with people enjoying or suffering through conditions that they themselves did not create. But the concept of reincarnation allows us to adopt a wider viewpoint, one from which we can see each person's situation as a result of his or her own choices in the past, however distant that past may be. The Cayce material at times emphasizes this delayed-reaction characteristic of karma by differentiating it from other forms of cause and effect. According to one reading, "Karmic is that brought over [from an earlier incarnation], while cause and effect may exist in the one material experience [lifetime] only" (2981–2).

An aspect of karma related to its operation over long periods of time might be referred to as the principle of continuity. Because we are co-creators with God, what we build tends to continue on in its effect until we do something to change it. This applies to what we create within ourselves as well as what we bring into manifestation in the outside world. We continue to be what we've made ourselves through our past choices until we decide to change ourselves by making other types of choices. From this angle, karma can be seen as memory. It is the soul's record of what it has brought into being in itself and in the external universe.

Viewing karma as the memory of the soul can help us grasp one of the most positive and hopeful of its ramifications. Because each of our activities leaves its stamp upon the soul, "that attained is never lost" (416–17). No effort on our part is ever wasted. It is never too late for us to begin

making creative decisions that will start us progressing in
the direction we wish to go. Because the record of our
choices continues on within the soul, we will in time reap
the results of all our constructive endeavors, even though
some of them may not come to full fruition during our
current incarnation.

The Purpose of Karma

Looking at karma as the good or bad result of choices we
have made can lead us to consider it as a reward or
punishment for our past actions. But such a view is mislead-
ing, for it overlooks the essential purpose of karma. As we
have seen, reincarnation is the process by which we can
forsake our rebellious ways and return to the Father. Karma
is the instrument through which we are enabled to determine
the direction we must follow in order to make this return
journey. It fulfills this function by revealing to us the results
of the choices we are making.

If we think of "good" karma simply as God's reward to
us for acting correctly, we are missing the point. Our
Creator loves us infinitely, always, regardless of our behavior. This love springs from *His* nature, not our actions. God
doesn't withhold His blessings from us until we earn them.
But when we show by our choices that we are willing to use
our abilities to express His love, the natural result is that we
will be given greater opportunities to proceed along this
divine path. This can involve, for example, an increase in
the resources and skills at our disposal, so that we can
continue our own spiritual development and manifest even
more of God's love to those around us. In this way we will
learn that by living in accord with the Father's plan for us,
we grow closer to Him, the source of all that is good. Thus
we will come to learn that by giving to others we ourselves
will have life in abundance.

It is perhaps an even greater mistake to regard "bad"
karma as God's punishment for our misdeeds. Karmic
misfortune is simply a tool for teaching us the results of our

unloving decisions. It shows us that in choosing to be ungodly we withdraw ourselves from God and all that He would provide for us. It can also give us a greater comprehension of the harmful way some of our actions affect others by causing us to experience these same effects in our own lives. This may enable us to develop the wisdom to choose not to repeat such mistakes in the future.

. The basic lesson unpleasant karma is meant to give us is an understanding of our shortcomings. When we act rebelliously, we separate ourselves from God. If there were no discernible effect of such choices, we would not be able to see what we were creating by them, and thus we would be unable to recognize the need for change. In such a case we would have no motivation to leave the ways of self and return to those of God. Unpleasant karma supplies us with this motivation by enabling us to experience personally the consequences of our rebellion.

With this in mind, we can see that the phrases "good karma" and "bad karma" are misnomers. Whether we perceive its effects as being pleasant or unpleasant, the operation of the law of karma furthers our spiritual education. Both types of experiences serve the purpose of showing us how to return to our Creator. In this way, even "bad" karma is an instrument for our salvation.

Thus all our experiences manifest God's love for us, beckoning us back to Him. The Cayce material makes this point over and over, stating in numerous places that "law is love. Law is God. God is love. God is law" (1942–3). As a signpost directing us back to our union with the Father, karma demonstrates the oneness of all force. Pleasant or unpleasant, it shows God's universal love at work in our lives. It is, if we make good use of the lessons it provides for us, one of the main provisions through which we will all eventually become reunited in loving oneness with God.

How Karma Operates

Recognition of the law of karma makes it evident that each and every one of us is responsible for his own situation in life. Through our past choices, we ourselves have built who we are and the circumstances in which we find ourselves. An obvious extension of this is that with our present decisions we are creating our own futures, the conditions we will encounter in our coming lives and the personal strengths and weaknesses with which we will meet those conditions. That which we term "good karma" arises from making choices that are in accord with God's plan, and what is commonly called "bad karma" results from the rebellious use of our free will. Let's look now at the mechanism by which our use of will gives rise to our karma, pleasant or unpleasant.

As we've seen, the soul bears the record of all it has experienced from the moment of its creation. Everything it has done and everything that has been done to it is carried forward in its memory, as are all the choices it has ever made. With each choice, each exercise of free will, we build within ourselves a pattern of action, a blueprint for a way of reacting to a given situation. These patterns, which become stronger each time we choose to act in accordance with them, may in time become habitual with us. Thus they influence our future decisions. In this way they have a continuity within us; they remain a part of us until we choose to change them by selecting alternative ways of acting. As one Cayce reading expresses it, "Seed ye sow becomes self" (261–15).

If in a given situation we repeatedly choose a way of acting that is harmonious with God's plan for us, we will in time find that we have created within ourselves a strength that will make it easier for us to continue along this proper path in the future. If, on the other hand, we habitually choose to give in to the dictates of self in a certain area, we build and reinforce a pattern that will increase our tendency to act in this way until something happens that causes us to

change. Most of us are personally familiar with some
pattern of action that we consider a "bad habit," and most
of us realize how difficult it can be to break such a pattern
once we've allowed it to become entrenched in our lives.

The patterns that we choose to imprint in our soul's
memory are not a property of the physical body. Therefore,
they do not pass away at physical death, but are carried
forward from one incarnation to the next. Such karmic
strengths and weaknesses affect us at many levels. They
influence the mental attitudes and the emotions we habitually
adopt and manifest. Our special talents, the abilities that
seem to come naturally and easily to us, are often the result
of efforts we've made in previous lifetimes. Even our
physical bodies bear at the cell level an awareness of and
responsiveness to the patterns we've built through our past
choices.

The strengths and weaknesses we've built into ourselves
help set the soul's purpose for entering into each physical
incarnation. They define the areas in which growth is
needed in our journey back to God. Whatever the purpose
of a specific lifetime, it will determine the conditions and
experiences we need to encounter during that life, since
certain situations are conducive to growth in certain areas.
Mind, which partakes of the spiritual as well as the physical, is the builder, the aspect of man that brings the spiritual
influences into manifestation in the material world. It pro-
duces in the physical life conditions that are suited to the
purpose of the soul.

This leads us to the reason for many of the karmic
conditions that arise in life. The soul remembers all the past
choices it has made. It knows how these choices relate to its
ideal, the standard which reflects the best that can be
conceived of. The soul recognizes which of its actions are in
harmony with that ideal, and which are in opposition to it.

Choices in accord with the ideal produce in the soul the
knowledge of a strength, showing which phases of life are
likely to be suitable for positive, constructive activity. Choices
that are contrary to the ideal, on the other hand, produce
awareness of weakness. Such knowledge can indicate to the

soul a need to experience the consequences of these actions, so a lesson can be learned and different, more loving decisions can be made in the future. In response to this knowledge of the soul, mind builds in the physical the conditions necessary for the individual to meet these karmic consequences. Since the patterns created by the soul's actions remain a part of it, the soul is drawn to these karmic conditions, according to the law that like attracts like.

We can see here the way in which karma can either expand our horizons or limit us. Choices made in accordance with our ideal tend to create for us opportunities to achieve spiritual growth by constructively applying the abilities we've developed. Actions motivated by self-will rather than divine love tend to bring conditions that allow us to experience the negative results of our behavior. Frequently these conditions are experienced as limitations on our abilities. The person who overindulges in food during one lifetime, for example, may find himself drawn to a body with disorders of the digestive system for his next incarnation. This not only shows him the consequences of his actions, it may actually make it all but physically impossible for him to continue on in his gluttony. In this way he may be prevented from reinforcing this negative pattern within himself until he is able to develop the strength of will to choose alternative modes of behavior. By forcing us to discontinue our negative actions, the restrictive aspect of many karmic conditions is another way in which the love of God is shown even in those conditions in our lives which we experience as being unpleasant.

Mental and Emotional Karma

Many of our mental and emotional traits are based on our soul memories of experiences in past lives. In itself, the concept that our past can influence the present characteristics of our minds is not a radically new idea. Several schools of standard psychological thought also seek to explain a person's mental or emotional state by referring to his past experiences, including ones that have been consciously forgotten. The theory of reincarnation merely allows us to consider the events of many lifetimes, rather than just one.

There are several ways in which our memories of events in past lives can give rise to unfavorable mental traits in the present. Perhaps the most obvious past-life explanation for a specific fear, for instance, would involve a subconscious memory of a relevant unpleasant occurrence in a previous incarnation. The person who falls to his death in one lifetime might come into his next with a fear of heights. Our aversions could have a similar cause. Someone who has a difficult incarnation in a certain area of the world may in his next lifetime show a distaste for the culture of that region. If the initial event in the past life was traumatic enough, the present reaction could be more extreme, producing phobias or other mental abnormalities.

The Cayce readings point to another possible past-life explanation for troublesome mental traits, one that could easily be overlooked. Instead of focusing on what was done to a person, several of the Cayce life readings emphasize what the subject himself did. The soul, with its memory of past actions, bears the imprint of the choices an individual made in previous incarnations that were contrary to spiritual development. It knows the areas of life in which the individual has repeatedly come up short. This can lead the soul to self-doubt in those areas, a distrust of its ability to make decisions that foster its growth. Because of the close relationship between body, mind, and soul, the doubt on the spiritual level naturally affects the mental attitudes and physical manifestations in the life. Doubt, the readings tell us, leads to fear. And from fear can spring dislike, hatred, anger, and many other undesirable patterns of thought. "If doubt has crept in, it becomes as the father of fear. Fear is as the beginning of faltering" (538–33).

Of course, not all the mental characteristics we bring with us from our previous incarnations are negative. The loving attitudes we've adopted remain a part of us and are ours to draw on as situations arise which call for their use in our current lives. The mental abilities we've developed are also carried forward and can be utilized constructively during this lifetime. And the areas of interest we've become involved in are another set of traits that can aid us this time around, by indicating the fields in which we're most drawn to work and suited to making positive contributions.

Various other aspects of our psychological makeup can also be the result of our past-life experiences. For example, the exhibiting of an introverted or an extroverted temperament might be a continuation of tendencies begun in a former incarnation. On the other hand, it could be a type of balancing measure, produced in response to the soul's knowledge that the individual had been going too far in the other direction. Today's introvert could be a soul that recognized the need for greater sensitivity after several lifetimes as an outgoing person, and so chose incarnation into a situation that would foster introspection; the extrovert could be someone who had in past lives been overly withdrawn, and so was attracted to circumstances conducive to a more open life-style, with increased opportunities for friendships.

There are always several possible past-life explanations for any characteristic we may possess, and there is no foolproof formula for determining which possibility is actually at work in any given case. The reincarnation theory simply states that these characteristics came from *somewhere*, whether in the current lifetime or a previous one. There is always a reason for them. And there is always the potential for them to be used positively, in a way that fulfills their purpose in our spiritual development.

Physical Karma

We sometimes think of man as consisting of three separate components—body, mind, and spirit. But in truth these three aspects form a single whole, for they are interrelated with and responsive to each other. Our physical characteristics are the material manifestation of what we have created in ourselves through our past choices. The statement that spirit is the life, mind is the builder, and the physical is the result indicates that our physical traits reflect our spiritual development, mental attitudes, and emotions. How we use our mind helps determine the form and condition our physical aspect—our bodies—will take. In the words of the readings, "To be sure, attitudes often influence the physical conditions of the body. No one can hate his neighbor and not have stomach or liver trouble. No one can be jealous and allow the anger of same and not have upset digestion or heart disorder" (4021-1).

To understand how input from the soul and the mind affects the body, consider the Cayce material's assertion that every cell of the body has awareness. Each is influenced by the memories of past lives imprinted upon the soul. Within the body, various endocrine glands serve as focal points of contact between the spiritual and the physical. These centers, which correspond to the chakras recognized by some of the religious traditions of the East, are the points through which the karmic memories carried by the soul come into physical manifestation. The glandular centers then act upon the body as a whole to produce the physical conditions, either advantageous or troublesome, that are most suited to the individual's spiritual development.

Favorable bodily conditions can be the result of physical efforts undertaken in a previous incarnation. A person who works to develop some part of the body not only builds strength into the physical, he also builds the pattern of that particular strength on the mental and spiritual levels. Though the body itself will eventually die, the pattern is carried on in those parts of the individual that survive death. Thus it can be brought forward into a succeeding lifetime, where it will once again produce a physical body that possesses that particular strength.

This concept is not substantially different from conventional wisdom. It's widely recognized that exercising a specific part of the body helps develop and strengthen it. The only new element introduced by this view of reincarnation is the existence of patterns in the aspects of the person

not subject to physical death. This allows physical characteristics built during one lifetime to be carried on into the next.

Here we have a possible explanation of favorable physical
traits that are present from birth or develop naturally at an
early age, seemingly without the person's doing anything to
merit such an advantage. Belief in reincarnation allows us to
see that, rather than springing out of nowhere, these strengths
were indeed built by the person using the power of his own
will; it's just that the building took place in a previous
lifetime. The development is recorded in the soul's memory
and carried on into another incarnation.

Physical problems also can have their roots in past-life
actions. Negative patterns relating to the body are carried
from one lifetime to the next as certainly as positive ones
are, and the body is as responsive to them as it is to the
more favorable ones. If a faculty of the body is misused, the
weakness-producing pattern is built into the mind. The
physical results of that pattern must eventually be met, if not
during that particular incarnation, then in a subsequent one.

Karmic physical problems are not always the result of
directly self-destructive behavior, however. Sometimes they
arise because a person has made choices that are harmful to
others. It may then be necessary for him to experience
physical disorders that will enable him to feel the consequences of his action, so that he can recognize the need to
start selecting more positive ways in which to act. Often,
but not always, the negative effects the person feels in his
own body will be the same as or similar to the difficulties
his behavior has caused others.

The Cayce readings make one statement related to physical disorders that many of us would find difficult to accept:
"That brought into materiality is first conceived in spirit.
Hence as we have indicated, all illness is sin; not necessarily
of the moment, as man counts time, but as a part of the
whole experience" (3395-2). Whatever the specific form of
the dis-ease, it has come into being because something is
not right with the person's spiritual development or mental
attitude. Mind, being the builder, has set up a pattern for the

physical vehicle that is in some way imperfect. As a result, the body that manifests in response to that pattern is also impaired.

Note that this is not a matter of God using illness to punish us for our misdeeds. Rather, the troublesome physical condition comes about as a natural consequence of turning away from God, the source of all life. There is a lesson somewhere that must be learned. The soul, with mind as the builder, acts through the endocrine glandular centers to produce the physical conditions necessary to demonstrate that in some way the individual's actions need to be changed.

Judging from the Cayce material, there appears to be a certain consistency to karmic illness. That is, certain specific misuses of will tend to produce disorder in particular areas of the body, although the readings describe a number of cases that don't seem to fit these tendencies. At times the relationship between a past mistake and the physical consequences described by Cayce is quite clear; at other times the connection is much less obvious.

Evidently there are many factors involved in producing illness, or any other karmic condition. About all that can be said with certainty is that if a person were in perfect accord with the universal law of love, the physical manifestation would be perfect. Where there is dis-ease, there is some flaw. But which of us isn't flawed?

External Karmic Circumstances

Our past-life experiences influence the external circumstances of our lives as well as our personal mental and physical makeups. The basic reason for this effect and the underlying mechanism by which it works is the same in regard to our situation in life as it is for our personal characteristics. The soul bears the entire record of its past, and so knows what it needs to experience in order to develop. Certain situations in life are likely to provide these needed experiences. Mind uses input from the soul to create in the physical the conditions that will foster spiritual growth. The soul is then drawn into those circumstances through the principle that like attracts like.

This attraction of the soul to a situation in which it can develop is in operation when a person is ready to experience birth into the physical. It influences both the body and the outer circumstances into which the soul will be born. By providing a physical body suitable for certain experiences, the laws of heredity are one of the means through which we are enabled to meet our karma. Likewise, the social, economic, cultural, and interpersonal environment we enter at birth is influenced by spiritual needs arising from the soul's past choices. Whatever situation the soul enters into, it will be one in which it can develop, using the advantages constructively and learning the necessary lessons from the disadvantages.

Among the most important of the external aspects of the karmic conditions we meet are the interpersonal relationships we develop throughout our lives. The major associations we enter into do not arise by chance: "There is never a chance meeting, or any association, that hasn't its meaning or purpose in the development of an individual entity or soul" (1648–2).

Whom we meet and how we respond to them is strongly affected by our relationships in previous incarnations. Our subconscious memories of our past-life experiences with other individuals influence our reactions to them this time around. If, for example, we experienced a close, rewarding friendship with a certain person during an earlier lifetime, we can expect our reaction to this person to be positive if we should meet in the current life. If we should encounter someone who in a former lifetime had betrayed us, our earlier experience with the individual might predispose us to an initial reaction of distrust, dislike, or fear.

Parent-child relationships are frequently the result of karmic ties. The Cayce life readings record several instances in which a child was born to the same parents it had had in the past. The basic premise is that the soul at birth is drawn into a specific family for some reason. This reason might be bonds of affection that were formed in a previous incarnation. It might be the soul's memory of an earlier incarnation in which this family group provided encouragement and support in its efforts to grow. Or it could be that the past-life relationship was a stormy one, leaving unresolved problems between the individuals. In such a case, the soul might be drawn into birth to the same family so that it would have a chance to work out these interpersonal difficulties.

Like parent-child relationships, those among siblings, marriage partners, friends, and fellow group members are at times recurrences of associations that had been established in the past. As with the parents, the previous experience may have been a positive one that the soul wishes to continue, or it may have been an unpleasant one that created interpersonal problems the person needs to meet and overcome. The latter possibility might explain some extreme cases of sibling hostility, marital incompatibility, and personal rivalry which, from a perspective that denies reincarnation, would seem to have cropped up from nowhere.

Perhaps this would be a good place to caution against adopting a fatalistic view of our interpersonal relationships. Our past-life experiences and karmic memories may contribute to determining whom we meet and our feelings toward them. But these experiences do not *control* whom we associate with nor how we react. The ability to decide these things is ours, through the use of our will. The Cayce readings emphasize that though our past-life experiences have their effect, each of us should "*know* that no urge, no experience is above the *will* of the entity" (1432–1).

We are not destined to marry a certain person, for example, just because of an attraction carried over from a previous incarnation. The urge might be there, but we have the power not to give in to it if we judge that the experience would be harmful. Similarly, we are not fated to react negatively to a certain person because of past-life animosity. We choose what we express in our lives. If our initial reaction is negative, we can change it. Giving us this opportunity may well be the reason we encountered the person in the first place.

In connection with this, when working out a troublesome relationship it's important to bear in mind that each soul is responsible for its own development. Each has to transform its own attitudes and actions if they're unloving, not the other person's. One person who asked Cayce about a possible "karmic debt" between herself and members of her family was told very plainly that karma is not a matter of debt between people; the issue is each individual's soul development, with the other people providing the opportunity to overcome any imperfect attitudes that had been built within the self: "It is merely self being MET, in relationships to that they THEMSELVES are working out . . . not karmic debt BETWEEN but a *karmic* debt of SELF that may be worked out BETWEEN the associations that exist in the present!" (1436–3).

Our task is not to make the other person into someone we feel we can love. It's to make ourselves into someone who can love him, even if he still bears a grudge against us and continues to try to hurt us. In this way we can make our lives into expressions of God's *universal* love.

One additional area of life in which karmic memories play a role is our choice of vocation and hobbies. The abilities and interests we've developed in our past lives are not lost at physical death. The record of them is carried in the soul from one lifetime to another. These memories can give us skills to be used in our life's work and our leisure activities and motivation for doing so. The Cayce material contains many examples of people who entered the same field in their current lifetime as they had been in during a previous one, often implying that their present success was due at least in part to their earlier efforts. Like our other attributes, the abilities we bring with us from our former incarnations are given us to be used constructively, so that they can contribute to our spiritual development.

This discussion has considered just some of the facets of our lives that can be influenced by our past experiences. It has not been intended to cover all the areas that are subject to karmic influences, but merely to provide some idea of how our previous lives can help shape the present one.

Every important factor in every aspect of our existence is caused by something, and frequently these causes lie in our former incarnations. There is a reason for every situation we confront. Whatever the circumstances in which we find ourselves, our condition is something that we ourselves have built, and something that can be used in the growth of our soul. Wherever we are, we can be assured that it's the right place from which to continue our journey back to God.

Karma and Grace

Our karma, as we have seen, is the result of what we've built through our use of free will. The choices we have made that are in accord with God's will have given us strengths that we can use to manifest the love of the Father and make our return to Him. Our rebellious choices have resulted in difficulties, which must be met as we retrace our steps back to our Creator. Even the difficulties have their purpose. Every trial we face is a challenge to us to reform. Each can be used positively, for it gives us an opportunity to gain spiritual strength by overcoming the selfish tendencies within us that have brought it into being. As one person was told by Cayce, conflicting inclinations "may be used as steppingstones, not stumblingstones, if the faith in the inner self—as to its relationships to Creative Forces or God—is held for a constructive experience rather than that for self-indulgence or aggrandizement . . ." (1494–1).

Overcoming our difficulties involves using the will to make loving, godly choices where before we had made selfish ones. This task is ours to do. Our shortcomings have been created by us; they must be redeemed by us. Our tool for doing this is the will, which is more powerful than the limiting karmic habit patterns we have built into ourselves. With it we can change our mental attitudes and the things we express in our physical lives.

Our past must be met and our imperfections eliminated. But we do not have to achieve this goal on our own. With His boundless love for us, the Father doesn't leave us to work out our redemption by ourselves. We have His help, in the form of grace, available to us always. Because this is so, we don't necessarily have to suffer through every unpleasant result of all our misuses of free will; for though our past mistakes must be faced, we can meet them in the grace of God rather than under the karmic law of cause and effect.

We sometimes speak of moving from the law of karma to the law of grace. But since both karma and grace can be used as instruments of our return to God, perhaps it would be more accurate to consider them as two facets of the one law of divine love. Karma gives us the opportunity to meet the effects of what we have created and make right the ungodly patterns we've built in ourselves, so that we can reattain our oneness with the Father. Grace is the aspect of God's love that promises divine forgiveness and assistance. It is the gift of His help, unmerited by us, in our efforts to overcome the unloving parts of ourselves. If we accept this offer of divine aid and use it in our lives, we will live under grace rather than cause and effect. Either of these avenues can lead us back to God; which one we will take is ours to choose.

Perhaps the following excerpt from the readings will help us to understand the relationship between karma and grace. One person was told that though karmic influence must be met, it should be remembered that "under the law of grace this may not be other than an urge, and that making the will of self one with the Way may prevent, may overcome, may take the choice that makes for life, love, joy, happiness—rather than the law that . . . causes the meeting of everything the hard way" (1771-2). Evidently, the effect of past rebellious choices that is built into the self remains present as an urge and must be met and overcome. But through grace this can be accomplished within, by making the will one with God's. If such a transformation within the self can be made, it eliminates the need to experience in physical life the unpleasant external results of misuses of the will; what has been created no longer has to be met "the hard way."

The key to availing ourselves of grace, as noted above, lies in making our will one with God's. We must replace the

imperfect karmic patterns we have created within ourselves
with the perfect pattern of divine love. This pattern, remember, has always been a part of us, given to us by the Creator
at our very beginning. When we use it as the basis of our
actions in each situation we encounter, we transform ourselves into more perfect expressions of the love of God. In
this way the situation will have fulfilled its purpose in our
spiritual development. Perhaps the best statement of what it
means to act according to the divine pattern is given by
Jesus in the New Testament: "Thou shalt love the Lord thy
God with all thy heart, and with all thy soul, and with all
thy mind. . . . Thou shalt love thy neighbor as thyself" (Mt.
22:37, 39).

One aspect of living according to the law of grace
deserves special mention. This is forgiveness. To avail
ourselves of God's forgiveness, we must be willing to
forgive others. This is indicated in the words of the Lord's
Prayer, in which we ask God to "forgive us our debts, as
we forgive our debtors" (Mt. 6:12). If we choose the law of
retribution in our dealings with others, we receive retribution; if we choose forgiveness, we receive forgiveness. The
spirit of God in ourselves which we seek to magnify in our
lives is the same divine spirit that is within our fellow man.
We cannot approach Him within ourselves while at the same
time turning away from Him in others. As one reading
points out, "If your brother is in the image of your Maker,
have you any right—ever—to find fault? or to speak unkindly? much less unjustly?" (262–109). God's help in our lives
is always ours to claim, but to experience the forgiveness
inherent in His love we must manifest it in our dealings with
those around us.

There is no all-purpose formula of specific measures that
will enable us to live in grace. But the Cayce readings do
indicate some general principles that will help us take
advantage of this aspect of God's love. On the spiritual
level, it is most important that we recognize and live
according to our ideal. Basically this involves formulating
an expression of the best, most perfect mode of life we can
conceive of and making it a part of us. Our ideal can be

used to guide our meditations as we seek attunement with the spirit of God within. It provides us with a standard by which to measure our motivations, desires, and mental attitudes. And it can direct what we choose to manifest through our physical actions, showing us an alternative to giving in to the imperfect karmic patterns and conflicting urges we may have brought with us from our past lives. If we habitually choose attitudes, emotions, and activities that are in accord with our ideal, our lives will become more perfect expressions of the love of God.

On the mental level, in order to live under the law of grace we must adopt attitudes that are consistent with it. If we want God's love to be active in our lives, we cannot be unloving toward others, for "there is no such thing as receiving without giving; for he that would have life must give life, he that would have joy must make joy in the lives of others, he that would have peace and harmony must create and make peace in self and in the relationships with others. This is the law, for like begets like . . ." (349–17).

Let's briefly consider some of the mental characteristics that will allow us to live in grace. The importance of an attitude of forgiveness has already been noted. Faith that grace is in fact available to us and can affect the quality of our being is necessary, since we can hardly expect to be able to use something if we don't believe it exists. We also need faith in ourselves, the knowledge that we can progress. Patience too is vital—patience with ourselves when we falter, and patience with others when they don't live up to our expectations. And, if we hope to use God's grace to help us deal with our karmic influences, we need to adopt an unfearing attitude toward karma; we need to know that even hardship can be helpful to us if we meet it in the right way, for through it we can learn to make better choices in the future and thus grow closer to God.

On the physical level, our challenge is to express our ideal motivation and loving attitudes through our actions in the world. Love fulfills the whole law. As we bring our lives into conformity with the law of love, we receive the grace of God that this law provides. A good guideline for living according to the law of love is given us in the Golden Rule: "As ye would that men should do to you, do ye also to them likewise" (Lk. 6:31). If we live according to this principle, we will be showing forth love, patience, cooperation, kindness, and helpfulness in our dealings with others. The Cayce material frequently refers to such manifestations of the spirit of love as fruits of the spirit, and of them the readings say, "Against these there is no law; they are the law—love, and life" (2716–1). Our present conditions in life are the product of how well we applied the law of love in the past. It may take time, but we can be assured that as we apply this principle in our present lives, we will be building for ourselves a future existence that is a reflection of divine love.

To recreate our lives on such a grand scale may seem a formidable task, but in this endeavor we have all the help we need. Our Father not only provides us with the opportunity to make His limitless love manifest in our lives, He has given us the Way in which we can do so. The Way is Jesus of Nazareth, through whom divine forgiveness is offered to each of us. In his life was the perfect embodiment of the love of God for man. Thus he became the law of love, and in becoming the law he fulfilled it. This is something each of us can do, if we will but follow in the path he has shown us.

By bringing the law of divine love into perfect manifestation in the earth, Jesus made that law available to each of us. Through him, every one of us can claim the grace of God. He has taken away the need for us to experience the action of cause and effect in the external circumstances of our lives, for he has brought the law of love within our reach. By living that law we can become, even as he, perfect expressions of the Creator's love. And that love fulfills the whole law, for it is the whole law.

Our part is to live the Way he has shown us, and even in this we have his aid. The following passage from the readings reminds us of one of Jesus' sure promises to us; it then rephrases this promise to clarify the type of help we will receive from Jesus in our quest to bring our hearts and minds, and thus our lives, into alignment with his: " 'If ye love me, keep my commandments, and I will come and dwell in thine own heart.' That is: 'I will so *fill* your mind, your *mental forces with the good,* until all else shall be driven away' " (294–71). Jesus not only has given us the pattern, showing us the Way; he also helps us to adhere to the Way, so that we may regain our oneness with the Father.

CHAPTER 3

Psychic Ability and Past-Life Investigation

The Levels of Consciousness

Our discussion of reincarnation and how it works is based on the assumption that the information which came through Edgar Cayce is valid. If this is the case, we have in his life readings a demonstration that events of our previous lifetimes can become known to us today. "Fine," one might say, "Edgar Cayce had this special ability to look into the remote past; but he was an extraordinary person, and an ordinary person like me can't hope to do what he did."

This attitude, however, is contrary to the overall tone of the Cayce material related to psychic information, in which "ordinary" people were repeatedly encouraged to develop their own psychic abilities. The readings frequently affirmed that such capacities exist in every one of us. One passage, for example, states that "there is innate in each physical individual that channel through which the psychic or the spiritual forces ... *may* function" (294–141). True, Edgar Cayce was special, in that his psychic ability was much more developed than is the case with most of us. But it is within the potential of each of us to cultivate similar faculties in ourselves.

Let's take a closer look at how Edgar Cayce's talent for discovering other people's past lives operated and the sources of information he tapped. This should give us some idea of how to go about developing our own ability to contact our former incarnations. A quick review of the levels of consciousness within each of us would be a good place to start.

At the center of our being is the superconsciousness, the direct awareness of God that was given to all souls at the moment of creation. Because this level of mind maintains contact with the omniscient, infallible Creator, it too is omniscient and infallible. Through our past choices of rebellion and separation from God, we have come to experience a sense of being cut off from our superconscious awareness. But we didn't destroy this aspect of our being, for it is of God and cannot be destroyed. It remains within each of us, an essential part of our nature. Its limitless, infallible knowledge is there for us, if only we can regain our ability to draw upon it.

The second major level of mind is the subconscious. This was built by us out of our experiences after creation. It has several sublevels. At the deeper ones we are not limited to our individual memories, for "what is known to one subconscious mind is known to another, whether conscious of the fact or not" (254-2). This concept of all minds being in contact with one another at the subconscious level is not unique to Cayce. It is compatible with Jung's theory of the collective unconscious, the body of images and symbols shared by all mankind; and various researchers have suggested subconscious contact between individuals as the basis of an explanation for telepathy, the transfer of thoughts from one person's mind to another's by nonphysical means. Since this shared sublevel of subconscious mind described by Cayce lies within each of us, we all have access to the information it contains.

For each individual, the subconscious mind also has its personal layers. Here are recorded those impressions of the individual's past which he no longer consciously remembers.

Some of these impressions, of course, are of events that happened during the current lifetime. At its deeper sublevels the personal subconscious also holds the soul memories of experiences from past lives. All these subconscious memories, whether from the present incarnation or an earlier one, remain a part of the soul.

The third level of awareness is the conscious mind, which can be thought of as the storehouse of the information that we know and are aware of knowing at any given moment. The conscious mind enables us to function in physical life. It is the level at which we operate during the normal events of our everyday waking life. Since we spend so much of our time here, we sometimes think that the conscious mind and the personal subconscious are the only levels of awareness we possess.

Just a little reflection will show that our subconscious memories can be retrieved by the conscious mind. The border between these two levels is not static, but fluid, with information continuously passing back and forth. As an illustration, just before beginning to read this sentence you were probably not consciously aware of what you had for dinner last night. That information passed from your conscious mind to the subconscious shortly after you finished your meal. But it can easily be brought back from the subconscious to the conscious once your attention is pointed in the proper direction.

Some subconscious information is harder to retrieve—for example, what you had for dinner a year ago on this date. How easily a specific memory can be brought back from the subconscious to the conscious depends on many factors, such as how recently the event has occurred, how important it was when it happened, how much has taken place since then, the strength of the individual's motivation to recall the event, and how practiced he is at retrieving information from the subconscious. But even though in a given case it might be difficult to achieve conscious recall of subconscious material, the information in the subconscious is ultimately available to us, if we only learn how to bring it forth.

Records of Our Past Experiences

It's very fine and quite obvious to say that we can recall past events from the current lifetime. But this doesn't account for memories from previous incarnations. In order for these to be available to us, it's necessary that there be a vehicle that doesn't pass away at physical death, so that it is able to carry memories from one lifetime to the next. This vehicle is the soul, which consists of spirit, mind, and will. The soul is who each individual was created as, and it is who each of us still is. Though it uses a series of bodies to express itself in the earth, it is not limited to these physical manifestations.

The soul is immortal, possessing continuity of both life and awareness. It bears the record of all we've ever done. These memories are carried in the deeper layers of the personal subconscious, which, like the soul itself, survives physical death. Among these recollections are the incidents, talents, interests, urges, and blocks that have left their imprint upon us during our past lives. All knowledge of our past experiences is brought forward as part of the soul.

This suggests a question that no doubt has occurred to most if not all people who have ever seriously considered the possibility of reincarnation: If I have lived before in the earth, why can't I remember having done so? And if my past experiences are in fact being retained as memories of the soul, why can't I recall them consciously?

Perhaps the cause of this forgetfulness will be apparent if we consider the origin and purpose of the conscious mind. This aspect of ourselves was evolved to deal with the physical world and the conditions surrounding us during the present lifetime. It tends to identify itself with the physical body and concern itself with the circumstances of life that affect that body. Because of this normally restricted focus of the conscious mind, it can be quite unaware of influences operating from beyond the boundaries of a single physical lifetime.

In a sense, we choose to be forgetful of our remote past

when we identify our essence with our physical being. Reincarnation is of the soul. If we lose our awareness of the soul, if we live our daily lives as if the physical is all that matters, we close ourselves off to the memories carried in the nonphysical parts of ourselves. If there is a screen between our conscious mind and our soul memories, it is one we ourselves have built.

Here is where we can find reason to believe we can regain conscious access to our past-life memories; for if it is our own attitudes and actions that have shut us off from these experiences, by making different types of choices we should be able to open ourselves up to them again. By turning within we can affirm the existence of the soul and establish our willingness to listen to and act upon its promptings. Presently we will be looking at several techniques for doing this. Each of them can make us more aware of the soul and more willing to allow it to become increasingly active in our daily lives. Thus the memories it holds, including those of our previous incarnations, will become more readily available to our conscious minds.

The individual soul is not the only place in which past-life experiences are recorded, however. The Cayce material tells us of the Akashic Record, which is also referred to in the readings as the Book of Life and the Book of God's Remembrances. The Akashic Record is the record of all every individual has ever thought or done, from the beginning of time. One reading describes it as "the record that the individual entity itself writes upon the skein of time and space . . ." (2533-8). As a universal record, the Akasha is lasting and is not limited in its scope to any single individual's experiences or awareness. It might be thought of as one manifestation of God's omniscience. It can be opened and read by someone who has attuned the self to the consciousness of the infinite—or, in other words, to the superconscious mind within.

Thus there are two possible sources of information about any individual's past-life experiences: the person's subconscious soul memories, and the Akashic Record. And there are two avenues by which this information can be obtained.

We can attune to the subconscious mind of the person whose past experiences we are seeking to discover. Or we can attune to the superconscious, to universal awareness, so that we can read the desired information from the Akasha.

Edgar Cayce was able to tap both of these sources. In order to reach either the universal superconscious awareness or the subconscious of another person, it is necessary to transcend the limits of the individual personality and the personal levels of mind. Evidently this is the reason for the specialness of Edgar Cayce's ability, for he had developed the capacity to enter "that condition where the physical self is laid aside . . ." (294–202). If we were able to do the same thing, and if we had attuned ourselves to the proper sources, we too could gain access to the type of information Edgar Cayce brought forth in his life readings.

Perhaps this would be a good point at which to inject a note of caution. Just because we have two possible sources of past-life information does not mean these sources are equal. There is a tendency among some people who are interested in psychic phenomena to regard all information that comes from outside the usual processes of conscious perception as the absolute truth. But the model of human awareness presented in the Cayce material shows that this is clearly not the case. Several people who obtained readings were given warnings similar to that received by one individual, who was told, "Getting outside of the realm of the material does not mean necessarily. . . angelic influence!" (314–1).

Superconscious awareness, being of God, is loving, omniscient, and infallible. The subconscious, on the other hand, was created by humans. Humans are fallible, and they are not necessarily benevolent. Therefore, the subconscious level contains much that is not of God.

We can probe the subconscious and come up with personal impressions that are beyond the normal range of our conscious minds—memories of previous incarnations, for example, and the mental images and attitudes we've built up around those experiences. But in all probability not every thought we had during our former lifetimes was valid, nor was every attitude we held helpful. And we can delve a little deeper and establish contact with other minds and receive information from sources outside our personal experience. But not every mind we contact in this way will be infallible, and not every outside source will have our best interests at heart in determining what to divulge. Only when we reach the superconscious level, the awareness of God within, can we be certain that what we receive will be valid and truly helpful.

The distinction between information received from the universal, superconscious awareness and that which can be obtained by contacting another being on the subconscious level is summed up in the following excerpt: "If it were individualized by a guide, it would become limited; while if universal it is in the hands of Him that is the Maker, the Giver, the Creator" (254–95).

This is not to say that information from the subconscious level should be dismissed out of hand, for in some cases it can be accurate and very useful. This is particularly likely with material about ourselves that is received directly from our own subconscious, for in such cases the danger of distortion or deception by outside influences is quite slight. But such information should not be accepted and followed blindly. In seeking guidance through nonphysical means we should be motivated by the most loving purpose we can conceive of, so that whatever we receive will be from the most godly source we are capable of contacting. And we should always evaluate any information we obtain to ensure that it is consistent with divine love and wisdom.

How to Contact the Sources of Psychic Information

The existence of the subconscious and superconscious levels of awareness provides a basis for the possibility of receiving information psychically. But is this possibility a realistic one, within the reach of ordinary, everyday people? According to the Cayce material, the realization of our psychic potential is closer to each one of us than we may think. The reason for this has to do with what psychic ability is: "Psychic means of the spirit or soul" (3744–1).

Each of us is a soul, so each of us has psychic ability inherent within. The soul has a God-given impulse to manifest itself. If we were aware of what it is trying to express, manifested psychic ability would be the natural result. Our task in trying to develop this ability is to overcome our identification with the physical, attune to and heighten our awareness of the spirit within, listen to its promptings, and make its operation an effective part of our daily lives.

Let's start by looking at some of the ways we can become more sensitive to information from our own subconscious. Here we'll be dealing with personal memories retained by the soul, including ones from our previous incarnations. These are memories we've forgotten how to reach, because we have chosen to overinvolve ourselves in conscious living and direct our attention away from the deeper levels of ourselves. It's important to bear in mind that in this effort we will not be going outside for information, since everything we're seeking is within. We're merely trying to remove the barrier between different aspects of our own being.

The first technique for contacting the subconscious we'll be considering is self-inventory and analysis. This forms a large part of the course on discovering our past lives presented in Part III of this book. Self-inventory and analysis involves simply using the conscious mind to ask questions about our present life and interpret the answers.

There are two main reasons this can help us discover something about our previous incarnations. One is that our subconscious memories affect our conscious attitudes and actions, so looking at how we feel and behave will give us some hint of the types of past experiences that could have produced these characteristics in our present selves.

The second reason we can expect our current life to reveal clues about our past is that mind is the builder. It creates life situations in the physical that give us an opportunity to use the strengths we've developed in the past and to learn the spiritual lessons we need to assimilate. Thus, by investigating our current circumstances, seeing where our strengths and difficulties lie, we can formulate a theory of what we may have done in the past to cultivate these strengths and produce the need to learn the lessons indicated by our problem areas.

Who we are at present has been created by our past choices and experiences. We can discover something of the type of person we've built and the kinds of experiences that might have produced this person by looking into such facets of our personal makeup as: the areas of the world that we find fascinating or unappealing; books and movies that have strongly impressed us; physical objects in our surroundings that reflect influences from another time or culture; the body we came into at birth; our early childhood memories; the types of people, objects, and situations that attract, repel, or frighten us; our talents and hobbies; and the patterns evident in our interpersonal relationships. There are clues to our past-life experiences all around us, if we will but take the time and effort to recognize and interpret them.

Another method of bringing material from the subconscious into conscious awareness is reverie. This technique, which is explained more fully in Session 2 of our course, involves quieting the conscious mind so that images can be received from the subconscious. Consciousness is not lost, but the logical and critical functions of the mind are temporarily suspended and the imaginative aspect is emphasized. Thus the type of reverie we'll be using is much like a common daydream. The main differences are that our reveries are guided to produce certain desired types of information, and that questions are used to focus the attention on this information so that it will be retained.

The reception of images from the subconscious should be familiar to us, for it is what happens when we dream. In dreams, the conscious mind is laid aside and awareness shifts to the activities of the subconscious. Scientific research has established that all of us dream, even if we don't remember doing so. With the wealth of subconscious material our dreams present, they can be a valuable source of past-life information.

Dream study, which can greatly enhance our ability to retain and interpret these images, is an important part of our course. In addition to helping us use the information we receive during sleep, over time it can actually stimulate this flow of material from the subconscious. This effect occurs because through dream study we let the subconscious know that we take the messages it sends us seriously enough to put some time and effort into trying to understand them. In Chapter 5 of this book there will be presented some hints for stimulating, recording, and interpreting dreams and recognizing the past-life clues they may contain.

Subconscious information can also come to us through meditation. Meditation, which is explained in more detail in Chapter 6, involves an attempt to attune to the spirit of God within by quieting and focusing the mind. With the conscious mind subdued, other parts of us can gain our attention. The subconscious is one of these other aspects of our being that can present information to us during meditation.

In fact, though, the subconscious is not actually the level we should be trying to reach here. Our true goal in meditation, in which we seek to attune ourselves to the Divine, is superconscious awareness. Remember, information from the subconscious is fallible. Only at the superconscious level can we be sure of receiving love and truth.

Let's move on now to consider some of the ways in which this superconscious awareness can have a more direct role in our lives and spiritual development. The superconscious mind, being omniscient, partakes of knowledge that is beyond the range of our personal experiences—and this is true even considering the events of all our previous incarnations. Yet access to this limitless store of information lies within each one of us. It is part of our divine heritage, resulting from the touch of the Creator that brought us into being.

Attunement to the superconscious can make available to us the Akashic Record, the record of all that has ever been done in time and space. Yet even this is not our primary purpose in seeking oneness with the divine spirit. The best reason for us to try to grow closer to God is simply so that we can be closer to God. Our companionship with the Father is one of the essential reasons for our creation and needs no justification outside itself.

Nevertheless, if we make His loving spirit active in our lives, we can trust that it will provide us with any information we need and are able to use. In one reading, Edgar Cayce used a rhetorical question to drive this assurance home: "Is there any knowledge, wisdom, or understanding withheld if ye have attuned thyself to that Creative Force which made the worlds and all the forces manifested in same?" (294–202).

It might be helpful at this point to look over some general guidelines for contacting the superconscious level. The first thing to bear in mind is that superconscious awareness will come to us as a natural result of soul growth. One attribute of the spirit of God within us is the impulse to express itself. If we sincerely seek to know the will of God and manifest it in our lives, the spirit will provide us with whatever comfort and guidance we need to continue on our path.

Patience and persistence will be required, for reaching this level of attunement to the spirit is not likely to be an overnight process for any of us. Faith is also necessary— faith that God is within, and faith that if we truly attempt to live in accord with His will, He will withhold nothing helpful from us. This assurance is given repeatedly in the Cayce readings, echoing the words of Jesus in the Bible: "Seek as children to know *His* love, His law, His bidding, and as ye seek so shall ye find . . ." (262–5; cf. Mt. 7:7, Lk. 11:9).

What we receive in our quest to develop psychically— which is to say, spiritually—depends on our motivation and on how we live. We can't successfully seek contact with the spirit of God, of love, if our intentions are selfish and unloving. Our motives should be harmonious with the highest, most godly mode of being we can aspire to. If they are truly loving, they will in some way involve our being a channel of good to others. We must apply what we receive through the spirit of love, because love must be expressed in action for others.

There are several specific ways in which we can obtain information from the superconscious. One of these is through dreams. As mentioned above, with the conscious mind at rest in sleep, we are able to receive images from the subconscious. But not all of these images have their origin in the subconscious. In sleep, the subconscious mind of the soul withdraws from the physical body. It is thus no longer subject to the limitations inherent in identifying with a single person, and it is able to obtain information from sources that transcend these personal limitations. One such source is the superconscious mind. In this way, the subconscious mind can function as an intermediary, relaying messages from the superconscious to the conscious. With practice, we can learn to remember these messages. The more sincere and persistent we are in seeking contact with the superconscious through our dreams, the more likely we'll be to actually receive information from this infallible source.

We've already noted that the superconscious is reachable through meditation and that it, not the subconscious level, is the true goal of this discipline. In meditation we seek attunement to the Christ Consciousness within. The more fully we achieve this attunement, the more able we become to express divine love in our lives. Since "psychic" is defined as being "of the soul," as the soul becomes more developed, psychic ability increases naturally.

One possible aspect of this development is the reception of past-life material. But this doesn't mean that we should meditate for the purpose of obtaining such information. When we seek contact with the Divine, it is only appropriate that we leave to God the decision as to what help or guidance we should receive. His loving wisdom is a much better judge of what information will be truly helpful to us than our conscious minds could ever be. If we really reach the spirit of God within, we will be given whatever aid or information we need, whether or not this includes knowledge of our previous incarnations.

With both dreams and meditation, which can bring us material from either the subconscious or the superconscious, consistency is important. For one thing, as we become more practiced in attuning to the superconscious, we will become more able to reach it. In addition to this, the more experience we have in receiving information from the superconscious, the more proficient we will become at recognizing it when it does occur. In time, we may develop a feel for which messages are truly guidance from the God consciousness within, and which are merely images from the subconscious— potentially valid and useful, but not necessarily so.

Mentioning dreams and meditation as means of contact with the superconscious might make it seem that we have to lay our conscious mind aside in order to receive such knowledge. This is not necessarily the case, for the spirit of God has an unlimited range of communication and activity. Thus the conscious mind can pick up messages from the superconscious. Among the forms such information can take are intuitive hunches, spontaneous revelation (in which the conscious mind just knows something to be true), and déjà vu (the feeling that we've experienced something before, even though, consciously at least, we haven't). Any of these types of experience might originate on the superconscious level, and any of them can give us knowledge of events from our former lifetimes. Once again, they occur as the natural result of soul development and the spirit's drive to express itself. Rather than being specifically sought after, these promptings from the superconscious can be stimulated by a sincere desire to know God's will, meditation and other practices to increase attunement, and loving, practical application of any knowledge we receive in our daily lives.

Seeking Psychic Information Through Outside Sources

Thus far in our discussion of how to obtain psychic knowledge, we've concentrated on searching for our own answers within ourselves. It is possible, of course, to receive such information through the help of outside sources. Thus some people, for example, may seek past-life information through hypnotic regression, in which the conscious mind of the subject is stilled by the hypnotist so that the subconscious memories of the soul can be reached. Others might consult a medium, a person who relays messages to the seeker from beings who are not inhabiting physical bodies at the time. Psychic channeling, in which the discarnate entity takes over the physical apparatus of the channel and uses it to communicate directly with the subject, is another possibility for those who choose to seek knowledge of their past lives through external sources.

It can be very tempting to try to discover our previous incarnations by such means, for at times the development of our own psychic abilities through spiritual growth can seem like a slow and difficult process. It would apparently be much quicker and easier to go to someone else who already has these faculties well developed and receive our answers from him.

The general attitude expressed in the Edgar Cayce readings toward seeking outside aid of this nature, however, is one of caution. We've already noted the potential for error in information that is received from the subconscious mind. It is difficult, if not impossible, to know for sure what level of awareness the outside source is attuned to. If it doesn't happen to be the superconscious, we have no assurance that the information we receive in this way will be correct and offered with our best interests in mind. The possibility that the outside source we choose will be mistaken in the information it provides, or will intentionally want to deceive or control us, is quite real, and we must be very careful in our evaluation of anything we receive through such means.

Edgar Cayce felt that most of the material that came through him was obtained from the superconscious level. And yet, awake or in trance, he never claimed that anyone should follow even his advice uncritically. The predominant tone of the readings on the subject of their own reliability is summed up in one passage in which he admonishes that the information conveyed through the readings ''may never be called tenets, but should *ever* [be presented as] that which has been applied in the experience of individuals as *producing* something in their experience" (262–61). Each person was thus told to disseminate only the material from the readings that he had applied and found to be productive in his life. In another reading, the subject was encouraged to "analyze that which has been indicated . . . and as ye have found this to be good, keep it in thy daily life" (294–197). It was the rightness of the psychic material, its ability to answer to the spirit of God within each individual, that determined whether or not it should be adhered to in life—not the fact that it came through Edgar Cayce.

We've mentioned before one of the drawbacks common to the various methods of obtaining past-life information through outside sources. This is the possibility that the other person is not attuned to the superconscious. This can lead to the material presented being either erroneous or inappropriate for use at the time. A second potential problem that can arise in such cases is the danger of distortion, either intentional or inadvertent, as the information is passed through the subconscious and conscious levels of someone whose motivations and accuracy cannot be completely assessed. Each of these possibilities exists whether the outside source is a long-time discarnate, a person recently deceased, or someone still living in the physical body.

Both these problems are greatly reduced when you rely on yourself to obtain knowledge of your own prior incarnations. Whether you attune to superconscious awareness or your own subconscious memories, the information you receive is coming from within yourself, through the faculties of your own soul. This means, first of all, that the material brought forth is much more likely to be helpful to you, since you yourself, on either the superconscious or the subconscious level, choose what is to be presented. And if perchance you should receive something you can't find an immediate use for, the decision of whether to accept it, reject it, or lay it aside for a while and come back to it later will likewise be your own.

The possibility of distortion is also lessened when you

serve as your own psychic. Consider that if another person obtains information from your subconscious, the material must pass from your subconscious to his, then from his subconscious to his conscious mind, and finally from his conscious mind to yours as he relays the knowledge back to you. That's quite a few levels of mind for the information to travel through, any one of which could misinterpret or slant the message it receives. And the complexity of the picture is increased if the mind of a third person is involved in the transmission of the material, as is the case in some forms of mediumship. On the other hand, when you turn within to receive information about your own past, the material is relayed directly from the deeper levels of your mind to your conscious awareness. The chances that it will be seriously distorted become much less.

There is a third factor to consider in deciding whether to turn within or to another for past-life information. As you endeavor to contact the deeper levels of your own mind—as you give time and effort to introspection, dream study, and meditation—you will be cultivating your ability to attune to the subconscious and superconscious. You will be growing, learning how to reach these aspects of yourself and use them constructively. As with any skill, with practice you will become better at it. In time you can expect to experience an increase in your psychic ability; and, more importantly, this growth will come as a natural part of your overall spiritual development.

Though relying upon outside help may get you some information about your past lives more quickly than seeking your answers within will, it cannot give you the same opportunity to develop the ability to express your inherent psychic potential. When we consider the possibility of receiving accurate, useful information and the growth that can be experienced through the process of obtaining this material, it becomes evident that ultimately you yourself are the best authority on the subject of your own past lives.

Evaluating Psychic Information

In the last section we touched on the issue of the reliability of psychic material, particularly that relating to our past lives. Whether a given piece of information has been obtained by seeking within or through the help of an outside agent, certain questions should be asked about it in order to evaluate its accuracy and usefulness. Among these questions are: Is this information coming from superconscious awareness or from a fallible source, such as the subconscious? If it's from the subconscious, is it likely to be true or false? If true, is it helpful, useless, or something I might be better off not knowing yet? In any case, what should I do about it?

The first test is one of validity. Here it's advisable to focus on your ideal and ask sincerely whether the information you have received is consistent with the best you know to be true. The conscious mind can be used to analyze this question. The unconscious should also be allowed to contribute its input, which can be obtained either in dreams, through meditation, or in the form of waking hunches—your intuitive feelings about the correctness of the material.

If you decide to use meditation to help you evaluate the information, the best method is to meditate for personal attunement to the superconscious, rather than focusing on the psychic material itself. When your meditation session is over and you have done your best to approach the spirit of God within you, then shift your attention to the information you're considering and listen for your response from within.

If your most honest conclusion is that the material you've received is not harmonious with the best you can conceive of, you would be wise to leave it alone— at least for a time, until you are able to see it in a different light. If, on the other hand, you decide that the material is valid, it is up to you to determine how you can make the best use of it.

This brings up the second point in the evaluation of psychic material—its usefulness. Even if the information you've received is true and consistent with your ideal, having it is not enough. Knowledge is given to us for a reason: to be used. As a great number of readings tell us, "To know and not to do is sin" (900–429). When presented with psychic information, ask if it will help you live your life as best you can. Will this knowledge help you express love more fully? If so, your next step is to decide how.

Finally, and most importantly, do something about it, and note the results of your actions. As Cayce stated in one reading, the reliability and usefulness of psychic material should be judged "by the results obtained in the end" (3744–2). Making constructive use of information we receive helps fulfill the very reason for our existence, because knowledge can be one of our most valuable tools for bringing love into our lives and into the world. But only if we use it.

CHAPTER 4

Purposes and Ideals in Past-Life Study

Individual Reasons for Seeking Past-Life Information

Among people who believe in reincarnation, there are no doubt many different reasons for wanting to discover what their past lives were. Even if we were to examine just a single individual, we would probably find several different sources of motivation for this search. Some of the possible purposes in seeking past-life knowledge are quite casual. One person might enjoy a sense of self-importance in believing that he was some great historical personage in a former incarnation. Another might seek to use such a claim to impress his acquaintances. Probably the most widespread motive for desiring past-life information is simply natural curiosity. Most of us would like to know who and what we are and why we have the characteristics we do. And for those who accept the concept of reincarnation, the range of such questions would naturally extend back to include earlier lifetimes as well as the current one. Just having knowledge of our past lives would be likely to bring some form of satisfaction to many of us. But at a certain point, the serious student of reincarnation would feel the need for a deeper reason for his efforts to discover his past. "Now that I have this information," such a person might ask, "what am I to do with it?"

Actually, there are many ways in which an understanding of our previous incarnations can be used. A number of benefits can be derived simply from believing in reincarnation, and others will become available once we begin to discover the specifics of our former experiences in the earth. In this chapter we will be looking at some of the ways reincarnation theory and information about our past lives can be helpful to us, and some of the ways in which we can use this information to live the best lives we can in the present. The intention here is not to convince anyone to adopt any specific reasons for seeking past-life knowledge or ways of using it. It's merely to present some idea of the possibilities, so that the reader can find his own purpose for engaging in this search.

Having a solid motive for trying to discover our former incarnations can help us in several ways. In the first place, it can serve as a stimulus for the flow of past-life information from our subconscious and superconscious awareness. Psychic is of the soul. When we seek to increase our psychic abilities, in whatever direction, what we are really trying to do is have the soul take a more active role in our lives. Since like begets like, our efforts to allow the soul to express itself will be more effective if our purpose is a spiritual one, one that will enable us to live better lives. The closer we can come to manifesting the quality of our superconscious awareness of God, the more likely we will be to receive material from this infallible source. Therefore, the reliability of the psychic information we obtain depends to a great extent upon the motivation with which we seek it.

Another measure we can take to ensure that the information we receive comes from the spirit of God within is to use whatever we learn in ways that are in accord with His purposes for creating us. We were created to be companions with God and expressions of His love. Whatever knowledge of our previous incarnations we receive is given us to be used in ways that are godly and loving. If we wish our quest for self-understanding to be guided by the spirit of God, we must use the understanding we are given to bring the fruits of the spirit into our lives, by helping others. For whatever knowledge we gain to bring wisdom and soul growth (and the Cayce readings clearly differentiate between knowledge and wisdom), we must use it constructively.

Having a spiritual purpose for seeking information about our past lives can also help us evaluate the material we receive. The individual who wants only to impress others with the famous persons he once was might be happy to discover he was George Washington in his last lifetime; at least, most former George Washingtons seem to be pleased with this identity. The person with the deeper motivation, on the other hand, is much less likely to be misled by information that doesn't contribute to his growth in wisdom. If our purpose in searching for past-life knowledge is founded in the desire to manifest God in our lives, and if the information we obtain helps fulfill that purpose, we can know that it proceeds from the spirit of truth.

Benefits and Uses of Past-Life Information

Even before we begin discovering the specifics of our previous lifetimes, there is a certain amount of aid and comfort to be found in the theory of reincarnation. Among the most basic implications of this concept is the assurance that death is not final, that we do in fact survive it and can return for future physical lives. Reincarnation can also make it easier for us to believe that God is loving, not capricious.

From a one-lifetime point of view, there is much in life that seems unfair. Reincarnation lets us see that injustices are only apparent, that the events that seem to be unfair actually do have a cause and can be used to achieve a positive result.

Belief in reincarnation can lead us to recognize that each of us is responsible for his own life. Whatever we are experiencing, we ourselves have created. Far from weighing us down, this sense of responsibility can give us hope. It can enable us to see that no matter how unpleasant our circumstances may be, they have a purpose; and if we meet them in the right way, they can help us achieve our ultimate goal of reunion with the Father.

Realizing that our past choices are what have created our current condition can increase our understanding of the present and the opportunities it holds. Because the results of our choices don't generally manifest in physical life immediately, this is one area in which a knowledge of specific experiences in our former lifetimes can be most helpful. This knowledge can allow us to see what past decisions of ours resulted in what current circumstances. It will thus enable us to identify which of our choices were constructive ones and which were mistakes. We will then know which types of action we should persist in and which patterns to change so that we can build a better future.

There are numerous ways in which specific items of past-life information can be useful to us. We're now going to look at some of the possibilities. The examples below are purely hypothetical. They are not meant to show all the potential uses of such material, nor to be taken as the only "correct" responses to the situations described. The important thing is that each individual makes the best use of whatever knowledge he has to fulfill his own purposes and ideals. The examples are given only to suggest a few ideas.

In using knowledge of our previous incarnations, our personal characteristics during former lives are more important than the specifics of our past identities. Knowing your name and when and where you lived during an earlier lifetime may satisfy your curiosity. But it is unlikely to be as helpful in the present as knowing the talents, attitudes, emotional predispositions, and shortcomings you brought with you from that lifetime to this one. It might be fun to discover you lived in Italy during the fifteenth century. It would be more useful to find out that during a recent incarnation you had great skill as a teacher but were completely unable to handle money.

Example 1 Suppose that during the present lifetime an individual had frequently felt the urge to take up painting as a hobby, but had never done so. After becoming interested in reincarnation and spending some time working with his dreams, he dreamed that he had been an artist during a previous life. The dream offered explanations for several other things he had noticed about himself, and it continued to ring true when he thought about it after seeking attunement through meditation. So he decided to accept it as valid, provisionally at least, and he formulated a past-life theory that stated he had indeed been an artist. How could this person use this information in his present life?

On the mental level, his feelings about his past might well convince him that there is a reason for his impulse, that it is not just an idle pipe dream. It could give this person confidence that something worthwhile can be done with this urge, providing the push he's needed to try developing his latent talent. His past-life knowledge could thus help enrich his present life and make it more creative.

Example 2 Suppose a person's activities during the current lifetime have always been severely limited by a chronic physical disability. This and other clues he has discovered about himself lead him to theorize a previous incarnation in which he had caused physical impairment to others in a way that is mirrored by his own present condition.

Here again, the improvement in the individual's current life would probably start with his mental attitude. Just knowing that there is a reason for his disability could help him overcome any feelings of bitterness he might have about it, any thought that life is against him. The person might find the courage here to try to use the abilities he does have more fully. At any rate, his past-life knowledge should make clear to him the type of mistake he'd made in the past, giving him the opportunity to change this negative pattern by developing greater sensitivity to the physical welfare of others. He could then begin to choose appropriate activities on the physical level that would express this improved mental outlook.

The important thing to note here is that just having this knowledge of his previous lifetime won't help this person meet his karmic condition successfully if he doesn't use it. Even after we've discovered valid information about our past, there is still work to be done if we really want to benefit from our study of reincarnation. Often, as in this example, the task of transforming mental attitudes and patterns can be quite difficult. But doing so is a vital part of spiritual growth and can enable us to create for ourselves a future less limited karmically by our past mistakes.

Example 3 During her present lifetime an individual has always enjoyed an abundance of material resources. She discovers in her current life several indications that in an earlier incarnation she had given much of what she had to help provide for the physical needs of others.

The lesson here is the flip side of the one from the previous example. Here the person is shown a pattern of past decisions that were loving and should therefore be continued. Mentally, her past-life knowledge could give her the assurance that money used in accordance with God's plan will in time be returned, with ample interest. If in the present she has any concern that her resources might some-day run out unless she hoards them, the information she has about her past could help her overcome her fear of poverty. This would enable her to maintain the generous pattern of action she had built in her earlier lifetime.

Example 4 Though this individual doesn't particularly like to admit it, she finds that her present attitudes toward a certain religious denomination are prejudiced. Her work with reincarnation leads her to believe that in a previous incarnation she had been severely persecuted by members of this faith and had died as a result.

There are several ways in which this information could help the person transform her mental outlook. Knowing the cause of any negative attitude can be an important first step in changing it. It can allow us to bring the power of our rational mind to bear on the problem. In this case, the woman's past-life information can enable her to see that what she's responding to is a situation from the past. It can help her realize that the cause of her reaction is within herself, and thus make it easier for her to avoid blaming the problem on present-day members of this religious group. Perhaps most importantly, it can show her that there is a need for her to forgive. She can then begin to take steps that will help her do so, whether this involves prayer, working to express a more positive view of this faith through her actions and words, or whatever she finds to be most effective in her individual case.

The common theme that runs through each of these examples is the need to do something with the past-life information that has been obtained. Enticing as the prospect of discovering our previous incarnations may be, we cannot live in the past. The current lifetime is the one in which each of us must function today. To be most beneficial, knowledge of our earlier lives should not be an end in itself. It is merely a tool to help us understand the present more completely, so that we can make the best possible use of our current incarnation. Our opportunity for soul growth is not in the past, but in the here and now.

Definition and Importance of Ideals

We've already mentioned ideals at several points in this book. It's high time now to take a closer look at exactly what is meant by this term. The Cayce readings define an ideal as "that to which an entity may, itself, ever look up, knowing itself to be gradually becoming a portion, but *never* may it be the whole. Something to look up to, or to attempt to *attain* to; not an idea [something one wants to accomplish], for then one reaches the goal! An ideal is that as is sought by, and developed to be, at an at-onement with same, a portion of same, but never the whole" (256-2).

The ideal is our individual formulation of a standard that will help us bring into manifestation the best we can conceive of in life. It is not some*thing* we wish to obtain, nor even a condition we hope to reach. It is, rather, a *way* of thinking and acting. The ideal concerns mainly why and how we do what we do. It is closely related to our soul's purpose in any incarnation, and should therefore be consistent with what we perceive as God's purpose in giving us life.

Having an ideal, a standard, gives us direction in life. It allows us to measure our actions to make sure they're taking us where we want to go. This is important once we accept the concept that each of our actions has an effect. Only by knowing what direction we want to head in and committing ourselves to it can we judge which steps to take in order to get there. The ideal can be viewed as each individual's personal image of his best possible self. The more elevated this image is, the greater a person's accomplishments are likely to be. The Cayce readings tell us that "that to which [an individual] may attain is limited only by self and that [which] self sets as its ideal . . ." (1510–1). So vital is our ideal, and the effort we make to follow it, in influencing the quality of our lives that one person was told, "The most important experience of this or any entity is to first know what *is* the ideal—spiritually" (357–13).

Recall for a moment the formula given by the Cayce material: The spirit is the life, mind is the builder, the physical is the result. Ideals work in the same direction, on all three levels. The spiritual ideal is the source, the motivation we wish to guide our thoughts and actions. The mental ideal relates to the attitudes we wish to hold in order to bring this spiritual ideal into manifestation, to build it into our lives. The physical ideal involves the actions that will express it in the material world. Since the whole point is to allow the spiritual ideal to permeate our body, mind and soul, the ideal on all three levels should flow from our perception of the spirit of God. It should reflect as much as we can recognize of our superconscious awareness of divine love.

The ideal we recognize is not static. Our perception and understanding of God's way changes as we develop spiritually. Our view of the best, most godly mode of life likewise changes. The readings recommend that we review our statement of the ideal periodically, in order to reflect this change. As we grow by applying what we perceive as the ideal, we'll be shown more of God's plan for us: "Use that thou knowest to do and the Lord will give thee the next step" (3654-1).

It may seem that we've wandered a bit from our topic of discovering our prior incarnations. Certainly it's possible for an individual to follow and get results from various procedures for obtaining past-life information without being the least bit concerned with setting or adhering to an ideal. But remember that according to the perspective of the Cayce material, past-life information, like any manifestation of our innate psychic abilities, should unfold naturally as part of our overall spiritual development. Our ideal, the source of our motivation and the pattern by which we attempt to live, is one of the most powerful tools we have with which to achieve our reunion with the Creator.

Setting an ideal that is grounded in the spirit is the first step in awakening the divine pattern within, the imprint of God that was given our souls in the beginning. As we apply the ideal that we know, we receive a clearer picture of the divine ideal. The pattern we seek to manifest takes on less and less of self, more and more of God. In time, through the power of Christ and our striving toward the ideal, we can come to know our spiritual nature and our relationship with the Father. And, as part of this knowledge, there will come the awareness of our entire past.

Formulating Your Ideals

The readings recommend several ways of organizing a statement of our ideals. The common elements among them are pencil and paper, for our formulation of ideals should be concrete, so that they will have definite meaning for us.

We're after something more here than just a nebulous resolve to "be good." As one person was told, "Do not confuse self in thine activities . . . but rather first analyze thyself, thy purposes, thy hopes, thy ideals. Not merely as in mind, but make them more concrete. Set them down. See what they look like. You will be surprised to find how few and yet how great they may be in thine own experience" (3062–2).

In the simplest format, a sheet of paper is divided into three columns. The first is labeled "spiritual ideal," the second "mental ideals," and the third "physical ideals." Appropriate entries, which will be described shortly, are then made in each column.

Some people find a circular diagram more helpful, for it makes it easier to show how the spiritual ideal can be applied mentally and physically to chosen areas of life. This diagram consists of three concentric circles. As shown in the illustration below, the outer two of these are divided into a

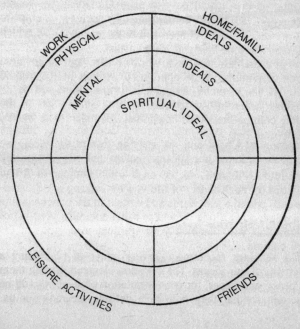

number of sections. The central circle is where the spiritual ideal will be written; the middle circle is for the mental ideals; and the outer one is for the physical ideals. Outside the outer border and corresponding to the divisions of the two circles are labels denoting the aspects of life on which the individual wishes to concentrate in the application of his ideals. The number and designation of these areas is strictly a matter of individual choice. Those shown in the illustration are meant merely as suggestions.

Whatever format you decide to use, start by identifying your spiritual ideal. This is the source, the motivation you want to direct your thoughts and actions in all areas of life. It should be an expression of the highest good you can conceive of. Select a word or short phrase that represents this quality to you and write it in the appropriate place.

Now go on to your mental ideals. These are the attitudes and qualities of mind that will allow you to manifest your spiritual ideal in life. They will therefore be consistent with it. If you're using the circular diagram, for each area of life you're working with choose a few mental attitudes which will express your spiritual ideal in that situation. Describe each of these attitudes in a word or two, and write these words or phrases in the appropriate section of the middle circle. If you're using the column format, there will be no divisions according to aspects of life. Simply list in the middle column the words or phrases that reflect your mental ideals.

Finally, formulate your physical ideals. These are activities that will express your spiritual ideal in materiality. For the circular diagram, decide on a small number of fitting activities for each aspect of life you're working on. Summarize each one in a few words and write it in the corresponding area of the outer circle. If you're using columns, your list of actions that will manifest your spiritual ideal goes in the third column.

For example, let's assume you've decided to use the circular diagram and focus on the four areas of life shown in the illustration above. First identify your spiritual ideal. This is a matter for careful thought, and perhaps some meditation. Suppose after due consideration you've determined that the best possible motivation for your life at this time would be to establish harmonious relations with everyone around you. You therefore choose the word "harmony" to represent your spiritual ideal, and write it in the center circle.

Now consider one of the areas you're going to be working with—"home/family," for instance—and decide upon the mental attitudes and patterns of thought that would bring harmony into your home life. These are your mental ideals in relation to your home and family. Let's say you arrive at cooperation, appreciation, and patience as appropriate qualities of mind. You enter these three words in the "home/family" section of the middle circle.

Move on now to your physical ideals in regard to home and family. Consider your mental ideals in this area, and come up with one or two actions that would express each of these attitudes. Suppose "cooperation" suggests to you that you help out more with the household chores; "appreciation" suggests both that you compliment your family members more often and that you take your spouse out to dinner once a week to show your gratitude; and "patience" suggests that you make more of an effort to control your temper around the kids. As words and phrases to denote these physical ideals, you might then write "chores," "compliments," "dine out," and "count to ten" in the home/family section of the outer circle.

You would then go on to the next aspect of life—say, "friends"— and determine the mental patterns and physical activities that would manifest harmony, your spiritual ideal, in this area.

Applying Your Ideals

Setting ideals and formulating them meaningfully is an important step in spiritual growth. But to really make a difference in our lives, our ideals must be applied. Their purpose is to guide us to express as much of God as we can conceive of. They provide us with a standard upon which we can base our choice of motives, thoughts, and actions. In this way, they can be applied on the spiritual, mental, and physical levels to help us make self-transforming decisions that are guided by the spirit of God within.

Spiritually, our ideal can help make our prayers and meditations more fruitful. The spiritual ideal we adopt should in some way motivate us to live in accord with God's will. In order for us to discover His will, it is necessary that we attune to the divine spirit within. Here is where our spiritual ideal can aid us, by providing a focus for our meditation that is consistent with the best we know. As we seek in this way to draw closer to what we recognize as God, He will reveal more and more of Himself to us. We will grow in our ability to make our will and our purpose one with His, allowing His spirit to flow through us and manifest itself in our lives.

On the mental level, our ideals can help us recognize the purpose of our life. As we grow through attunement and application of what we know, our understanding of God's purpose for giving us life will increase. This will enable us to recognize and choose attitudes, thoughts, and emotions which are harmonious with that purpose. And, since mind is the builder, we can expect that in time the physical circumstances of our life will also come to reflect God's loving will for us.

Our challenge on the physical level is to live our ideals by choosing actions that manifest our spiritual and mental standards. This may well involve changing ourselves and our behavior patterns in certain ways to express more fully the best we know in life. Such a transformation is likely to be gradual, requiring consistency and active patience, that quality which enables us to keep trying, even though the initial results of our efforts might not be all that we would hope. In this way, we can achieve spiritual growth by making a steady series of small improvements in how we live our lives. Taking just a small step each day will eventually bring us to our desired destination— provided the steps are in the right direction.

Using Ideals in Past-Life Study

There are several ways in which our ideals can be used to direct our general approach to past-life study and how we use the specific information we receive. On the spiritual plane, they can clarify and guide our purposes for trying to discover our previous incarnations, so that our work here doesn't become just an exercise in idle curiosity. At the mental level, our ideals can help us evaluate the information we receive. They give us a standard to measure it by, allowing us to ensure that the knowledge we gain is being used to create the quality of mind we wish to develop. And physically, our ideals enable us to weigh how we're using our past-life information, so that we can make our application of this knowledge consistent with what we truly want our lives to express.

Our ideals can help us make the most positive use of our karmic strengths and meet our karmic weaknesses constructively. We can be guided by them to utilize our talents and resources in ways that reflect the best we know. In cases where we have brought forward conflicting urges from our previous incarnations, our ideals can aid us in resolving the conflict by making decisions based on our own highest standard. And they can help us overcome the karmic mental blocks of confusion, doubt, and fear. If we have a clear picture of our ideals and adhere to them, the strengthened sense of purpose we develop will give us the power to overcome confusion and self-doubt. This in turn will enable us to confront our fears successfully. Doubt, remember, is the father of fear. As doubt is eliminated by our knowledge that we are moving in the direction that will accomplish our soul's purpose, the influence of fear in our lives will in time grow less and less.

Our ideals can become an extremely powerful aid in our efforts to meet the karmic patterns we have built within ourselves. These patterns must all be met, but they can be met either under the law of cause and effect or through the law of grace. As we bring our spiritual motivation, mental attitudes, and physical actions into closer alignment with our ideal, our lives become more expressive of God. The pattern with which we meet life's circumstances grows closer to the Christ Pattern, the perfect model of divine love. We develop the ability to live in accordance with this pattern of love rather than in ways that are influenced by the karmic patterns we have built. And in this love is the fulfillment of the entire law. Thus, through the power of Christ within, we become able to meet what we have created under the law of grace rather than that of cause and effect.

Let's look at some examples of how this might work. Once again, these are totally hypothetical. They are not meant to prescribe what anyone's ideal should be on any level or how it should be used. The purpose of these examples is only to indicate some of the ways in which our ideals might guide us as we confront the karmic results of our past choices. In each of these cases, imagine that the individual described is using the circular diagram illustrated on page 75 to formulate his ideals, and that one of the areas in life he's decided to apply his ideals to is the karmic condition he's meeting.

Example 1 Suppose that someone has selected as her spiritual ideal "oneness with God." This person has a serious long-term physical disability which she feels is the result of past-life actions. She decides to use her ideals to help her meet this condition.

Through meditation and conscious thought she determines that the mental attitudes of patience, faith, hope, and joy will reflect her spiritual ideal of oneness when applied to the problem area. She adopts these attitudes as her mental ideals and enters them in the appropriate area of her circular diagram.

To choose her physical ideals, she asks herself what actions would manifest these attitudes in relation to her condition. She decides that prayer, making better use of the abilities she does possess, encouraging others who have physical problems, and smiling more often would be fitting activities, so she selects them as her physical ideals and writes them in her diagram.

Having formulated her ideals, she makes a consistent effort to hold to these attitudes and manifest these actions in relation to her disability, doing all in a spirit of oneness with God. Thus she grows closer to becoming the person she wants to be and fulfilling her soul's purpose.

Note that the disability itself is not necessarily eliminated. But by using her ideals the individual has turned the problem presented by this karmic condition into an opportunity for soul growth. In this way the purpose of her experiencing this circumstance in life is fulfilled. By meeting her disability constructively, the person has used it to help her in her effort to regain oneness with God. She has transformed this potential stumbling block into a stepping-stone and made her experience with it a positive one.

Example 2 In this example, let's suppose a person has chosen brotherhood as his spiritual ideal. This individual is someone who has been quite wealthy all his life, and he's decided to use his ideals to help shape his attitudes and activities regarding his money. His goal in doing this is to ensure that this favorable condition that resulted from what he built in his previous incarnations will work toward his spiritual development during the current one.

He settles on generosity and compassion for others less fortunate as qualities of mind that will help him use his material abundance to express brotherhood, and he adopts these two attitudes as his mental ideals in this area.

His mental ideals suggest to him physical ideals of making his financial resources available to his friends by helping them with loans when needed, and tithing, or donating a fixed portion of his income, to the needy.

Assuming this individual is able to hold to the mental and physical ideals he has chosen, he will indeed be using his wealth to manifest brotherhood. And in adhering to his spiritual ideal, he will be progressing by making his life an expression of the best he can recognize.

Example 3 Here let's assume that a person who has chosen love as his spiritual ideal is nevertheless beset by intense feelings of rivalry with one of his colleagues at work. Through his efforts to discover his past lives he comes to understand that the rivalry he feels toward this person stems from an earlier incarnation in which they had been fierce competitors in business. This knowledge, though helpful, does not in and of itself enable the individual to eliminate his negative feelings toward the other, so he decides to use his ideals to help him overcome the hostility he has built within himself.

He seeks attunement to his spiritual ideal in meditation, then considers the situation logically and arrives at friendliness and cooperation as two states of mind that will help him manifest love toward the other person.

These mental ideals suggest to him asking the other person out to lunch, saying only positive things about him to others, and offering to help him at work as loving activities in this area of life, and he adopts them as physical ideals.

If this individual is sincerely able to hold these attitudes and perform these actions in a spirit of love, he will be taking a step toward awakening the Christ Pattern within and using it to take the place of the karmic pattern of rivalry that had been built. Even if the other person doesn't respond in kind, the first individual will in time overcome the karmic condition that was part of himself. He may succeed in replacing his mental hostility with love before it has a chance to manifest as serious discord in his physical life. He will then have met himself under the law of grace, rather than through cause and effect.

In using our ideals to help us meet what we have built in the past, we have important work to do on each of three levels. We must allow our spiritual ideal to set our basic purpose and direction, and we must commit ourselves to following it. As completely as possible, we must choose the attitudes and thought patterns prescribed by our mental ideals. And we have to act in accordance with our physical ideals if our spiritual one is to be manifested in our lives. All three elements are necessary in order for us to use the past-life information we gain to make our present lives the best we can conceive of.

PART II

Practices for Use Throughout the Course

CHAPTER 5
Dreams and Journal Writing

The Purpose and Process of Dreaming

Dreaming, as most of us realize, is a completely natural activity. This conclusion is supported by scientific experimentation, which has established that we all have a need not only to sleep, but to dream. But just because dreaming is natural doesn't mean that it is totally mundane. The scope of our dreams extends far beyond the limitations of our everyday physical existence. The Edgar Cayce readings indicate both the ordinary and the special aspects of dreaming in their description of it as "a *natural* experience! It's *not* unnatural! Don't seek for unnatural or supernatural! It is the natural—it is nature—it is God's activity! His associations with man, His *desire* to make for man a way for an understanding!" (5754–3).

In order to see how dreams can be at the same time a natural activity and a godly one, let's take a look at what happens when we sleep. In sleep we lose consciousness of physical conditions around us. Awareness, which during our normal waking hours depends upon the operation of our five physical senses, becomes diffuse throughout the body. With the physical consciousness laid aside, other aspects of our being can become more noticeably active. This is because sensory input from the physical world is no longer monopolizing our attention, as it frequently does during waking life.

One part of ourselves most active in the dreaming process is referred to in the readings as the sixth sense. The sixth sense partakes of the intuitive forces and is an attribute of the soul. Being of the soul, it is not restricted to the limitations of the conscious mind and physical body. It has access both to our soul memories and to universal awareness, or to the subconscious and superconscious levels of mind. While we sleep, the sixth sense receives impressions from these two sources, and these impressions form the basis of our dreams.

The purpose of this process, as given in the reading quoted above, is to provide for us a God-given means of increasing our understanding. This underscores the nature of dreams as a source of information and guidance to us. As stated in another reading, "All visions and dreams are given for the benefit of the individual, would they but interpret them correctly..." (294–15). The material offered to us in dreams can relate to conditions in the physical body, our conscious mental processes, those of the subconscious, or projections from the spiritual forces to the subconscious; in other words, our dreams can inform us about any part of ourselves we might be concerned with.

In order to make use of this aid, we must become receptive to it. The challenge lies not in obtaining the guidance, for it is all available within ourselves. Rather, the difficult part seems to be in consciously recognizing the information we do have. This requires being attuned and attentive to that faculty of our own soul, the sixth sense. Attunement to the soul forces within can thus increase the amount of material that reaches our conscious level through dreams.

Attunement can enhance not only the quantity of the information we receive, but also the quality. A dream can either instruct us or mislead us, depending on what level of awareness it comes from and how we interpret and use it. Dreams can be based on impressions either from the omniscient and loving superconscious, or from the subconscious, which might contain misinformation. Attunement to the spirit of God within, along with a sincere motivation to make the best possible use of the best information available, can help us reach the highest parts of ourselves and receive the most valid material through our dreams.

Even in cases where the message of the dream is accurate, there is the possibility that what it is telling us will be misinterpreted by the conscious mind. In this connection, attunement to the intuitive and spiritual forces within—getting better acquainted with these parts of ourselves, so to speak—can make the conscious mind more able to discern the true meaning of our dreams. Finally, being attuned to our ideal can be very important in our evaluation of the material we receive and our interpretation of it. If we consistently focus our minds on the best we know, we will become more adept at determining which interpretations of our dream messages will help us live in accordance with God's will for us.

The Role of Dreams in Past-Life Study

In the dream process, the sixth sense brings us material from the subconscious and superconscious levels. The subconscious mind contains, among other things, our soul memories of past-life experiences, and superconscious awareness is omniscient, with access to the Akashic Record of all that has ever been done in time and space. Both these dream sources, then, have the potential to provide us with psychic information, including memories of our previous incarnations.

Because many of us don't have recognizable past-life dreams all that frequently, we may tend to think that it is a relatively rare event for the sixth sense actually to receive this type of material. But according to the Cayce readings, this isn't true. While we sleep, a major function of the sixth sense is to compare our day's activities with the ideals that have been established by our souls through many lifetimes, and our dreams are representations of these comparisons. Thus our sixth sense picks up some input from our past lives as a matter of nightly routine.

It's true that a depiction of an ideal from a previous incarnation might not be recognized as a past-life dream in the same way as a portrayal of an event from an earlier lifetime would be. But our reception of nightly messages from a part of us that has regular access to past-life knowledge demonstrates that our dreams have the potential to show us more of our earlier incarnations than is commonly realized, if we could only consciously remember and identify this material.

We mentioned earlier that attunement to the spirit within can help us get the most out of our dream life. The reverse is also true: understanding our dreams can aid attunement. In presenting comparisons between our current activities and established ideals, they provide us with important guidance as to our present application of these standards. This can help us see the importance of living according to the best we know and strengthen our determination to recognize and adhere to our ideal. And by giving us an indication of our former incarnations, our dreams can make us more aware of our continuing existence and spiritual identity and give us a clearer understanding of our relationship with God.

Dreaming is one of the safest and most natural ways in which we can receive reliable, relevant knowledge of our earlier lives. Far from being an extraordinary occurrence, in presenting past-life information to us and giving us guidance, dreams are fulfilling their normal function. The availability of this material is the natural result of the ability of the sixth sense to contact our personal soul memories and superconscious awareness.

Though some dreams may involve communication from an outside source at the subconscious level, the dreaming process is primarily an internal one. Unconscious aspects of you yourself select the material and present it to your conscious mind. This makes the dream relatively safe from outside distortion. And because dreams are largely a comparison of your ideal with your current behavior, you can be sure that whatever information and guidance you receive is relevant to the present. You choose the material that is most likely to be helpful in your present situation and relay it to yourself at the time when you are best able to understand and use it.

What conditions are most likely to evoke a past-life dream? One of the strongest possibilities is the need for such information in our present life. The purpose of dreams is to give us understanding, and when the needed understanding can be gained most readily with the help of past-life material, we have the greatest chance of receiving this type of guidance, provided we are open to it.

A second likely stimulus to dreams of a former lifetime is the occurrence of an event that echoes something we have experienced in a prior incarnation. Meeting a person we have known in a previous experience, being in a situation similar to one from our remote past, and finding ourselves in a place we had lived in before are examples of the types of happenings that can call up our distant soul memories. The process is similar to the familiar one of having an experience that causes a recollection of an earlier event in the current lifetime that hadn't been thought of consciously for a long period of time. Evidently the soul's memories of our previous incarnations can be activated in the same way. Note that a past-life dream that is brought on in this way is highly likely to be relevant and useful in the current situation. Our memory of the earlier, similar condition, how we responded to it, and what the results were can guide us in choosing the best reaction in the present.

Recognizing past-life material in our dreams when it does occur can be a bit difficult. For some people, there may be times when an entire past-life drama is portrayed in a dream. But usually information about our previous incarnations will not be so obvious, and a few hints about what to look for might be helpful.

Usually the dreamer will be able to identify himself as a specific character in any dream. If this character is different from the dreamer's current identity in terms of such characteristics as race, nationality, or sex, it's an indication that the dream might relate to another lifetime.

Sometimes an entire dream can be set in a different time or place, and this can be one of the more noticeable clues as to past-life content. More often, however, the indication will be just a single element of the setting, such as architecture, costumes, or even a contemporary object that the dreamer associates with another location or period. Details like these can easily be overlooked, but with a bit of practice and self-training at being alert to them, we can greatly improve our ability to pick them out.

One possible indication that a dream concerns an earlier incarnation is the dreamer's intuitive feeling that this is the case. When this occurs, it would be a good idea to look at the content of the dream with special care, to see if there are any other elements that would support this conclusion.

Within the larger context of dream study and soul growth, it would be well to consider past-life material as a tool, rather than an end in itself. The main goal in working with any dream is to grow in self-understanding and the ability to live our present lives as well as we can. Knowledge of our earlier lifetimes can often contribute greatly to the self-understanding and guidance a dream makes available to us, and we should make every effort to recognize and use such information when it is present. Still, the primary question to be asked is, How can this dream help me to make the most of my opportunities now? Answering this question and applying our answer constructively will ensure that the central purpose of any dream is fulfilled.

The Importance of a Dream Journal

Now let's look at some specific measures that can enhance the quantity and quality of information we receive through our dreams and help us use this information to best advantage in our daily lives. The hints given below certainly do not constitute a complete listing of everything that might be done to help us work with our dreams effectively. But following these suggestions will get you started in the right direction to derive the most value from your dreams.

In the following sections, we'll be focusing on remembering our dreams, recording them, interpreting them, and using the messages they bring us. Keeping a journal in which to record your dreams is a vital part of each of these four aspects of dream work. Your dream journal should be convenient, so that you can make your entries easily, and kept in a specific place, so that you can retrieve and refer to your previous records readily. For most people, a separate notebook or a section of one reserved for just this purpose serves quite well.

There are several ways in which a journal will prove useful in your dream work. To start with, just having a journal is likely to increase the flow of dreams you remember, for by making the effort to obtain one you demonstrate to your unconscious self that you're seriously interested in hearing what it has to say.

The journal can also help you with needed self-discipline as you start this project. If when you wake up you merely think about your dreams, you may find yourself glossing over important details or putting your dream work off "until later." If, on the other hand, you provide the means and the time to record your dreams upon awakening, your efforts in this area are likely to be much more complete.

Recording your dreams can be a great help in cases where the meaning they are intended to convey is not immediately apparent. It would be quite difficult to arrive at a valid interpretation of such dreams later on if one were relying entirely upon memory. But if the dream has been written in a journal, it will be much easier to return to it, reread it, and, after a period of logical and intuitive reflection on it, arrive at a conclusion as to the message it had presented.

In many cases we will receive a series of dreams on the same general subject, either during successive dream periods in the same night or spread out over a number of nights. In such instances having a record of our dreams can be invaluable, for it allows us to compare an earlier dream

about a given area of life with a later one, and each dream
will help us gain some insight into the meaning of the other.

The dream journal is likely to prove particularly useful in
conjunction with past-life study. This is because, as was
mentioned earlier, for most people it is comparatively rare
to receive a single dream that gives a comprehensive picture
of an earlier incarnation. It's much more common to receive
this information a little bit at a time, with various details of
the prior experience being scattered among several dreams
spanning a period of weeks, months, or years. To have any
hope of fitting these pieces together, it's necessary for us to
have a record of them that we can rely on to be accurate.

Enhancing Dream Recall

Let's suppose, now, that you've determined to start working with your dreams and you've obtained a suitable notebook to serve as your journal. What can you do, first of all,
to help you receive useful information in your dreams and
enable you to remember the material you do receive?

1. Maintain a seeking and open attitude. As sincerely and
fully as possible, adopt a willingness to be shown whatever
your subconscious and superconscious have to offer you.
You can't expect these deeper parts of yourself to provide
you with guidance unless you're prepared to follow it.

2. Make a habit of seeking attunement in meditation.
Through this practice you will become more able to recognize the voice of the spirit, and this skill will make you
more aware of its promptings in your dreams and waking
life as well.

3. Before going to sleep, give yourself the suggestion
that you will remember your dreams. Don't try to preprogram
their content here; just affirm to yourself that you will be
able to recall what you've dreamed when you awaken.

4. Keep your journal and pen beside your bed. This will
do two things. It will impress upon your unconscious mind
that you are serious about your effort to work with your

dreams, and it will make it as easy as possible for you to record them in the morning.

5. After you awaken, stay physically still for a few moments while you mentally review the details of your dreams. One of the biggest obstacles to dream recall is physical stimulation. If you move around before fixing the dream firmly in your mind, you will be giving your brain increased input from your senses, and this can crowd your dream impressions out of your awareness.

6. Record the dream immediately. Here again, the idea is to get the dream written down as accurately as possible before your consciousness is distracted by the physical conditions and events around you.

7. If you don't have time to write your dream down when you awaken, tape-record it. You can transcribe the dream into your journal later. If you find yourself using this method very often, it would be a good idea to keep the tape recorder beside your bed.

8. Be consistent in your dream work. This is another way of letting your entire self know that you're committed to this endeavor.

9. Use whatever guidance you receive through your dreams in your daily life. As you use the understanding you have, more will become available to you: "In the application of truths known greater truths may come to the knowledge . . ." (97–2).

Recording Your Dreams

Once you've received a dream that you can remember upon awakening, your first step in working with it is to record it in your journal. Below are some suggestions that will help you make journal entries that are as useful as possible to you. After a time you may discover that some slight variation from these recommendations works best for you. If such is the case, feel free to change the format of your entries in any way that will better suit your individual needs. These ideas are meant to be taken as helpful hints, not ironclad rules.

1. Start by noting the setting of your dream, describing the time and place in which the action occurs.

2. Summarize the story as a whole. Record the main sequence of events, identify and describe the major characters, and state who is doing what.

3. Make note of any individual symbols that stand out.

4. Describe any emotions you feel in the dream. Include a statement of the type and intensity of the feelings and any condition, event, or character in the dream that seemed to bring these emotions out most powerfully in you. This is an important part of your journal entry, for the feelings evoked by any particular symbol or occurrence in a dream can greatly modify its meaning to you.

5. Date each journal entry. If you should happen to receive a series of dreams related to a single condition in your life, knowing the date of each dream can help you understand how the situation and your perception of it evolved, and it can help you gauge your progress in dealing with the condition as a whole.

A second reason for dating the entries in your journal is that at times our dreams will preview events coming up in our daily lives. In fact, the Cayce readings tell us, "Any condition ever becoming reality is first dreamed" (136–7). If you should experience such a dream, the dated journal entry will help you verify its precognitive nature, which in turn can lead you to understand more fully your own psychic ability.

6. Make note of any special problems or conditions going on in your waking life at the time of the dream. One of the most powerful factors determining the content of a dream is relevance to the dreamer's current situation. Considering your dream in relation to your major concerns at the time you have it can in some instances show you at a glance the area of your life the dream as a whole relates to, and this makes it much easier to discern the meanings of its individual elements.

7. As you go through the steps in interpreting your dream given below, record any insights you gather as to the dream's meaning.

8. You might also want to keep a record of the guidance you feel your dream was offering you, what you actually did about it, and the results of your action.

Interpreting Your Dreams

This brings us to the step in dream work that many people find most intimidating—interpreting the dream. "I don't know anything about psychology," such a person might say. "How can I expect to figure out what this dream means?" What this individual is overlooking is that, though he might be lacking academic credentials regarding the study of the mind, he is the world's greatest expert on the one subject that matters most—himself. Our dreams are messages from ourselves to ourselves about ourselves. The Cayce readings consistently take the view that the person best qualified to interpret any dream is the dreamer, for he is the one most knowledgeable about his own life. Self-confidence is not only an extremely helpful attitude, but also an entirely appropriate one to have as we go about unlocking the meanings of our own dreams.

The attitudes of openness and objectivity are also important in dream interpretation. We must be sincerely open to whatever guidance our dreams may contain if we hope to understand their true meaning. And we must be objective, not looking for just what we want to see; we have to be willing to recognize what the deeper parts of ourselves have determined we need to know, even though these messages may at times be not entirely to the liking of the conscious mind.

Once our attitudes are set, the first step in interpreting any dream is to discover its general meaning. To do this, read through the section of your journal entry summarizing the dream as a whole and try to identify the area of your life the dream relates to. With some dreams this may be relatively easy, for it may be spelled out explicitly in the dream content.

In other instances it could be harder. You may have to come up with a number of alternative phases of your life the dream could be about. Think about each of these possibilities for a moment, and then turn it over to your intuitive self. Still your mind, focus on one of the areas the dream might concern, and listen for a reaction from within yourself as to whether this is truly the subject of the dream. Consider each of the alternatives in this way. Your gut feeling here is likely to be more accurate than decisions based on logic would be. With a bit of practice, you will become more and more sensitive to your inner promptings regarding your dreams, more and more able to identify their major topics correctly.

After you've decided which area of life the dream is about, consider the feelings the dream brought out in you. This can help you recognize the general thrust of the dream's message—for example, whether it's meant to admonish you to change a destructive pattern of thought or action, to encourage you to persist with a positive one, or to warn you about an approaching difficulty. Seeing the basic purpose of a dream will be of aid to you later, as you are deciding how you should respond to it.

Once you've determined the dream's general area of concern and its purpose, the next step is to look at the specific symbols that seemed important in the dream. You'll find that having related the dream to a certain area of your life will make it easier for you to pin the individual symbols down, because their meanings will also pertain to the given topic. To discover what the symbols represent, consider how the images relate to each other within the dream, and pay special attention to elements in the portion of your waking life that the dream as a whole deals with. What we're after here is a correlation between the dream and your daily life, so any waking information you have in the relevant area can be used to help you arrive at the meanings of the dream's parts.

One thing to keep in mind here is that these are *your* symbols. They are intended to carry a message to you. What the dream images might signify to someone else is unimportant; what they represent to you is everything. Don't be too concerned about checking someone else's "dream dictionary" to find a standard meaning for a given symbol. Check yourself to discover its personal meaning for you, using both logical analysis of the dream's subject matter and sensitivity to your own intuitive reactions.

One more hint for deciphering dream symbols might be helpful. Just as dreams are sometimes repeated from night to night, symbols sometimes appear and reappear in a series of dreams. If you find that a certain image is present in a number of dreams, there is a chance—not a certainty—that it has the same significance in each dream. If you think you know what it represents in one dream, see if the same meaning fits in the other ones as well.

There are several things you can do if you have problems understanding the message of a dream. One of these is to pray. The dream, remember, was provided through your sixth sense, an attribute of your soul. Through prayer we express the desire for the forces of the soul and the spirit of God to become more active in our lives. By doing so we stimulate the soul's natural impulse to communicate with us, while at the same time increasing our sensitivity to the material it gives us. This may lead to our receiving a restatement of the message of the dream, either in meditation, through waking intuition, or through another dream, one that we can understand more easily.

It can also help us grasp the meaning of a difficult dream to go back and read our journal entries of the other dreams we received at about the same time. Because messages are sometimes repeated from one dream to another over a certain period, reviewing all our dreams from that time can make us aware of any dominant themes present throughout that period. This will give us a chance to recognize any dreams related to the one we're having trouble with, and we can then use our understanding of the related dreams to help us discover the meaning of the one we've had difficulty figuring out.

Finally, if nothing else works, you might try simply leaving a certain dream alone for a while. Let your subconscious turn it over for a few days, then return to it. You might find that your perspective on the dream will have changed enough to allow you to grasp its meaning when you look at it afresh. Or maybe in the intervening time you will have received a second, more understandable, dream on the same subject that will enable you to gain an insight into what the first one was trying to tell you.

Applying Your Dreams

There is a tendency among some people who are interested in their dreams to feel that once a dream has been interpreted their task is done. This outlook does not encourage us to make the most constructive use of our dreams. Whatever the message of a specific dream may be, it was given to us for a reason. In some way, it is meant to add to the quality of our waking lives. Remembering, recording, and interpreting our dreams won't make much difference in our lives unless we apply the understanding we receive through them.

In deciding how to apply the material presented in a dream, focus first on the area of life the dream relates to. Determine, if you can, the alternative actions in your waking life that the various events in the dream suggest. Consider all the different alternatives that are open to you in the relevant area of your life; try to correlate each with the content of the dream, and see what the dream has to tell you about the likely outcome of each one. Pay close attention to any feelings that were evoked by the dream, for these can tell you whether a certain response to the situation is to be desired or avoided.

When you have decided upon a course of action based on your interpretation of the dream, check it over logically to see if it is consistent with everything you consciously know about the situation in your waking life. Next, evaluate this response in terms of your ideal. Will acting in this way truly manifest the spiritual standard you wish to have as the guiding motivation in your life? You may wish to use meditation for attunement to your ideal to help you reach the right conclusion here. If the action you had originally considered taking doesn't measure up, go back and consider the other alternatives suggested by your dream, to see if any of them is likely to yield a more positive result.

Finally, do something about the guidance you've received. Even if your interpretation of the dream is slightly off, you will not go far wrong as long as your actions are in accord with your ideal, the best that you know. And we have the assurance that as we act on the best conception we have, greater understanding will come our way.

Example

The entire process—remembering and recording the dream, interpreting it, and doing something about it— might at this point seem to be an exceedingly long and involved one. Actually, in many cases you might well be able to record and arrive at the meaning of a dream in less time than it took you to read this chapter.

To give you a better idea of what a dream-journal entry might consist of, let's look at how a very short, simple dream might be recorded, interpreted, and used. This again is a hypothetical example. Bear in mind that our imaginary dreamer's interpretation might not match what you or anyone else would make of the dream, but it's what the dream means to the person who has it that counts.

(Date):
Setting: In my car, on the road, at dusk.
Action: I'm driving down the road, alone. It's getting dark outside. I notice that one of my headlights is getting quite dim.
Symbols: Car, headlight.

Feelings: Vague uneasiness, foreboding; not a strong fear,
    but I feel that if I don't do something about the
    headlight something serious might happen.

Waking conditions: Concerned that I'm running behind sched-
    ule on my project at work; feeling a bit run-down
    physically.

(The rest of the entry need not be completed immediately
upon awakening. But it would be a good idea to do it while
the dream is still reasonably fresh in mind.)

Interpretation:

General area: Did a mini-meditation to see if the dream
    concerned the job—didn't seem to click; strongest
    feeling is that it's about my health; suppose it could
    actually be about the car.

Feeling: With the foreboding, maybe there's something wrong
    with either my health or the car I'd better check out
    before something more serious develops.

Symbols: If about health: car—body; headlight—eye. If
    about car: self-evident.

Possible application: Get eyes examined; check headlights.

Response: Checked headlights—seem to be okay; made
    appointment with eye doctor for tomorrow.

The important thing to notice in the above example is that
the dreamer did something about the message he received.
In a sense, recalling the dream, writing it in the journal, and
figuring out its meaning are all intermediate steps, leading
up to the point where we actively respond to the information
we have received. Regardless of their specific content, our
dreams are given for our benefit, to provide us with direction. What we do about the guidance they present determines how completely they fulfill their purpose.

CHAPTER 6
Meditation

Purpose of Meditation

There are a number of systems of meditation in existence, each with its own central purpose. The techniques used in the different systems vary, depending upon the goal each school of thought seeks to achieve by meditating. To some, meditation is a means of withdrawal from the concerns of physical life. The adherents of these points of view typically adopt meditation practices aimed at suspending the functioning of the conscious mind. For others, meditation is a way of developing certain abilities, frequently psychic or occult in nature. This leads them to focus on those capabilities in meditation, perhaps using visualization in an effort to stimulate the development of the desired powers.

The purpose of meditation as presented in the Edgar Cayce readings is simply to enable us to draw closer to God. "You have the meditation because you desire to be attuned with Creative Forces. You don't have the meditation . . . because you want to feel better, but to attune self to the infinite!" (1861–18). The goal here is not to escape from the body and conscious mind, but to attune them to their spiritual source. This form of meditation is not musing, or daydreaming, or blanking the mind. It involves stilling the mind and focusing it on the spirit of God within. The energy of the spirit can then flow through the mind and the body and express itself in every aspect of our lives.

Meditation of this sort is not undertaken to get any specific benefits or special abilities, psychic or otherwise.

It's not a matter of getting, but of becoming. The quest is to be closer to God and to become a better expression of His love. As we approach this goal, we become better channels for the divine energy of spirit. We grow more conscious of the activity of the spirit in our lives, more aware of our own souls. As this happens, our psychic abilities will develop naturally, for psychic is of the soul.

We can see here why meditation plays such an important part in increasing our recall of previous incarnations. It heightens our awareness of the messages we receive from the spirit within. According to the perspective of the Cayce readings, we do not meditate for past-life recall in itself, or for any other manifestation of psychic powers; and we do not try to preprogram our meditation sessions to produce this type of information. But as we make a consistent practice of meditation, our memories of our earlier lifetimes will increase naturally as part of the larger process of soul growth. As we approach the source of divine wisdom within, we will receive from it whatever information we need, whenever we need it and are able to use it.

The great importance of meditation in our spiritual quest derives from our history as souls. We were created as spiritual beings, each made in the image of God and bearing His imprint. In the beginning we had perfect superconscious awareness of the presence of our Creator. But we used our free will to rebel against God, and thus we separated ourselves from Him. We built flaws into what were to become our subconscious and conscious minds and into the physical bodies in which our souls would eventually incarnate.

But the imprint of God within us, being divine, was not destroyed. At the deepest level of mind, our superconscious awareness of our oneness with God is still retained. It's just that with all the unloving patterns of thought we've built into our subconscious and conscious minds, we don't often pay attention to it anymore. To become all that we as children of God can be, we must regain our awareness of the Creator.

Meditation helps us do this by quieting the body, the conscious mind, and the subconscious mind so that we can listen to the voice of God within. Its effectiveness is based on the certainty that He in fact abides within us, and that the divine spirit, which always seeks to express itself, will manifest through our lives if we let it.

Definition of Meditation

Meditation, as described in the Edgar Cayce readings, involves communication with God. Many people consider communication with God to be synonymous with prayer, and to them the distinction between meditation and prayer can be unclear. But though these two activities are related, they are definitely different from each other. To see where this difference lies, let's examine the definitions of prayer and meditation given in a few passages from the Cayce readings.

"Prayer, in short, is appealing to the divine within self, the divine from without self, and meditation is keeping still in body, in mind, in heart, listening, listening to the voice of thy Maker" (5368–1).

"For thy prayer is as a supplication or a plea to thy superior; yet thy meditation is that thou art meeting on *common* ground!" (281–28).

"Prayer is the concerted effort of the physical consciousness to become attuned to the consciousness of the Creator... *Meditation* is *emptying* self of all that hinders the creative forces from rising along the natural channels of the physical man to be disseminated through those centers and sources that create the activities of the physical, the mental, the spiritual man..." (281–13).

Perhaps the central difference between prayer and meditation is that in prayer we are active, in meditation we are still. In prayer we actively seek God's help and guidance; we ask a question of God, so to speak. In meditation we sit in silence and wait for His answer. Meditation is based upon the knowledge that the body is the temple of God, and there is where He will meet us, "on *common* ground!" (281–28).

The third quotation above emphasizes this difference

between the activity of prayer and the stillness of meditation. Prayer is a "concerted effort" (281-13) to bring ourselves into attunement with God, so that His spirit can become active in our lives. In meditation, the "*emptying self of all that hinders*" (281-13) the rise of the creative force, we get the ungodly parts of ourselves out of the way so that the divine activity we have sought in prayer can take place.

Both prayer and meditation are means of attunement to the voice of God. In prayer we work with self to achieve this alignment, seeking to make of the physical consciousness an instrument more attuned to the Creator, and therefore more able to communicate with Him, both within ourselves and without. Meditation is not so much a process of *self*-transformation. In it we lay aside the separated parts of ourselves and focus on the voice of God within, allowing His spiritual energy to flow through us and work the transformation in us.

Obviously, prayer and meditation are closely related to each other. They are two complementary phases of a total process of attunement to God and communication with Him. Thus, to be most effective, each should be used with the other. A "meditation" session, in other words, should combine both prayer and meditation. Prayer in which we dedicate ourselves and invoke the presence of God is the best means to lead us into meditation. In this way we invite God into our consciousness. Then in meditation we wait in silence to receive Him and hear His words. When we are done meditating, it's a good idea to close with prayer as a way of using the energy that has been raised. The most sensible and powerful sequence for our session of communication with the Creator is prayer, followed by meditation, and more prayer.

The Forces Raised in Meditation

Looking once again at the elements of our being might help us gain a clearer understanding of how the energy raised in meditation affects us. We speak of man as having three basic aspects: spirit, mind, and body. But we must bear in mind that these three are not separate from one another. Each interacts with and influences the other two. The relationship among them is given in the formula: spirit is the life, mind is the builder, and the physical is the result. In meditation we seek to attune our physical and mental attributes to the spirit of God within.

The body contains within it focal points of contact with mind and spirit. The nervous system is the physical center of connection between the body and mind. The body's points of contact with spirit are focused in specific centers related to the endocrine glands. There are seven of these centers. Starting with the one situated lowest in the body, they are associated with: the gonads, the cells of Leydig, the adrenals, the thymus, the thyroid, the pineal gland, and the pituitary gland. The forces of meditation are raised through these centers, from which they are disseminated throughout the body.

The spirit is the spark of God within us that gives us life. It is always present, seeking to express its relationship with the Creator. In meditation we still the body and mind and focus on the spirit, enabling us to become more aware of the spiritual forces within. This allows the energy of spirit, working through the focusing of mind, to be expressed in the physical.

Our ability to allow this spiritual force to flow through us is the natural result of our origin as co-creators with God. Like the spirit of God, whose expression in materiality resulted in the formation of the physical universe, our individual souls have creative power that can be manifested physically. In meditation there is a flow of this same creative energy from the spirit to the body in ways that are patterned by the mind.

This results in an actual physical effect, which can be felt by the meditator as a vibration of the whole body, as vibrations running up and down the spine, or as sensations of lightness or slight dizziness. These feelings indicate that creation is taking place within the body. The Cayce readings tell us that meditation "properly done must make one *stronger* mentally, physically..." (281–13). This increase in physical energy can be manifested as healing, which can either affect the body of the meditator himself or be disseminated to others.

Because of the reality of the forces raised in meditation, proper motivation is crucial. We might be tempted to think that since this energy is from the spirit, its effect in the physical would have to be good. But this is not the case. Ultimately, all energy comes from God. Nevertheless, if our purposes are selfish, destructive effects can result from our use of the energy we receive through our food, that of the atom, or any of the other sources of power in the physical universe. Similarly, the energy raised in meditation, even though it is of the spirit, can have negative effects in the physical if our motivation in using it is unloving.

Meditation changes us. How depends upon mind, the builder, which determines the way in which spiritual energy manifests in the physical. Our motivation and what we select as the focus for our minds in meditation set the pattern that we raise. If this pattern and the purpose for which we raise it are in accord with our superconscious awareness of God, help and value will be transmitted to our consciousness. If our pattern and purpose are out of harmony with the spirit of God, confusion and turmoil will be. In order to ensure that the forces raised in meditation will be manifested constructively rather than destructively, we must select a motivation and a focus for meditation that are founded in our spiritual ideal, and we must avail ourselves of the protection that is found in the Christ.

Entered into in this way, meditation becomes for us a source of spiritual development. Our application of the energy raised will be loving, constructive, and practical. Proper meditation helps each aspect of our being fulfill its function in God's plan for us: Spirit becomes more active in our lives; mind becomes more effective at channeling spiritual energy constructively; and the body, the physical result, becomes a better instrument for expressing divine love.

Preparation for Meditation

There are many things we can do in preparation for meditation to help ensure that the experience will be beneficial to our body, mind, and soul. In this section we will be considering the ongoing practices that can work over a period of time to make us more willing to accept the divine help and guidance that meditation makes available to us and more able to apply it in our lives. The specific techniques that we can use to lead us into the meditation session itself will be taken up in the next part of this chapter.

To a certain extent, our preparation for meditation is a matter of individual choice. Each person makes attunement according to his own development. When it comes to specific exercises of mind and body, each of us should do what he requires of and what works best for himself. Nevertheless, some general guidelines do apply. Certain spiritual purposes, mental attitudes, and physical conditions are conducive to communing with God and expressing His love in our lives. Others are not.

On the physical level, preparing for meditation involves adopting general practices of good health. Attention should be paid to such matters as diet, exercise, rest, and moderation of personal physical habits. Through these means we can purify the body, making it a better instrument to manifest our ideal and to use the forces raised in meditation constructively.

At least as important is purification of the mind. If we're truly seeking to attune to the voice of God within, we should know what it is we recognize as God, so that we can choose habits of mind that are consistent with our conception of Divinity. First of all, we must believe that God is and that He communicates with us. The mental attitudes we adopt should reflect what the Cayce readings refer to as the fruits of the spirit—such qualities as love, mercy, humbleness, kindness, and gentleness. We should put away from us hatred, greed, malice, and selfishness. Above all, we must maintain an interest in the welfare of our brother, for he too is of God; to be out of harmony with our brother is to be out of harmony with our Maker.

On the spiritual level, our motivation in entering meditation is a prime factor in determining what we will derive from it. The promise "Seek, and ye shall find" can work either to our benefit or to our detriment, since what we are likely to find depends on exactly what we are seeking. To find God, we must sincerely want to make our will one with His. To hear His truth, we must be willing to be shown what is truly the best and to follow the path we are shown. Our best motivation for entering meditation is the desire to grow closer to God and to consecrate ourselves to His will.

Along with the proper motivation, recognizing our spiritual ideal and focusing on it during meditation can help us contact our superconscious awareness of God within. Remember, not everything outside the realm of the physical and the conscious mind is of God. By using some aspect of our ideal as our focus in meditation, we can make sure that we are attuning ourselves to our best understanding of the divine spirit. This will make it more likely that what we meet will be true and helpful. In selecting our meditation focus with care, we are not trying to preprogram the experience we have or the information we receive; we are simply doing what we can to ensure that this experience proceeds from the best source.

Meditation Techniques

Now let's look at some specific techniques for preparing for the meditation session, entering the silence, and using the energy that is raised. Of the preliminary steps listed below, setting your ideal, having a sincere desire to seek God, and adopting a loving attitude toward others are necessary in order to attune yourself to the spirit of God within. The other measures can be considered optional, and few people would use all of them. Don't feel you can't meditate just because there may be some things among the preparatory steps you are unable to do or feel uncomfortable doing. Still, it would be a good idea to try each of these techniques out for a period of time, so that you'll be able to evaluate sincerely which of them work for you.

Preliminary Steps

1. Set your ideal. This is a formulation of the highest motivating spirit, mental attitudes and patterns of thought, and physical activities you can conceive of. It will help you reach and build the best parts of yourself.

Once you have set your ideal, for use in meditation compose a brief statement of your spiritual ideal or some aspect of it that you're particularly interested in seeking attunement to. Such a statement, called an affirmation, is to be used as the focus toward which you will direct your mind in meditation. The affirmation you choose to use should be suited to you; it should be an expression of some aspect of your ideal that you want to magnify, in words that are meaningful and moving to you.

To give you an idea of the type of statement that might be used as an affirmation, here are some samples based on material from the Edgar Cayce readings. Each of these is a paraphrase of an affirmation Cayce suggested for use in meditation.

"May Your will rather than mine, O Lord, be done in me and through me. Let me always be a channel of blessings to those that I contact in every way. Let everything I do be in accord with what You would have me do. And whenever You call on me, may my answer be 'Here I am; send me, use me' " (based on 262–3).

"How excellent is Your name in the earth, O Lord! If I would have fellowship with You, I must show brotherly love to my fellow man. Though I may come in humbleness, if I have anything against my brother, my prayer and my meditation do not rise to You. Help my efforts in my approach to You" (based on 262–21).

"Our Father, through the love that You have manifested in the world through Your Son, the Christ, make us more aware that God is love" (based on 262–43).

2. Set a regular time and place for meditation. Choose a place that will be free of distractions and a time that fits your daily schedule. Consistency in your practice of meditation is the key.

3. Prepare the external setting for meditation. Some people feel that cleaning the room in which they will be meditating gives them a heightened sense of dedication and the specialness of this practice. Others have found that certain external influences can stimulate and enhance their attunement. Among the influences mentioned most often in this regard are: incense or other fragrances, flowers, music, certain types of lighting, and certain stones or crystals worn about the body. If you choose to try the latter, you should be aware that various minerals affect different people differently, and that their effects also depend upon where on the body they are worn. A mineral that is helpful for one person might be ineffective or even detrimental to someone else.

4. Cleanse the body with water.

5. Assume a comfortable position. Cayce recommended either sitting in a chair with the feet on the floor or lying on the back. In any case, the spine should be straight and the clothing should not be binding. If you choose to meditate while lying down, the hands should be clasped over the solar-plexus area.

6. Many people find a simple head-and-neck exercise described in the readings to be helpful. In the most common form, each of the following steps is repeated three times before going on to the next step; the head should be returned to an upright position after each movement of steps *a* through *d*.

a) Drop the head forward. b) Let the head fall to the rear. c) Drop it to the right shoulder. d) Lower it to the left. e) Drop the head forward and slowly rotate it in a complete circle, starting to the right. f) Rotate it in a complete circle to the left. Return the head to an upright position.

7. Breathing exercises are highly recommended, and

those suggested in the Cayce material are also quite simple. For one of them, breathe in through the right nostril and out through the mouth. Do this three times. Then breathe in through the left nostril and out through the right nostril, also three times.

8. Some people find chanting to be a powerful aid to attunement. Several suitable chants are described in the readings. In one of them, the recommended combination of sounds is "Ar-ar-r-r-e-e-e-o-o-o-m-m-m." This should be repeated several times, in such a way that its vibrations are felt to be raised in and through the body.

9. Reading the Bible or other inspirational material can help you get into the right frame of mind for meditation.

10. To the best of your ability, adopt the mental attitudes appropriate for seeking contact with God. That is, make an effort to attune your mind to your spiritual source. Prayer is a very effective means for accomplishing this. Different types of prayer can help you in each phase of this mental attunement.

> a. Put away hatred, greed, malice, and selfishness. A prayer of forgiveness, for others and for yourself, would be most fitting here.
> b. Take on love, mercy, humility. Consecrating yourself in prayer to the will of God can help you attune your mind to the Creator more completely, and thus draw closer to Him.
> c. Take on a sincere desire to communicate with your God, and believe that He will in fact meet you within the temple of your body. Saying a prayer of invocation, inviting His presence into your life, will help prepare your consciousness to receive Him.
> d. In prayer, throw about yourself the protection of the Christ, that your communion may truly be with God.

11. For many individuals, saying the Lord's Prayer is the most deeply moving final step in preparing to enter the silence. Many use it as the affirmation on which they focus their mind during the meditation itself.

Entering the Silence

In your mind, repeat your chosen affirmation several times in order to evoke a sense of the spirit you wish to raise. The repetitions here are meant not to cause you to lose consciousness, but to help you focus it. The words of the affirmation in themselves are not important; the meaning they express is. Once your mind is focused on this essential meaning, the words will have served their purpose and you can stop your mental recitation of the affirmation. In silence, hold your mind on the quality it expresses. Do not try to analyze it logically. Just focus your awareness on this spiritual essence, which you have chosen to raise and magnify in yourself through your meditation.

As you enter the silence, let yourself feel a sense of oneness with the creative force of divine love. Still holding to the essential quality of your affirmation, listen for the still, small voice within. Some people actually hear a voice in their meditation, while others experience through meditation a sense of rightness, in which they can recognize that they have indeed communed with their God.

When you notice that your mind is wandering from the quality you have been trying to hold, use the words of the affirmation once again to bring it back. Be patient with yourself in this, not harsh. Meditation must be learned. You will find that with practice your ability to remain focused on the essence of your affirmation will increase. Meditation gives us a good opportunity to learn the virtue of active patience described in the Cayce readings, for to get very far with it we must be gently persistent with ourselves; we must keep trying.

Using the Energy

As we meditate, an actual energy is being raised; there is "actual *creation* taking place within the inner self!" (281–13). In meditation, the creative force rises from the spiritual center associated with the cells of Leydig to that of the pineal, located at the base of the brain. From there it moves to the pituitary center, which can be felt as the "third eye," just above the bridge of the nose. The force can then be disseminated from the pituitary to the other centers throughout the body. Through the creative power of mind, it can also be sent out to other people.

Since in meditation we are seeking attunement with God, who is love, this creative energy should be used lovingly. We know that meditation done properly will bring helpful effects to our own minds and bodies. Before ending our meditation session we should share these benefits with others. In doing so we ensure that the physical result of the spiritual energy we have raised is a manifestation of love. There are several ways in which this sharing can be done.

One of these is through loving prayer. There is power in prayer, power that can be used to help others. Prayers of healing and of protection allow us to use the spiritual energy of meditation in ways that will be helpful to those around us.

As we do so, however, we should make sure that in our prayers we do not seek to infringe upon the other person's free will. Unless a person has expressly asked for our prayers for help in a certain area of his life, it would be inappropriate for us to try to use the power of meditation and prayer to bring about a specific transformation in the person's actions or condition. That is, this energy should not be used in an attempt to make someone else's life conform to what we think it should be. Unless we have received a specific request, it is better in our prayers simply to surround the other person with love, and to rely on the wisdom and power of God to supply him with what he truly needs.

A second way of sharing the beneficial effects of our meditation is through loving thought toward others. On the one hand, this practice uses the creative force of meditation to build loving attitudes and habits of mind within ourselves. And on the other, since all minds are in contact with one another at the subconscious level, our thoughts of love can be communicated to the other person. Thus, perhaps without even being aware of it consciously, the individual may begin to feel more of the divine love in which he is constantly held, and may develop a greater understanding of the presence of God in his own life.

The spiritual energy raised in meditation can also be disseminated through loving physical actions. We've noted that proper meditation makes us stronger physically; in other words, it makes our bodies more effective instruments for expressing love in the material world. This we can do simply by helping others. If we are sincere in our purpose to meet God in our meditation, we will want to manifest the results of this contact in our daily lives. The power of this communion will not achieve its full potential to transform our entire being if we feel and use it only during the meditation session itself. To be most fruitful, this energy must be applied and given out in our day-to-day activities.

Effects of Meditation

Meditation has the power to transform every area of our lives. The energy that is raised as we sit in silence has a definite effect on our physical bodies. Over time, the practice of attuning our minds to the spirit of God within will give us a greater understanding of our true nature. And by allowing the spirit to become more active in our lives, we enable ourselves to become more aware of and more expressive of the spiritual dimension of our own being.

On the physical level, the energy raised in meditation can cause certain immediate sensations in the body. Different bodies react in different ways, and so different individuals may feel different physical effects. Some may feel none at all. It should be emphasized once again that the true purpose of meditation is to draw closer to God, not to experience various physical sensations. Nevertheless, these sensations do give evidence that in meditation something is happening. Among the effects that various people have noted are a vibratory or rocking motion in the body, a pulsation in the lower spine, vibrations moving up and down the spine, fullness in the head, slight dizziness, lightness, coolness on the head or forehead, sensations to the eyes, popping noises in the head, and a feeling of moving up and out of the body.

As has been mentioned, there are also more long-term physical effects of meditation. As the image of divine love is raised within us, divine power is also raised. The consistent practice of meditation makes the body more receptive to and able to use energy from the soul. This manifests as physical energy that can be used in daily living.

The energy raised in the body through meditation can be used in healing. Its benefits can be given out to others so that their physical condition can be improved. The readings tell us that this gives us the possibility of practicing healing via the laying on of hands, and that "*healing* of *every* kind and nature may be disseminated on the wings of thought . . ." (281–13).

One of the greatest mental benefits we may receive through meditation is the divine guidance it makes available to us. The readings repeatedly assure us that in the voice of God within us we have a source of all that we could possibly need to know: "It is not who will ascend into heaven to bring us a message—not who shall come from over the sea that we may hear and heed—for Lo, the answer to *all* thy problems is in thine own heart!" (262–121). If we listen for the still, small voice of God within, whatever information and direction we need will be forthcoming.

As we gain practice in listening, we'll experience a growth in our intuitive powers, the ability to hear and recognize His voice. A prerequisite of this development is that we be sincerely willing to follow whatever divine guidance we receive and use it in the service of God. With this commitment on our part, our contact with the source of all wisdom will enable us to make self-transforming decisions in every phase of our lives. Some meditators may experience this guidance as a feeling of rightness about a certain course of action; others may hear an actual voice in meditation. Either possibility is a manifestation of an awakening in self to communication from the spirit within.

It would be well here to inject a note of caution, that we not be overawed by the possibly spectacular form such a manifestation may take. The experience of hearing an actual voice in meditation might be overwhelming to some. But we should remember that not every manifestation from the nonphysical realm is of God. The voice that is heard might be relaying a message from the Creator, or it might be from some other power, not necessarily a reliable one. It is necessary that we enter the silence protected by the Christ and that in it we attune ourselves to our spiritual ideal. Doing so will enable us to receive our direction from the highest possible source. And when we feel we have received guidance in meditation, we should evaluate it in relation to the highest standard of our ideal, so that we won't be led astray.

Another beneficial effect meditation can bring us on the mental level is an increase in self-understanding. Attuning to the deeper parts of ourselves will help us get to know them better. When used in harmony with our ideal, meditation and constructive application will bring us experiential knowledge of our spiritual nature. Through it we can achieve recognition of our soul's purpose in life. In this way, we can come to realize our full potential and fulfill the purpose for which we were given life.

The knowledge of our soul that meditation gives us will be accompanied by development of our psychic ability, for psychic is of the soul. As we attune to the still, small voice of God within, we will become more aware of our relationship with Him, and the powers inherent in the divine imprint upon our souls will become more active in our lives. Once again, it's important to remember that it is closeness to God that we are seeking in meditation. We are not meditating for the purpose of developing our psychic abilities; they will develop naturally as we grow closer to God. In time, we will begin to notice them becoming more evident, not only during our meditation sessions, but through our dreams and in our waking life as well.

As part of this psychic awakening, our increased awareness of the soul will bring with it a greater knowledge of the soul's record. Thus meditation, when used in conjunction with self-inventory and dream study, can be a powerful stimulus of past-life recall. Note that we don't have to meditate with the express purpose of receiving knowledge of our former lifetimes; it will just come as the natural result of our growing closer to God, the source of all knowledge.

Spiritually, the effects of meditation can be most profound. With time, it can enable us to become aware of passing into the presence of God, becoming aware of our oneness with the Whole. Meditation thus gives us knowledge of the spirit of God within and a sense of our personal relationship with Him. This awareness of our union with the Father, and the ability to express it through our activities, can be seen as the main point not only of meditation, but of life itself.

In meditation, by attuning to our highest conception of life in harmony with divine love, we permit the power of our ideal to flow through us. As we leave meditation and express this in our daily activities, we allow God's spiritual aid, the gift of life, to become active in all that we do. In ways that are patterned by mind, the spiritual energy flowing through us becomes manifest in our physical lives, thus transforming us at every level.

With consistent application, we grow in our ability to use the spiritual gifts made available to us by the flow of this energy through us. We begin to awaken to our full potential as children of God, and our lives and selves take on a whole new quality. We may not be delivered from all the cares of the material world, but we will be able to meet these circumstances by drawing upon the source of spiritual power within. This will bring peace, joy, and true happiness into our experience. Our lives will become more productive, creative, fulfilling, and loving. Ultimately, our union with the Father will be fully realized, our nature as beings created in His image fully manifested. We will regain our original status as companions and co-creators with Him and become once again, totally, the expressions of divine love that we were intended to be.

PART III

How to Discover
Your Past Lives

Introduction

General Description

You are about to set out on an exciting adventure in self-discovery. Through the information, instructions, and exercises presented in the following pages, you'll be taken through a comprehensive course in remembering past lives. In fact, this program, based upon insight and examples found in the Edgar Cayce material on reincarnation, is among the most complete experiences in past-life recall offered anywhere.

Actually, the Edgar Cayce readings are filled with various ways to remember past lives. In the upcoming sessions, you'll see how memory of another life can come through spontaneous recall, and you'll discover the ways in which past-life clues can be identified in your dreams. You'll begin to recognize the influences and patterns in your daily activities that may have originated in other lifetimes. You will learn how meditation can be used to enhance recall. As you work with the questions and inventories, you'll begin to notice where your taste in clothing, furniture, and decorations is influenced by your previous lives. You'll also see how past-life involvement affects your job, your talents, and your personal relationships. And, as you begin to get in touch with your former experiences in the earth, you will

121

gain a greater understanding of the troublesome patterns and habitual emotional responses that are part of your life today.

This course provides a chance for you to use both the analytical and the subjective aspects of your mind. In some of its sessions you will be given instructions and information interspersed with periods for reflection and answering the questions in the various exercises. Other periods have been set aside for reveries—guided experiences in using your imagination—which will quicken your unconscious memories.

Many of the techniques and exercises that are part of this program have previously been tried by others seeking to develop their own recall of previous lives. At various places in the following pages you will find mention of these people and the past-life clues they have obtained by using this material. These references should serve to give you an idea of the sort of information that the exercises can make available to you, the kind of conclusions that can be drawn from this information, and the ways in which these insights can be used to improve the quality of your present life.

Course Overview

You might be interested now in taking a quick, preliminary look at the material that will be covered in each of the course's fourteen sessions.

Session 1—Awakening Memories:
In this session you'll learn how sounds, sights, and conditions around you can awaken unconscious memories of past lives.

Session 2—Wardrobe Fantasy:
In this session you will be introduced to reverie, a guided experience that will help you exercise your ability to imagine.

Session 3—Tracing the Laws of Reincarnation:
This segment will use case histories from the Edgar Cayce life readings to demonstrate how the laws of reincarnation work.

Session 4—You and Your Surroundings:

Here you'll explore your tastes in living quarters, furnishings, and decor to discover the past-life clues they hold.

Session 5—A Trip Around the World:

This segment will put you in touch with your personal impressions, biases, and feelings about different cultures of the world. The questions in this part of the course will be one of your major sources of past-life information.

Session 6—Hereditary and Environmental Influences:

Here we will be investigating how heredity and environment fit in with past-life influences. You will discover how "reading" your body and remembering your early childhood can help you gain information about your previous incarnations.

Session 7—Analyzing Your Emotional Reactions:

Brief instructions and a comprehensive inventory will help you see how your emotional reactions, both positive and negative, may be reflecting past-life experiences.

Session 8—Constructing Past-Life Theories from Present-Life Clues:

In this session we will examine how patterns of activity begun in previous incarnations can continue on into the present, and how present situations can be related to former experiences. You will have an opportunity to practice developing past-life theories based on current circumstances, matching your answers with actual case histories from the Edgar Cayce readings.

Session 9—Exploring Your Talents, Hobbies, and Interests:

This session will combine reveries and exercise questions to help you identify past lives as they are reflected in your talents and hobbies. It will also help you recognize and develop your hidden abilities.

Session 10—Discovering Past-Life Clues Through Dreams, Meditation, and Your Religious Feelings and Experiences:

Here you will receive guidance in looking for past-life material in your dreams, enhancing your recall through meditation, and examining your religious experiences and feelings for information about your previous lifetimes.

Session 11—Identifying Patterns in Your Life:

In this section you will be helped to discover the major patterns in your life and to learn how these patterns spring from past-life experiences.

Session 12—Past-Life Reverie:

This session uses guided reverie to bring unconscious past-life memories to the surface.

Session 13—Forming Your Own Past-Life Theories:

In this session you will be taken, step by step, through the process of putting together the information you've gathered throughout the course. The aim here is to help you identify the connections among the individual clues you've come up with thus far, and to give you a chance to formulate theories that will clarify the past-life origins of some of the influences you are feeling in your present life.

Session 14—Your Future Life:

Here you will receive, through reverie, a glimpse of the future life you are building today.

Suggestions for Using This Course Effectively

As with any program of instruction, the more you put into this course, the more you are likely to get out of it. You can give this material a quick, cursory reading, which will probably yield a smattering of clues about your previous incarnations and some inkling of how to discover these clues and use them in your present life. Or you can give it a more in-depth treatment, involving a thorough evaluation of the ideas it suggests and the questions it asks. If you take this approach, there will naturally be a greater chance that you will obtain the full potential value of the material. Following the recommendations below will help you to derive the most benefit from your search for self-knowledge.

Your experience in this endeavor will be most valuable if you follow the instructions as they are given in the text and complete the exercises in the order they are presented. Keep in mind that there is no rush to finish this book. It's important that you cover this course at a pace that is comfortable for you. The greatest benefit will come from taking time to think and reflect about each portion and allowing yourself to become gradually more aware of everyday influences that may be echoes of past lives.

In order to preserve any past-life clues that you may uncover and any insights you are able to obtain from them, it is advisable that you write down your answers to each exercise. This will be helpful to you in several ways. There is something about putting words on paper that makes most of us pause to think, to reflect. Writing your answers to the exercises will help ensure that you give each of the questions the thoughtful consideration needed to unlock its full value.

In addition, you will find that the early sessions of this course yield a surprising number of individual past-life clues. Many of these details will be necessary for the completion of later exercises. Even items of past-life information that seem insignificant when they are first noted can have great importance when related to other clues that may be brought out in subsequent exercises. To read through the text, answer the questions only in one's head, and then be able to remember all those answers when they are called for later on would be a task well beyond the great majority of us. For this reason, the accurate recording of your insights and responses is essential. And, to aid in easy retrieval of these clues and prevent their getting lost, it is strongly recommended that you keep your responses together in one special place—a notebook or a section of one used only for this purpose, for example.

If all this is starting to make the program seem like a heavy schoolroom assignment to you, try to loosen up a bit. Yes, this work is serious; but it should also be enjoyable. Your experience with this course will be most rewarding if you maintain an attitude of excited and open-minded anticipation, letting your natural interest in discovering your past and enriching your present be the driving motivation behind your efforts. If at any time you find yourself regarding your work on this project as a routine commitment, that's a pretty good indication that you should put it aside for a while. Let it simmer on the back burner of your subconscious for a few days, until you are able to return to it with a refreshed outlook and renewed interest.

The material in this program has been divided into sessions, each of which covers one area of past-life inquiry. This does not necessarily mean that each session, and only that session, is to be covered in a single reading period. Some of our chapters are quite short, and you may feel able to finish one and go on to the next without stopping for rest. Others are more involved, and you might discover that several sittings are necessary to complete them. Allow yourself to proceed at whatever rate you find to be most suitable. Keep in mind that this program is meant for *you*, and it should be used in a way that answers your needs, not someone else's. Be flexible in the number of time periods you devote to each session, the duration of each one, and the amount of time you take off between sessions.

Similarly, a certain amount of flexibility is also recommended as you work with each of the exercises in the course. Though you should consider each question carefully, do not feel obligated to make up a response if you come across an item you are unable to answer. And by all means, don't hesitate to make note of any insights you may have that seem significant or interesting to you, even if they are not specifically called for by the questions in the section on which you are working.

As the first few exercises begin to yield clues to your former incarnations, you may find yourself tempted to try to formulate theories to explain these items of information, constructing specific past-life scenarios to account for them. While you should certainly note any such ideas that strike you as being valid, try not to be overly concerned about putting the pieces together as you go. Time and instructions for creating theories about what your previous lifetimes might have been will be provided in the final sessions of the course.

Recording your dreams between sessions can be very helpful to you. Dreams are among the most useful vehicles we have for receiving messages and recovering memories from the unconscious, and the Edgar Cayce readings contain numerous references to their usefulness in tapping this source. It is suggested that you begin recording your dreams right away and continue to do so throughout your work with this course. Instructions on how to unlock your dreams so as to recognize and make use of any past-life information they may contain will be given in one of our later sessions. You may also want to refer back to Chapter 5 for a more thorough discussion of the nature and meaning of dreams and some helpful hints on keeping a dream journal.

If you proceed through this course slowly, you may be able to find some time to keep a record of insights that come to you in your waking life, as well. Among the situations that arise in our daily life are many that can be seen as having their origins in our remote past, and as you gain experience in working with recall of your former lifetimes you will become more adept at identifying these situations and meeting them constructively. Perhaps you have a mate or a close friend with whom you can talk over any ideas or theories you may have regarding your previous incarnations. Such discussions are another everyday activity that can greatly enhance our understanding of our past.

Past-life recall can also be increased through the regular practice of meditation. In meditation we direct our attention away from the normal processes of our conscious minds and attune to those aspects of ourselves that we are ordinarily not aware of. This activity renders our unconscious store of memories more accessible to us, thus making it more likely that we will experience and recognize influences from previous incarnations. If this attunement to the unconscious becomes habitual to us, we can expect the resulting past-life clues to become more evident not only during the meditation periods themselves, but in our dreams and our waking life as well. But this is not usually a short-term process; just a few sessions of meditation are unlikely to produce a noticeable increase in our recall of former lifetimes. For this reason, if you feel that making a regular practice of meditation would be helpful to you, now would be a good time to start. A more detailed description of the nature and techniques of meditation has been presented in Chapter 6.

Perhaps the most important single factor in allowing you to obtain the greatest benefit from this course is practical application. As working with this material helps you to grow in the understanding of your past experiences and present potential, try to use this increased understanding in your daily activities. Do remember that the purpose for awakening past-life memories is to enable you to have a better, more productive, more creative life now. Simply having a memory of a past life is not enough if it does not have some practical use today.

Summary

For quick reference, a summary of the above suggestions might prove helpful to you.

1. Follow the instructions given in the text, and complete the exercises in the order they are presented. Work at a pace that is comfortable for you, and allow time for reflection.

2. Write your answers to each question and keep them together for easier reference later on.

3. Try to maintain a fresh, adventuresome attitude toward your work with this material.

4. Consider each question carefully, but be flexible in tailoring your efforts to suit your own individual needs.

5. As you gather past-life clues during the early sessions, don't worry about putting them together to form complete theories of your previous incarnations. This will come later.

6. Record your dreams, preferably in a separate dream journal.

7. Be alert for insights that can be gained from situations which arise in your normal waking life. Consider making a record of these also, and talk them over from time to time with a mate or trusted friend.

8. Set aside time for regular meditation.

9. Apply what you learn constructively in your daily life.

Good luck on your new adventure.

Session 1
Awakening Memories

Have you ever stepped outside on a warm spring night and found that the balmy air and the light fragrance of early blossoms awakened feelings almost too deep to describe? Or maybe you've had the experience of hearing a particular song from the past come on the radio, and all of a sudden that song transports you to another time and place. You not only remember what you were doing when you first heard the song, but you can even remember what you were thinking and feel what you were feeling then.

The sounds, sights, and smells around us—they are such powerful influences on our memories and emotions, and so individual in their effects on us. The same song can bring a happy memory for one person and a painful recollection for another. One person might feel a restless sense of adventure at the sound of a train whistle in the night, while another feels lonely desolation. Even the most common, everyday experiences can produce very different feelings in different people. For example, when you hear a telephone ring, do you experience anticipation? Annoyance? Some other reaction? Or maybe nothing at all? What is it about the sounds, sights, and smells around us that brings forth such a variety of responses from people? Is it something in these perceptions themselves that causes us to react differently from one another, or is it something in us?

Just the briefest reflection will tell us that we respond differently because *we* are different. As individuals with unique experiences and memories, we go through life responding to the world around us on the basis of what we've seen, done, and felt in the past.

In the same way that we are constantly unconsciously associating sounds around us with earlier memories from this lifetime, we may also be reacting to stimulation that triggers past-life emotions and attitudes. Becoming aware of these automatic responses to sounds, sights, and experiences is one very fruitful way to uncover memories of previous lives.

Most of the time, such reactions arise without any obvious connection to a specific set of past-life circumstances. In order to get an idea of their origin, we must observe them carefully and consider them in conjunction with other clues to our remote past. In other instances, an automatic response of this sort can evoke a definite, readily identifiable experience from an earlier incarnation. According to the information in the Edgar Cayce readings, the recall that comes when we spontaneously react to events in this life is perhaps the most accurate memory of all.

Often, people who came to Edgar Cayce for readings reported such spontaneous responses, wondering if they were actually the result of past-life memories. Their readings confirmed that these responses had indeed been glimpses of former incarnations. Since these individuals were ordinary people, not necessarily possessing psychic gifts, we can assume that we, too, may happen upon times when actual memory of a past experience comes to mind.

At times these memories, or fractions of memory, seem to be like pieces of film that have been inserted somehow into our normal thoughts—bits and pieces of memory that fleetingly pass through our mind as we go about our daily routines. Sometimes they catch our attention; often they go almost unnoticed.

In some cases a spontaneous reaction will be triggered by a particular thing which we can identify. For example, one woman reported that whenever she heard a certain type of singing, she seemed to experience herself watching Jesus' triumphant entry into Jerusalem. Her Edgar Cayce reading said that she had been present at that event and thus confirmed her experience as an actual memory. Mr. Cayce told her that this experience in her former lifetime had so impressed itself upon her that it was brought to mind very often.

Others who had readings from Edgar Cayce also found that unusual emotional reactions were clues to past-life influences. For example, one woman asked why she had such a noticeable tingling sensation each time she heard the words of Jesus. She was told that she had actually heard his voice in a lifetime in Palestine. Another woman had felt much fear and dread whenever she heard the sounds of ice slides or of horses running over snow. Mr. Cayce explained her emotional responses to the sounds by telling her that in a previous life she had died in the icy waters of the Ohio River. Another person was told that his sympathetic understanding for people who were suffering from tuberculosis was the direct result of a lifetime in which he had had the same condition.

Those who are lucky enough to be able to travel to other countries often tell of unusual happenings that may be related to memories from the distant past. Some people experience a vague sense of having been there before. Others feel a sense of belonging, a sense of peace, as if they were coming home. Many travelers find that they have an unexplainably acute sense of direction. They know what is around the next bend, know what is down that certain side street. Still others experience uneasiness, tingling sensations, sadness, or despair; some even find themselves crying intensely for no apparent reason.

One woman was on a tour of Israel and reported such an experience at Caesarea. She had particularly looked forward to visiting this historic spot, as she had always been interested in the Bible and the early Church. It was a beautiful day, and she felt great. As she stood just inside the entrance to Caesarea, the tour guide paused and was explaining the various happenings that had taken place there throughout history. She found his description vaguely interesting, though it wasn't anything that particularly intrigued her.

She noticed, however, that all of a sudden her stomach was upset and she had become quite shaky. She brushed it aside and went on with the tour inside the ruins. However, the feeling became worse, and finally she decided to leave the tour and go back to the bus. After spending a few minutes on the bus, she told herself that regardless of how she felt, she simply couldn't miss this tour.

By the time she caught up with the group, they had gone over to the amphitheater at Caesarea. As she looked down into the coliseum, she burst into uncontrollable deep, convulsive sobbing, which she was unable to stop for more than an hour. She was totally surprised by this and had no idea what had caused it. Certainly nothing that was said could have brought about such a reaction. She was also embarrassed at such a display of feeling, as she was not an overly emotional person. She has no explanation as to why this reaction occurred.

Her husband has reminded her that she feels particularly close to the teachings of Paul in the Bible and often will defend Paul to those who take issue with some of his stands. Another related clue might be that she does not enjoy sports which are held in our coliseums today. Perhaps one explanation would be that she had been one of the early Christians in Caesarea, had known or worked with Paul, and had been persecuted there in some way. We might also theorize that she probably did not enjoy some of the sports and activities that went on in the coliseum during that period, which was at the height of Rome's power.

It seems as if our interest in and fondness for certain countries might also indicate a past life in those places. Even circumstances beyond our control, such as a business trip, a military assignment, or a chance layover, give us opportunities to open the door to old memories. Maybe we "just happen" to travel to countries where we have lived before.

One young woman recently made plans to take a trip to Egypt. At first it seemed that the plans came out of nowhere. The opportunity presented itself, and she jumped at the chance. When she was telling her grandparents about the trip, they reminded her that one of her great-uncles had traveled to Egypt in the 1950s and that items he had brought back were scattered throughout her house—a vase, a footstool, several copper and brass bowls, and a picture of her uncle on a camel. The young woman suddenly realized that those items had always intrigued her. In fact, she noted that one of her earliest memories was of a small brass container engraved with hieroglyphics. Suddenly she began to wonder if her trip to Egypt was as spontaneous as it had seemed.

Even without extensive travel, sights near to home can trigger recall. The Cayce readings report that often we tend to incarnate in localities close to where we have lived previous lives. The readings told the parents of one young boy that in a past life he had been associated with George Washington. They were told that if they would take him to Mount Vernon, to the kitchen and to the bedroom where Washington had died, he would remember many things. When the parents took the four-year-old to Mount Vernon, the bedroom was roped off. They were able to visit the kitchen, however, and when they got there the child said, "I know where I am. I'm at Mount Vernon."

One woman who lived in Virginia was told that if she would go to the town hall at Williamsburg and look out a particular window, she would remember standing there in a previous life, watching for her lover and catching her first glimpse of him from that window. Another was told that if she went to a fort near her home on a moonlit night in August and listened she would hear her own voice from a lifetime there. Sometimes just a facsimile of a previous experience can be enough to trigger recall. One person was told in a Cayce reading that sitting on the sands anywhere would evoke memories of an incarnation in Persia.

Movies and television provide an opportunity for each of us to travel to far-off places. In addition to documentaries and travelogues, the authentic backgrounds to many historical movies and on-location programs enable us to steep ourselves in other cultures and customs. All of this serves to kindle in us sparks of memories.

Books and stories also have a way of reaching us and transporting us to other countries and other periods of time. We can pick up valuable clues as to where we might have spent some of our prior lifetimes by noticing the types of countries we like to read about. The Cayce readings encouraged those who wanted to recall past lives to study certain areas and countries in which they were interested. Not only history, but geography, maps, and pictures of scenery were recommended to foster recall. One person, for example, was told to study the history of the early Church and he would find that his memories were more accurate than the recorded accounts.

Sometimes we can start with a hint of a past-life experience and then expand that inkling through study. One person who has worked with recalling former incarnations finds that her dreams will suggest countries she has lived in. She enjoys learning the languages of those countries and finds that she encourages further remembrance by doing so.

Whenever you feel you have had an experience in a certain time or place, use your imagination to fill in the details of those past lives. One individual was told in his Cayce reading that his ability to imagine certain places stemmed from a previous lifetime he had spent there. The reading encouraged him to ask himself to make up details concerning those locations as a way of prompting even more recall. Another person was advised to imagine what the people in a particular setting from the past had had for dinner; this would be a surprising stimulus to old memories.

Exercise A

Without even being aware of it, most of us have definite feelings about certain places. Of course, this could be the product of earlier conditioning in the present lifetime. But often the roots go deeper than that.

Let's get in touch with your feelings and your imagination now. Take a few moments to consider this question:

If you could visit any foreign country in the world, where would you go?

Now, if you have your place to visit in mind, it is time to use your imagination to fill in some of the details of what you would expect to find there. Take as much time as you need to let your mind explore. Don't worry about the accuracy of your image of this country; what is important is *what you expect to find*. Allow yourself to free-associate, and cover a wide range of areas of life. When you are through constructing your mental picture of your chosen country, answer the following questions:

1. Where did you choose to visit?
2. List some of the things you imagined you'd find there. Let yourself come up with a variety of impressions from a number of different facets of life. Consider such things as places, objects, moods, types of people, colors, painting and architecture, music, and any other aspects of this country that suggest themselves to your imagination.
3. List some of the feelings these things awaken in you. Do you find a range of feelings—some good, some not so good?
4. What stories have you ever read about this place? How did they make you feel?
5. Do you like movies and/or television programs set in this country? Note any that stand out and the emotions they evoke in you.
6. Do you associate certain foods with this country? Do you have a taste for these foods?
7. Are there items in your home that remind you of this place? What are they, and where in your home are they located?
8. Are there other areas of your life in which an interest in this country is expressed? Consider such items as articles of clothing and other elements of personal adornment (hairstyle, for example), a liking for the music you associate with this country, an interest in reading nonfiction books or news items about it, an enjoyment of museum exhibits or other cultural displays that portray this area, etc.
9. Have you ever known people who have traveled to this country, who have lived there for a period of time, or

who were born there? How did you feel about these people
and about your relationships with them?

10. Have you ever visited this country yourself? If so,
list a few of your strongest impressions from your trip. If
not, list some of the things you associate with this area that
make you feel you would like to go there.

11. Is there any particular period from this country's
history that holds a special interest for you?

12. Take a few minutes to make up a little story about the
type of person you might have been if you had lived in this
country during a previous lifetime. Once again, rely on your
imagination rather than your factual knowledge of the area
to fill in the details. Allow your mind to free-associate and
explore a wide scope of possibilities. When you've made up
your story, you might want to jot it down for future
reference.

13. Are there any other comments you'd like to make
concerning this exercise?

Were there some questions you were unable to answer?
Sometimes the questions we cannot answer are as important
as those we answer readily. Often, for example, people
report that they don't know what foods come from the
countries they've chosen. This is a good opportunity to use
the imagination and try to see what comes spontaneously to
mind. Another possible approach is to use this uncertainty
as a point of study. If your past-life puzzle pieces start to
point to a specific country, this might be a good reason to
explore the foods of that country, perhaps through reading
and studying, learning a new type of recipe, or even
broadening your range of restaurants for a special night
out.

Exercise B

Let's try another exercise in imagination, but this time
we'll stay in our native country. Think about the following
question:

If you could visit anywhere in your own country, where would you go?

Now imagine some of the things you would expect to find there. Again allow your imagination to include things, moods, people, colors, music—whatever comes to mind. Take as much time as you need to identify these impressions you associate with the area you've selected. Then, when you're ready, begin answering the questions below.

1. What part of the country did you choose to visit?

2. What did you imagine you'd find there? Once again, allow yourself the full range of expectancy and give yourself permission to surprise yourself.

3. Do these things evoke any special feelings, either pleasant or unpleasant, in you?

4. Do you associate certain types of people with this area? How do you feel about about these people?

5. List any memorable stories you've read and any movies and television programs you've seen about this region, along with any vivid emotions they may have brought out in you.

6. Do you associate any special foods with this part of the country? Do you like this kind of food?

7. Are there any items in your home that remind you of this area? What are they, and where are they located?

8. Are there any other facets of your life which show your interest in this region?

9. Have you ever actually visited this portion of the country? If you have, what are your strongest memories of your trip?

10. Is there any phase of this region's history that is of particular interest to you?

11. As part of a game this time, use your imagination to make up a little story about visiting this area and recalling a past life there. Allow yourself to be as clever as you can. Include as much detail as you'd like, or be as fast and as simple as you wish. When you're finished, take a minute to jot down the story.

12. Do you have any additional thoughts or comments you'd like to make here?

Many people find that these two exercises yield a lot of memories, feelings, and observations. Processing them is one of the most important parts of the exercise. There are several possible ways of doing so. If you are working on this course with a group of people or with a friend, or if you are working alone but have a mate or trusted companion with whom you can share some of your past-life clues, this may be a good time to stop reading for a while and talk about some of your feelings. If you are more comfortable working alone, you may find several ways to reflect upon your responses to this workshop. Maybe you'd just like to allow yourself to relax and let your mind drift. You may want to close your eyes and take a nap. You may prefer to write a few paragraphs about your experience. Or maybe you'd rather write a letter to an imaginary friend relating some of the feelings and clues you've discovered in your preferences for certain areas and in the stories you've made up.

In analyzing your responses, be sure to look for tendencies that are similar to current-day situations. One woman, for instance, imagined herself as an Indian squaw in Colorado, going about her daily tasks. She associated this with her delight even today in finding kindling and pieces of firewood as she goes on walks in the woods. Her present enjoyment of an evening fire is similar to feelings she imagined having during the Indian lifetime she fantasized. Another person, who imagined herself in a British manor house in the mid-1800s, was surprised to associate her love of sweets and desserts with the English tea tray that she was enjoying in her story.

Our stories can also present very useful suggestions to us when they portray conditions that do not parallel those in our daily lives. For example, one woman reported feeling serenity in her made-up tale of a lifetime in Italy. She realized her hectic present-day life-style might borrow from the appreciation for the fine arts that she had learned there.

She decided that she might include visits to art museums and concerts in this lifetime to invite some of the serenity and well-being she had discovered from her story.

When awakening memories from any past experience, you need to use good judgment and discretion as to what you choose to awaken. If a certain remembrance brings hopefulness and helpfulness into your experience, try to incorporate it into your life-style. If memories are brought out which are not helpful to you this lifetime, lay them aside. Past-life memories and talents are best used to enhance the present life. You should not use them as escapism or as a detour from the road you have chosen for yourself this lifetime.

Session 2
Wardrobe Fantasy

In the last exercise, you used both your imagination and your thinking ability to get in touch with some thoughts, feelings, and impressions about two chosen places. Now we're going to take imagination a step farther. In order for you to derive the greatest benefit from this exercise, it's necessary that you become really comfortable with allowing your imagination to flow. We're going to use a special type of fantasy, called reverie, to give you a chance to practice imagining. Before beginning this specific exercise, however, let's take a brief look at what this form of fantasy is and how we can use it in our search for self-understanding.

Throughout this course we will be striving to maintain a balance between thought and imagination, between the conscious and the unconscious aspects of the mind. The conscious mind is surely an important tool, and we will be using it extensively to gather and analyze past-life clues.

But it is not all there is to our mental makeup, nor is it the only facet of the mind available for use in our quest.

Recall that it is the unconscious mind that is the very storehouse of our memories of previous incarnations. As we work with these remembrances on the conscious level, the unconscious is also stimulated into activity. Our problem here lies in getting this unconscious material to the surface, where it can be recognized and used. Reverie is an important technique in enabling us to do this. Through it we make the images from our own unconscious more accessible to us, which can allow us to achieve insights quite different in nature from those we are likely to obtain through the use of analytical thought alone. But what exactly do we mean by reverie?

The dictionary defines "reverie" most simply as "daydreaming." Though this process of daytime fantasizing is familiar to all of us, it is easy for us to overlook its potential usefulness. The trouble with daydreams is that, for most of us, they tend to be undisciplined and lacking in direction. Thus they are not a particularly reliable vehicle for us to use if we have a specific goal that we'd like to reach.

In order to have any confidence that we can actually use our daydreams to achieve a definite purpose, we must guide them along a path we'd like to follow. This is the aim of the several reverie experiences that are part of this course: to give direction to our fantasies, so that we can enjoy and take advantage of the freedom of imagination they give us in a way that we've determined will be most useful. For our purposes, then, let's define "reverie" a bit more narrowly than the dictionary does, and use the term to mean "a guided experience in imagining."

To further clarify what reverie is, perhaps it would be helpful to look at a few things that it's not. Though there is a certain similarity between the unconscious images it can evoke and those that arise during nighttime dreams, reverie is not sleep. In reverie you will not lose consciousness or your awareness of conditions around you. You may become so relaxed that you fail to pay any attention to your surroundings, but you will continue to be awake and able to respond to anything that requires you to do so.

Reverie is also not a form of hypnosis. It involves no submission of your mind to any outside influence, no loss of your ability to think independently. To be fruitful the experience must be based upon images from *your* unconscious mind, not ones imposed upon you by some external source. You will not lose control of your thoughts, and you will be able to end the fantasy at any point you wish.

Now let's go over some of the ways in which you can ensure that the reverie experience will be as beneficial to you as possible. Relaxation, both mental and physical, is the key to the whole process. First, relax your mind. As you embark upon your fantasy, lay aside the critical, analytical function of your mind. Give your conscious mind a rest, so that your unconscious can come to the fore and create for you a new reality from the wealth of material it holds. Leave behind the restrictions of your usual view of the world, and allow your reverie the freedom to present you with images beyond those your conscious mind habitually entertains.

Next, relax your body. Physical comfort and relaxation is absolutely essential for the reverie experience to unfold. In preparation for these sessions, get yourself into a comfortable sitting or reclining position. Close your eyes, breathe slowly and deeply, and let any muscular tensions you may be feeling slip away from you. One technique that can help you do this is described toward the end of this section. Whatever method you choose, try to reach a point where you are able to forget your body and let your thoughts flow.

As you enter into each reverie, you will be directed to see yourself in a specific setting. Remember—relax. Don't work with your conscious mind to construct an image of the situation. Simply take the image that comes to you from your unconscious, accept it without logical criticism, and notice the details that appear before your mind's eye. Don't limit yourself to just the sights in your new surroundings; become conscious of the sounds, smells, and touch sensations as well. Take note of as many of these details as you can, for they are important. It is by focusing on them that you will become able to immerse yourself most completely in your fantasy world.

Seeing yourself in your reverie surroundings, as in a movie, is a good beginning. But to realize the full value of the experience, a different viewpoint is needed. Rather than just observing a mental image that includes a character you identify as yourself, try to become part of the scenario in your mind. That is, use your imagination to shift your perspective so that with your mind's eye you are seeing the scene as if you were actually in it. Feel in your imaginary body the sensations of any movement or activity you picture yourself doing. And, as completely as possible, adopt the mental state you would have if you were actually engaged in the fantasy activity. Think the thoughts you would be thinking and feel the emotions you would be feeling if you were performing the actions involved.

At various points in some of our reveries you will be asked certain questions. Do *not* interrupt the experience to write down your responses. The questions will be repeated and there will be time to answer them on paper after the fantasy has reached its conclusion. These questions appear in the body of the reverie only to guide you to direct your attention toward certain details that will help you understand the significance of the fantasy as a whole. Merely take mental note of these details so that you can recall them once the reverie is over. The time to analyze and write about them will come later.

Stay with each reverie as long as you can. Allow time for the experience to unfold at its own pace and reach its natural conclusion. Don't worry about keeping to any specified time periods that may be suggested in the text; such recommended durations are meant as general guidelines only and should be adjusted to suit you and your involvement in each individual fantasy.

If the reverie fulfills its purpose, at its conclusion you will find yourself feeling refreshed, relaxed, and contented.

More importantly, you will emerge from your experience
with a new understanding of yourself, a greater awareness
of how you have become the person that you are, and an
expanded vision of the possibilities open to you in your
present life.

There is a problem inherent in using a book to guide you
through a reverie, however. In order to get your directions
from the printed page, you must use your conscious mind to
pick up the instructions you are to follow, and this can be a
serious distraction from the flow of images from the unconscious. If you try to proceed line by line—reading one line
of directions, following it, reading another line, and so
on—your fantasy experience will continually be interrupted.
You may find it extremely hard to truly immerse yourself in
it, for most of us can't shift gears, from the logical aspect of
the mind to the imaginative and back again, that completely
and effectively.

It might be a bit of an improvement to read and try to
remember a larger chunk of the material, follow it without
referring back to the book, and then go on to the next
chunk. At least this would cut down on the number of
interrruptions of your fantasy. But this seems like an awful
lot of work to expect of the conscious mind, which is, after
all, the part of us that's supposed to be at rest during
reverie. In adopting this technique we run the risk of
forgetting one or more key phrases of the directions, thus
affecting the completeness of our experience. And there is
also the danger that in memorizing the instructions we might
find ourselves consciously preprogramming our responses to
them, which would limit the range and spontaneity of the
images presented to us.

While either the line-by-line or the large-chunk method
could be used in a pinch, there are a couple of superior
alternatives available. One of these is to call for help. If you
have a trusted friend with whom you would be willing to
share your involvement in this course, he or she can be
asked to read the reverie material aloud while you yourself
undergo the experience. Your friend would thus become

your guide, while you would be free to lay your conscious mind aside and concentrate upon the images that arise from your unconscious.

The other option is for you to prepare a cassette tape recording of yourself reading the guidance material for each fantasy. When it comes time for a reverie, the only potentially distracting work you will have to do is to turn the appropriate tape on at the beginning of the session and turn it off at the end. In between, you will be able to relax and let your unconscious do its job without any intrusions from your physical body or conscious mind.

Regardless of which method you choose, do not neglect to prepare for each reverie session. This preparation consists mainly of mental and physical relaxation. In order to help you with this, there are given below two routines for relaxation, one for the conscious mind and one for the body. These can be incorporated at the beginning of the material for each reverie experience. You can read them over yourself and follow their suggestions before beginning your fantasy; you can have a friend read them to you aloud if he or she will be guiding you through the reverie; or you can record them on each tape of reverie material if you are using the cassette method of experiencing these exercises in imagination.

Of course, there are many techniques of relaxing the mind and body. Those that follow will take you through just one of the possibilities. Try them out once or twice as they are given, to see how well they work for you. Then by all means feel free to modify them in any way that will make them more effective. With a bit of practice you may find yourself able to reach a state of relaxation without any verbal guidance whatever. But whether you ultimately decide to use the given relaxation text, a different one, or none at all, do take time before beginning each specific reverie to put your mind and body at ease.

At frequent intervals in the relaxation instructions below and in the descriptions of each fantasy, you will find various durations of time inserted in parentheses. These are to indicate suggested pauses and their lengths. The purpose here is to give you time to perform the different steps in relaxation or to direct your attention to the specific images that arise in your reverie. Some pause at each of these points will probably help you use your fantasy to greatest advantage, but here again you should be flexible. The amounts of time stated are merely suggestions and should be altered if they are either too long or too brief to meet your individual needs. Don't limit your reverie to a timetable; change the timetable to fit the dimensions of your reverie.

The first block of material below is to help you relax mentally. The second is to help you relax physically. The following sequence is recommended for each reverie session:

1. Get settled in a comfortable position.
2. Relax your mind.
3. Relax your body.
4. Experience the reverie.
5. When your fantasy is over, take a few moments for quiet reflection on it.
6. Answer the questions asked about it in the text.

For mental relaxation

It's time now to begin to prepare yourself for a period of quiet relaxation. Get as comfortable as you can, and quiet your thoughts as much as you are able. (5 seconds) You're safe and secure and ready to let your imagination take you on a little adventure.

Be assured that as you enter into peaceful reverie, you are not going to lose consciousness. You're not even going to lose control of your thoughts. You'll be perfectly aware of what's going on around you, although you'll be so relaxed that you may easily choose to ignore any distractions. (5 seconds) Know, however, that if anything happens in your surroundings that makes it important for you to react, you will be fully awake and able to do so.

You're simply going to enter a state of mental and physical relaxation that will allow your unconscious mind to

present you with its thoughts. All you have to do is sit back
and notice the thoughts or pictures your unconscious mind
suggests to you.

For physical relaxation

And now let's take a few moments to allow your body to
become as relaxed as your mind is. Close your eyes and
take several slow, deep breaths. Slowly, deeply, easily—
breathe in (3 sec.) and out. (3 sec.) Again—in (3 sec.) and
out. (3 sec.) One more time—in (3 sec.) and out. (3 sec.)
Continue breathing slowly and naturally.

Now gently shift your awareness from your breathing,
and focus your attention on your feet. (5 sec.) Now, from
that point of awareness inside your feet, tell them to relax.
Feel any tensions you may be holding there. As you find
those taut muscles, voluntarily tense them (3 sec.) and
relax. Let the tension melt away. (5 sec.)

Slowly, gently, move your awareness up your legs, finding any taut muscles. (5 sec.) Tighten your leg muscles as
hard as you can (3 sec.) and then relax. (5 sec.) On up the
legs, hips, buttocks (5 sec.)—tense (3 sec.) and relax. (5
sec.) Now your abdomen and lower back (5 sec.)—tense (3
sec.) and relax. (5 sec.)

On up to your chest and shoulder blades. (5 sec.) Pay
special attention to your shoulder area. Become aware of
any tensions you are holding there. (5 sec.) Push your
shoulder blades together, hold them tense (3 sec.)—now
relax. (5 sec.) Shrug your shoulders up tight, hold them
tense (3 sec.)— now relax. (5 sec.) Feel all of the tension
flowing out, flowing off your back, as you're bathed in a
glowing golden light of relaxation. (5 sec.)

Now that your neck and shoulders are relaxed, become
aware of your facial muscles. (5 sec.) Your eyes are closed—
but are you squinting? Is your jaw tight or relaxed? Let your
facial muscles relax entirely. (5 sec.) The eyes are closed,
but not squeezed shut. (5 sec.) Your jaw is comfortably

relaxed. (5 sec.) Your scalp feels loose. (5 sec.) Your whole body is relaxed. (5 sec.)

Take just a moment to monitor your breathing. With your mind's eye, watch your lungs slowly filling with each deep, even breath that you take. And watch your lungs empty as you let each breath out. Don't try to control your breathing; just breathe normally and naturally, peacefully. (10 sec.)

You are now totally relaxed, ready to forget your body for a while. You are at peace, able to let your thoughts flow, and ready to lose yourself in them.

(At this point, you can move on to the contents of the specific fantasy experience you are working with.)

One of the qualities that makes reverie such a valuable technique is that each such exercise in imagination can be repeated many times over, with each repetition yielding different and useful results. For example, in our first guided excursion into fantasy you will be reaching into an imaginary garment bag, taking out a suit of clothing, and examining it to discover what it can tell you about yourself. This exercise can be done several times over, each time producing a different imaginary costume and a new set of insights. In a reverie toward the end of the course, you will be viewing a scene from one of your past lives. Obviously, each of us has many such scenes available, so it would be possible to experience this fantasy again and again and still obtain fresh, helpful information every time.

As you gain practice in using your imagination in this way, you might reach a point where you would feel comfortable designing a reverie of your own for a different part of the course, a section for which the material in this book does not specify a fantasy exercise. Do not hesitate to do so whenever you feel an experience of this sort will be helpful to you. You might even notice ways in which the reverie technique can be applied to areas of your life that have nothing to do with recall of previous incarnations.

And now it's time to leave the theory of reverie alone for a while and move on to our first actual experience in guided fantasy. We're going to start with a short, uncomplicated reverie, one that will help you to become confident in your ability to envision circumstances with your mind's eye. As we go through this fantasy experience, don't try to do anything with your conscious mind; remember, that part of you is to be at rest. You're not going to try to remember a past life. That will come later in the course. For now, all you are going to do is practice using your imagination. Just picture in your mind the things that are described to you. This is pure fantasy.

Before heading into the body of the reverie itself, it would be a good idea for you to go through the procedures for mental and physical relaxation given above. Then let your unconscious take you into this imaginary scene.

Wardrobe Fantasy

See yourself in the center of a very large, empty room. It's a pleasant, sunny room, filled with light. (5 sec.) There is nothing in this room except a large wardrobe closet. (5 sec.)

See yourself walking over to the closet. (5 sec.) Reach for the handle. Slowly, you open the doors. (5 sec.) Inside you see a rack full of closed garment bags. (5 sec.) Reach in and take one of the hanging bags out. (5 sec.) Open it up. (5 sec.)

Inside, you find a costume—a complete outfit of clothing. (5 sec.) As you slowly remove this garment or costume from the bag, examine it carefully. What is it? (10 sec.) What does it look like? (10 sec.) How does it feel in your hands? (10 sec.)

Now put the outfit on. (5 sec.) As you put it on, you notice that it fits perfectly. How does it feel, now that you have it on? (10 sec.) There's a mirror behind you. Look at yourself in the mirror. (5 sec.) How do you look in this costume? (10 sec.) Is your appearance changed in any way? (10 sec.) How do you feel about yourself in this attire? (10 sec.) Does it bring out any particular attitudes or emotions in you? (10 sec.)

And now, as you stand there, one more question: Where are you going, or what are you going to do, now that you are wearing this outfit? Take a few moments to think about this.

Exercise

Once you've allowed your fantasy to reach its conclusion and given yourself some time for quiet reflection on the experience, answer the following questions.

1. What did your costume or garment look like? Feel free to draw a sketch of it or to describe it with words—whichever you prefer.

2. How did it feel in your hands as you removed it from the garment bag? How did it feel once you had it on?

3. How did you look when you were wearing this outfit? Did your appearance differ in any way from the way you look now? In answering these questions, consider not just the clothing itself. Also make note of such details as any jewelry you pictured yourself wearing with it; any associated changes in your style of personal appearance, such as how you wore your hair or the length of your fingernails; and any changes in your body structure when you had this costume on.

4. Did wearing this outfit bring out any feelings about yourself? Did it evoke any particularly noteworthy attitudes or emotions? Do you recognize any of these as part of your current makeup?

5. Where were you going, or what were you doing or about to do, in this attire?

6. Do you associate this costume with any particular place, period of history, or group of people?

7. Did your experience leave you with any additional thoughts or impressions that you'd like to make note of?

Session 3
Tracing the Laws of Reincarnation

We may have hunches about past lives. We may have theories about experiences in another time or place. Some of us may even have vivid past-life dreams or flashes of waking recall. But what do such experiences really mean? Can they teach us anything about ourselves and how to live *this* life more fully? Unless we can answer yes to these questions, the study of past lives may be nothing more than an interesting pastime, an indulgence of curiosity about ourselves that has little practical value.

But suppose, on the other hand, that the study of past lives is actually a look into the inner workings of the universe we live in, a glimpse into the purpose and orderliness of life. If this is so, then this investigation is a very important avenue to the answer to two of the most important questions mankind has ever asked: Why is life the way it is, and why am I the way I am?

Through the study of past lives, we can gain insight into how life works, how to make the most of our positive traits and talents, how to meet the obstacles life seems to throw in our way, and how to overcome our faults and weaknesses.

Throughout this course, you'll be approaching past lives from two sides. From the first angle, you'll be using past-life theories to help you understand the way life works. And coming at it from the opposite side, you'll be using that understanding of the way life works, or the laws of reincarnation, to develop theories about your own past lives and about the experiences you may have had in any lifetime. Your understanding of the laws governing the reincarnation

150

process will be a very important foundation, then. It will become the framework that makes sense out of the past-life clues that you'll gather as you go through the exercises in this course.

Just what are the laws that govern the soul's movement from life experience to life experience? We'll be looking at these on two levels: the basic laws or premises that describe the reincarnation process, and the specific laws that influence the particular experiences we have from lifetime to lifetime.

First, then, let's examine the basic premises. Anyone who has tried the reincarnation theory on for size has encountered the basics. In a nutshell, it suggests that life is eternal, purposeful, and orderly; and that we have experienced and will continue to experience life as human beings many times. The very fact that you are working with a course on how to remember past lives suggests that this philosophy appeals to you or rings true in some way.

Let's take a look at some of the things that reincarnation implies. When we say that life is eternal and that we have lived before in other human bodies, we're really saying that who we are is nonphysical. We might call our true self the soul. The soul goes through many experiences, each one having its impact, leaving its mark on our identity. The person you are today is the sum total of all the experiences you've ever had. Therefore, the person you are today is helping to shape the person you will be in the future, both later on in this life and in future incarnations.

Possibly the most attractive aspect of the reincarnation theory is its emphasis on free will. Free will is supreme in the reincarnation scheme of things. In one sense, we could even say that the purpose of life—of all our lives—is to grow to our highest potential by learning to make the best choices as we go through daily experience. With the people and circumstances that come into our lives, we have the opportunity to learn love, to develop talents and abilities, to grow in understanding—in short, to become all that we, as children of God, are capable of being.

Now, of course, choices build on one another, with a

choice leading to a circumstance, and that circumstance leading to another choice. The resulting chain of choices makes our life what it is at any given moment. Because we can't change our circumstances instantaneously, we sometimes mistakenly think we're not free.

Suppose you have spent your whole life developing the ability to play tennis. You've made choices about taking lessons, spending time in practice, maybe even selecting as friends people who share your interest in sports. It would be unrealistic to expect that you could make a sudden choice to oil paint instead and instantly produce a masterpiece. But you could decide to start working on developing your artistic skills and so start building a whole new chain of choices. Similarly, it would be foolish to say that you were predestined to be a tennis player instead of a painter, knowing that you yourself had made decisions much earlier that set your life along an athletic direction.

It works the same way with reincarnation and free will, except that the time span is usually longer. You may have made choices in other lives that you don't even remember. But it will be these choices, and not fate, that determine the family you are born into, the circumstances you meet in life, the talents and traits that you possess.

This process of making choices and then experiencing the results of those choices is really what karma is all about. Karma is the operation of the law of cause and effect. As such, it is the main dynamic around which your experience from life to life turns. And let's get one thing very clear at the outset: Karma is not punishment for misdeeds, it's not the merciless judge and jury that sentences us for every failing, nor is it a mysterious force that comes along and knocks us down because of some long-forgotten sin.

Karma is simply the law of cause and effect in action. It suggests that everything we think, everything we do and say—constructive or destructive—is a cause that will in due time have its effect. As we sow, so shall we reap. We alone determine whether our karma is pleasant or unpleasant.

Let's take a closer look at how this works. In doing so, we will be moving from our discussion of the basic premises behind reincarnation into an examination of the specific laws by which it is governed.

There are several ways that we experience cause and effect. The first aspect of karma has to do with the simple rule that no effort is ever lost; the effect of the effort continues. This means that the things we learn, the talents we work to develop, and the efforts we make at getting along with other people all carry a certain momentum. Until some situation arises in which we choose to change them, we will continue to carry over personality traits, talents, interests, and attitudes. So we might call the first law the Law of Continuation.

There is a second way in which we experience karma. Because our purpose in reincarnating is to grow and learn from our mistakes, we must sometimes experience the results of our poor or destructive choices. This is the only way we get to learn firsthand that certain actions and thoughts are not conducive to our growth. Just as even the most loving parent must at times allow a child to make a mistake in order to learn from it, our God allows us to make mistakes and experience the consequences. God does not punish us when we treat other people unkindly, do something dishonest, or misuse the resources that have been put at our disposal. But under the law of cause and effect, those actions must bring certain consequences that will help us learn not to repeat our mistakes. Let's call the second law the Law of Consequences.

At times we can experience the consequences of our past mistakes very directly. This is like the eye-for-an-eye, tooth-for-a-tooth law of the Old Testament and many ancient cultures. For example, one young woman who had a reading from Edgar Cayce was told that the repeated disappointments she was experiencing in her love life were the direct result of an earlier incarnation in which she had discouraged many suitors by not keeping her word to them. The Law of Consequences can bring conditions into our lives that help us to see what it's like to be on the other side of the fence.

Sometimes physical harm done to others may result in physical consequences. One example is the case of a blind man who was told by Edgar Cayce that he had blinded others with hot pokers in an earlier incarnation in Persia. A word of caution here, though. We can never look at another person's handicap or unfortunate circumstances and assume that he or she is paying for some past misdeed. In fact, there are always so many possible past-life reasons behind a person's situation that we can never judge from the outside what the actual cause may be. What's important is that we gain a sense in our own lives of why we experience the things we do.

The Law of Consequences also brings us the results of the constructive choices we make. For example, the person with the good and happy home may have done much to create a home for the homeless in another life. The person with the ability to make friends easily may have continually offered comfort and encouragement to those around him during a prior incarnation. The person with a healthy body may have nursed others in a previous experience.

Sometimes the consequences of our choices can be some-what less direct, or even symbolic, in the form they take. Consider, for example, the woman who repeatedly found herself drawn toward, yet resentful of, people in authority. Her Cayce reading told her that this was a result of a lifetime when she had been a lady-in-waiting to a queen. Or take the case of the man who had in an earlier lifetime in Egypt worked on building communications with people of many languages and cultures in order to do business with them. He was told that in this lifetime he could make money investing in airlines. We can see how in the modern age air travel brought the rewards of what this man had tried to do in his earlier, Egyptian incarnation.

There is one more law we can trace through the development of souls from lifetime to lifetime—the Law of Compensation. According to this law, we all go through multi-faceted experiences in order to become balanced, well-rounded individuals. In keeping with this law, we may incarnate into many races and religions. In order to become balanced, we may have to experience opposite extremes from time to time. This apparently happens with our sexual identity, for example. During our countless lifetimes in the earth, most of us have incarnated in the bodies of both sexes in order to incorporate into our identity the best traits of each sex. Other polar opposites—such as meekness and courage, intellectual and physical development, an outgoing nature and an introspective one—may each be experienced in turn to round out the character.

Before going on to see how these laws can be traced in patterns described in the Cayce life readings, let's list and briefly summarize each one. This will provide you with a quick review and easy reference.

The Law of Continuation: Personality traits, talents, interests, and abilities tend to continue from lifetime to lifetime-until some situation arises in which we choose to change them.

The Law of Consequences: We experience the consequences of our choices. Constructive choices bring positive consequences, and destructive choices bring negative ones that will teach us not to repeat our mistakes.

The Law of Compensation: In order to balance personal traits, we may experience opposite extremes—such as masculinity and femininity—from lifetime to lifetime.

Now let's take a look at a few case histories. In each instance, the person's past-life experience is described, along with his or her current circumstances. It's up to you to determine which law is in operation. Answers are given immediately following the last case, number 7.

Don't think of this as a test; it's merely a tool to aid in your comprehension of these laws. It's not necessary for you to write your answers or count up your total score of correct responses. What is important is that you consider each case carefully, note any of the laws that you misidentify, and reach an understanding of how those principles actually work.

Case 1: This man was an Italian living in America. His life reading said that he had been an early Italian explorer at the time of Columbus and had been drawn to the Americas to become involved in various associations with other people. He was now back in North America, apparently reexperiencing some of those associations in his business dealings. What law might you say predominates in this story?

Case 2: This woman was told that she had been of the tribe of Mound Builders in North America in a previous incarnation and that her biggest contribution to the general welfare during that lifetime had been in assisting people to build their individual homes. During her modern lifetime, her home—preferably in a natural or rural setting, as opposed to a city—would be of central importance. Which law do you feel is at work here?

Case 3: Here we have the story of a young girl who had lived in England just after the Holy Wars. She had become a religious recluse, using her hands to labor very hard in a convent. In her current lifetime, her hands showed remarkable physical beauty and she had the ability to create beautiful things with them. What law might be in operation here?

Case 4: This man had been an executioner during the French Revolution. His reading said that even during that life he had hated himself for his role. In his modern-day lifetime, he hated persecution of all kinds and was even sensitive to the destructiveness of faultfinding. What law do we see here?

Case 5: Again we have a man, this time one who had lived after the destruction of Atlantis. He had been a leader who led a group of survivor–refugees into a new land and settled it. His one failing was in sexual excess, which apparently made him many enemies among the people who inhabited the land he settled. In his current lifetime, he was sterile. What law do you see operating here?

Case 6: This woman was told of a lifetime as a Greek athlete. Today she had great admiration, to the point of worship, for the ideal body form. Which law is at work here?

Case 7: Finally, there's the case of the woman who at times had the sensation of choking physically and found it hard to catch her breath. When she asked about this in her reading, she was told that in an earlier life she had choked back her emotions. What law might we see here?

Answer 1: This seems to be a case of continuation. We see the man repeating his Italian nationality and once again being drawn to the Americas. We see him almost picking up where he left off in the earlier lifetime.

Answer 2: Here again, continuation is the most straightforward explanation. The thing that the woman valued so highly continued to be of value for her. We might even read in a little of the Law of Consequences here and imagine that she would have a particularly pleasant home because of what she had done for others in the earlier experience.

Answer 3: Here we see a case where the Law of Consequences brought this soul the results of its labors in an earlier life. The beautiful hands were a symbolic representation of the way she had used her hands to live out her faith. And her ability to create with her hands was a direct and practical consequence of the effort she had put in earlier.

Answer 4: This is probably a case of compensation. After having experienced the extreme as an executioner, this man was balancing himself by avoiding all contact with persecution and faultfinding.

This case is particularly interesting because it is not necessarily what we might expect to be the karma of a former executioner. We may see the man's apparently mild karma from several different perspectives. On the one hand, the fact that even during the French incarnation he had realized that what he did was wrong and had come to regret it so deeply may have eliminated the need for him to experience a more traumatic consequence of his deeds. On the other hand, he may have learned his lesson in some other lifetime before the current one. His reading indicates that later on in the French lifetime itself he fell victim to the counterrebellion, and so he may have experienced at that time the direct consequences of his destructive actions.

Answer 5: This might be either the Law of Consequences or the Law of Compensation. We're not told in the reading exactly why his excesses caused problems with the native people. If he broke their moral laws or social customs, we might see his current sterility as a symbolic payment for his misdeeds. Perhaps he fathered many children who were not properly cared for. In that case, we might see his sterility as compensation—one extreme balancing out another.

Answer 6: Here we have a clear and simple case of continuation, in which the attitudes and traits of the past continue to be a part of the individual character.

Answer 7: This is the Law of Consequences, with a symbolic twist to it.

From these examples, it's easy to see how the things we like and don't like in the present, the talents we do and do not have, and the relationships that go smoothly and the ones that are difficult can all be clues to understanding our past lives. We have also seen, as these laws operate, that what we have sown in another life we are reaping now, what we gave then we are gaining now, what we did to others then is being done to us now, and what we were then we are meeting in others now.

Karma can therefore be blessings, or it can be problems which subtract from our blessings. It is a perfect system of justice, in which each one of us, certainly and inevitably, faces or experiences in some form what we have done—both good and bad—to others.

Understanding these karmic laws also raises some questions: How can we use our credits to the best advantage? What can we do about past failures? How do we keep from making the same mistakes over and over again? How much do we yet have to face?

You are familiar with the fact that more than one law can be in operation at the same time. For example, the laws of aerodynamics overcome the law of gravity, and planes take off from runways daily. Gravity is not annulled, but it is counteracted by another law. Or perhaps as a child you filled a bucket with water and swung it full circle without spilling a drop. Centrifugal force overcame the law of gravity.

Just so, the Cayce readings say that the law of grace will counterbalance karma and that we can choose to live under the law of grace. What exactly is this law of grace? Simply stated, it is the Golden Rule: Do unto others as you would have others do unto you. As we apply the Golden Rule in our dealings with others, we move from karma to grace. In other words, we live under the law of grace to the extent that we treat others according to the Golden Rule.

Session 4
You and Your Surroundings

One of the ways to identify your past lives is to look at what surrounds you. Our homes, for example, reflect much about us that we don't often realize. Here is where we unconsciously surround ourselves with those things we're comfortable with. Not only our homes, but also personal items, such as clothing and jewelry, reveal much about our past lives. The style of home we like, the furnishings and accessories we buy—or would like to buy someday—and even the patterns and designs we like can give us clues to influences from our prior lives.

Exercise A

We're going to use a selection of pictures now to look for evidence of your past. On the pages that follow, you will find a series of drawings. As you look at each one, become aware of the feelings and thoughts that come to mind. Do you like the style, dislike it, or have little or no response to it? If you have a strong reaction to any of the pictures, make a note that best describes your feelings. State whether your reaction is positive or negative, and include any comments you'd like to make about the items. When you've finished going through the drawings and moved on to Exercise B, you will find each of the items identified there.

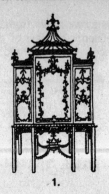

1.

2.

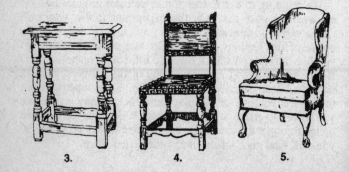

3.   **4.**   **5.**

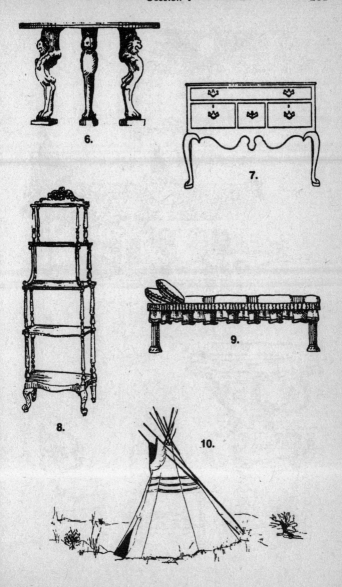

6.

7.

8.

9.

10.

11.

12.

13.

14.

15.

16.

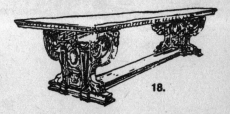

17.

18.

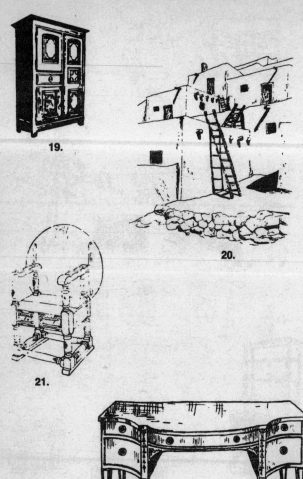

19.

20.

21.

22.

23.

24.

25.

26.

27.

29.

28.

30.

31.

32.

33.

34.

35.

36.

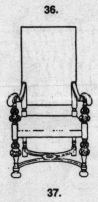

37.

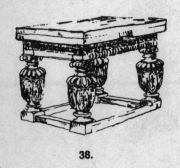

38.

39.

40.

41.

42.   43.   44.

45.

46.

47.

48.

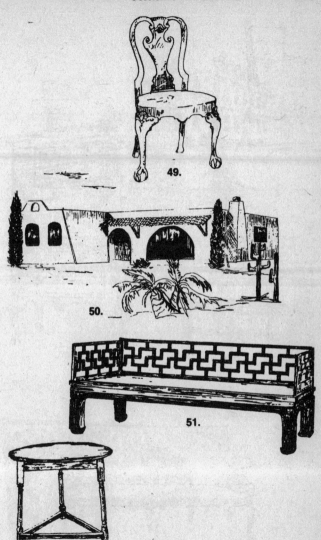

49.

50.

51.

52.

53.

54.

55.

56.

57.

58.

59.

60.

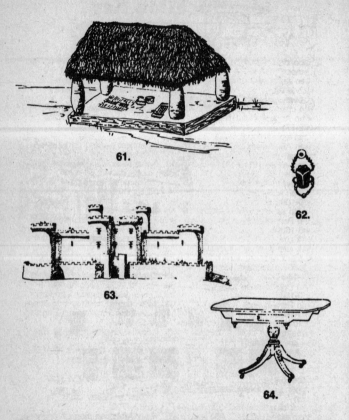

61.

62.

63.

64.

Illustrations 1, 14, 23, 24, 27, 42 and 45 reprinted from *The Book of Furniture and Decoration* by Joseph Aronson. Copyright 1936, 1941, 1952, by Crown Publishers, Inc. Used by permission of Crown Publishers, Inc.

Illustrations 3, 4, 5, 6, 7, 8, 9, 11, 13, 15, 17, 18, 19, 21, 22, 26, 28, 29, 30, 32, 33, 34, 37, 38, 39, 40, 43, 44, 47, 48, 49, 51, 52, 54, 55, 56, 57, 60, 62, 64 from the American School of Interior Design, 423 Cardinal Drive, Little Falls, New Jersey 07424.

Illustrations 2, 10, 12, 16, 20, 25, 31, 35, 36, 41, 46, 50, 53, 58, 59, 61, 63 by Karen L. Fili.

Identification Key

You and Your Surroundings

1. Chippendale wardrobe, Chinese influence (1718-1779)
2. Queen Anne period home (1702-1714)
3. Jacobean oak table (1603-1688)
4. Dutch chair with decorative studs
5. Queen Anne upholstered chair (1702-1714)
6. Roman table (1000 B.C.-500 A.D.)
7. Queen Anne lowboy (1702–1714)
8. American Victorian "whatnot" for holding curios (1840-1880)
9. Greek bed (1100-350 B.C.)
10. American Indian teepee
11. Egyptian winged hawk (4500-1090 B.C.)
12. Spanish architectural design
13. Italian Renaissance table (1300-1600)
14. Greek chair (1100-350 B.C.)
15. Greek pitcher (1100-350 B.C.)
16. Aztec architectural design
17. Louis XIII sideboard (approx. 1624-1642)
18. Italian Renaissance table (1300-1600)
19. Italian Renaissance armoire (1300-1600)
20. Pueblo home of the Taos Indians
21. Jacobean oak "monk's" seat or table chair (1603-1688)
22. Hepplewhite desk (1786)
23. French Provincial chest (1723-1774)
24. Jacobean stool (1603-1688)
25. Victorian period architectural design
26. Greek folding stool (1100-350 B.C.)
27. Roman table (1000 B.C.-500 A.D.)
28. Colonial fireplace and ovens (1608-1720)
29. Louis XVI sofa (1774-1793)
30. Early Colonial trestle table (1608-1720)
31. English Tudor manor
32. Sheraton kidney-shaped desk (1751-1806)
33. Victorian sofa and stool (1840-1880)
34. Chippendale chair (1718-1779)
35. Polynesian pile dwelling
36. Early American log cabin
37. William and Mary armchair (1689-1702)
38. Elizabethan table (1558-1603)
39. French Provincial sideboard (1723-1774)
40. Queen Anne cockleshell— used as accent carving on furniture (1702-1714)
41. Swiss mountain chalet
42. Hepplewhite chair (1786)
43. Chippendale tea table (1718-1779)
44. Egyptian chair (4500-1090 B.C.)
45. Spanish chair
46. French Provincial home (1723-1774)
47. Early colonial cabinet with hutch (1608-1720)
48. Queen Anne upholstered sofa (1702-1714)
49. Queen Anne chair (1702-1714)
50. Pueblo Indian style home
51. Couch with Chinese key design
52. 18th-century "poor folk" cottage-style table from Ireland, England or Scotland
53. Colonial American architecture, 18th century
54. Queen Anne highboy (1702-1714)
55. Jacobean gateleg table (1603-1688)
56. Neoclassic, Louis XVI sofa (1774-1793)
57. William and Mary table (1689-1702)
58. Early American plantation house (1734 and later)
59. Colonial architectural design
60. Short-legged Chinese table
61. Mayan house
62. Egyptian scarab or beetle (4500-1090 B.C.)
63. 13th- and 14th-century castle
64. American Empire pedestal drop-leaf table (1795-1830)

Exercise B

Arranging the pictures of items from different areas and time periods so that they are interspersed among each other, as was done in the foregoing exercise, is one way of making it easier for you to give each drawing careful individual attention. But it does make it a bit difficult to detect recurring patterns of responses. These patterns of similar or repetitious reactions to a number of items from a single region and period of history can be a valuable clue when it comes to formulating past-life theories.

For this exercise, you are to go back over the drawings you've just examined. This time, look at all the pictures from each historical setting to see if you have an overall reaction to that group of items as a whole. To help you with this, each of the items is identified below. The identifications are not given in the numerical order in which the illustrations were presented in the previous exercise; rather, they are grouped according to the area and period of each item's origin. When you have finished considering each set of pictures, answer the questions that follow.

A. These items are from various ancient civilizations.
   Egyptian (c. 4500–1090 B.C.):
      11—winged hawk
      44—chair
      62—scarab, or beetle
   Greek (c. 1100–350 B.C.):
      9—bed
      14—chair
      15—pitcher
      26—folding stool
   Roman (c. 1000 B.C.–A.D. 500):
      6—table
      27—table

B. The following articles are from non-European cultures.
   Chinese:
      51—couch with Chinese key design

60—short-legged table
(Item 1, though of English make, shows Chinese influence and perhaps should be considered here as well.)

Polynesian: 35—pile dwelling
American Indian:
Mayan: 61—house
Aztec: 16—architectural design
Pueblo-type: 20—home of the Taos Indians
50—house
North American plains: 10—teepee

C. These articles are of continental European origin.
European, many localities (c. thirteenth and fourteenth centuries):
63—castle
Italian Renaissance (1300–1600):
13—table
18—table
19—armoire
Dutch: 4—chair with decorative studs
Swiss: 41—mountain chalet
Spanish:
12—architectural design
45—chair
French:
Louis XIII (c. 1624–42): 17—sideboard
French Provincial (1723–74): 23—chest
39—sideboard
46—home
Louis XVI (1774–93): 29—sofa
56—sofa (neoclassic)

D. These items are from the British Isles.
Tudor (c. sixteenth century): 31—manor
Elizabethan (1558–1603): 38—table
Jacobean (1603–88): 3—oak table
21—oak "monk's seat" or table-chair

                            24—stool
                            55—gateleg table
        Irish, English, or Scottish (eighteenth century):
                            52—"poor folk" cottage-style table

E. The following styles of furnishings originated in England. They also influenced developments on the European Continent and in North America, however, and thus might shed light on possible past involvements in those settings as well. The dates show when each style was most popular in England.

William and Mary (1689–1702): 37—armchair
                                57—table

Queen Anne (1702–14):   2—home
                        5—upholstered chair
                        7—lowboy
                        40—cockleshell, used as accent carving on furniture
                        48—upholstered sofa
                        49—chair
                        54—highboy

Chippendale (1750–79): 1—wardrobe, with Chinese influence
                        34—chair
                        43—tea table

Hepplewhite (1760–95): 22—desk
                        42—chair

Sheraton (1790–1810): 32—kidney-shaped desk

Victorian (1840–80): 25—architectural design
                        33—sofa and stool

F. Our last group of articles is from the English North American colonies and, subsequently, the United States. Colonial period (c. seventeenth and early eighteenth centuries):
                        28—fireplace and ovens
                        30—trestle table
                        47—cabinet with hutch
                        53—architectural design
                        59—architectural design

Early American (c. eighteenth and nineteenth centuries):
    36—log cabin
    58—plantation house
American Empire (1795–1830): 64—pedestal drop-leaf table
American Victorian (1840–80): 8—"whatnot," for holding
                                                    curios

Consider your responses to each group of items from
Exercise A in turn, and answer the questions below. List any
pattern of reactions that you yourself feel is strong enough
to be significant. You may find that you would like to
answer more than one area or time period for some of these
questions, while other questions you might want to skip, for
lack of any noteworthy reactions to the items they concern.
Either of these options is perfectly fine.

1. Do you have any repeated or similar positive reactions to the items from any of the ancient civilizations?

2. Do you have any pattern of negative reactions to the
items from any of these ancient civilizations?

3. Did any of the non-European cultures evoke a strong
positive reaction in you?

4. Did any of them cause a significant negative response?

5. Do you have any reaction, positive or negative, to
the continental European items as a whole? List any regions
that you feel these reactions might be focused toward, and
state whether your reaction to each of these areas is positive
or negative.

6. Do you have a pattern of responses to the items from
the Italian Renaissance? Is it favorable or unfavorable?

7. Do you have an overall reaction to the articles from
France? Is it positive or negative?

8. Is there a pattern in your responses to any of the
specific French periods? Is it favorable or unfavorable?

9. Considering the drawings listed in groups D and E
above, do you feel an overall reaction to the British items?
What is the nature of this reaction?

10. Did any of the styles or periods of British articles
give rise to a pattern of responses? Was it positive or
negative?

11. Do you feel a general reaction to the items from the colonies and the United States? Consider group E, above, as well as group F. Is your reaction favorable or unfavorable?

12. Do you have an overall response to the articles from any of the American periods shown? Is it positive or negative?

13. Do you have any additional comments you would like to make regarding this exercise?

Exercise C

While the drawings in these exercises are only a small sampling of the various periods and styles we see around us today, you probably found certain pictures that you really liked and some that you really disliked. Do any of the drawings reflect your own taste or resemble items found in your own home? Did you see the dream home you would like to have?

The questions below will guide you in looking around your home and among your personal effects to see if you can discover evidence of other times or places reflected in your surroundings. Look carefully at the decorations, patterns, and styles that you find there. You'll be amazed at many of the details you never observed before. Do you have remnants of a particular incarnation that you now recognize in your home? It can be fun to notice aspects of yourself that you have previously been unaware of.

1. Do you notice any strong influences of other times and places in your house and its furnishings? Which articles reflect these influences, and where in your home are they located?

2. How do you feel about these objects?

3. Take a moment to imagine your dream house and its furnishings. Does it show a predominant influence from any geographic or historical setting?

4. Does your taste in clothing, jewelry, and other person-

al effects indicate a possible connection with any particular region or historical period?

5. Have you ever had an especially strong emotional attachment to a specific material object? Do you associate this object with any other time or place?

6. Let's look at some other ways in which your taste in physical surroundings might indicate possible past connections: Do you feel a strong reaction, either positive or negative, to objects in the homes of others that remind you of a certain region or era? Do your reading or television and motion-picture viewing habits reveal an interest in the artifacts of any specific culture? If you visit cultural or historical museums, is there a section devoted to any particular time or place that you find especially fascinating?

7. Has this examination of your taste in material surroundings and personal effects suggested any other comments you'd like to make?

Before moving on to the next section of this course, we might find it helpful to look at some of the observations other people were able to make based on these exercises. In regard to the series of pictures presented, one woman noticed that she responded positively to all the drawings of furniture from the Queen Anne period in England. Upon looking around her she discovered that not only her own home, but also the homes of other family members, reflected this style. She went to the library, where further reading on this period revealed a great deal that tied in with her theory of a life during this time in England.

For instance, she has always insisted on furniture made of walnut—no other wood would do. She found that walnut was used so much during the Queen Anne period that it became known as the "Age of Walnut" in the furniture world.

This woman particularly likes small tables and loves to play cards. She associates drinking tea with this pastime. She discovered that during the Queen Anne period card games became very popular, and many small tables were designed for cardplaying and the tea-drinking that went along with it.

She loves tall clocks and beautiful mirrors, but her favorite piece of furniture is the Queen Anne upholstered wing chair. She reported that everyone in her family has a wing chair but her, and she has always felt deprived because she didn't have one.

One fun piece of trivia she discovered concerns a habit of the men during this time. Chairs were armless, which allowed the skirts of the ladies to fall in graceful folds and also helped the male dandies to arrange their long coattails. It was the habit of young men of this period to turn these chairs around and sit on them backward, resting their arms on the tops of the chair backs. The woman noted with amusement that her beloved grandfather always sits on chairs backward, resting his arms on the back of the chair.

One man realized that he reacted very negatively to anything French that reflected the Louis XIV through Louis XVI periods, yet he had a very comfortable feeling about the things identified as French Provincial. This puzzled him, since both were French and from the same period. In reading, he discovered that the grandeur and extravagance of the monarchs of that time were paid for by the high taxes and oppression of the people, and this oppression helped sow the seeds of the French Revolution. At the same time the homes and furnishings of the provinces of France reflected homier life.

As he thought about this, the man realized that he had always associated the Louis XIV influence with the very rich, and he held a certain amount of resentment toward anyone who could afford such luxuries. He theorized that he might have taken part in the French Revolution, or that at least he could have been someone who experienced and resented the oppression of the people. He also felt he had lived somewhere in the provinces of France during that time and had enjoyed the comforts associated with a simple, modest home life. The interesting thing is that the man reports he's better able to overcome his feelings of resentment now that he understands he's holding on to something that no longer exists, except within himself.

Another woman noticed that she was very uncomfortable in one room of her home. It had a hardwood floor, with a braided oval rug and early American furniture, which she had bought just because it was on sale. While others found this room attractive and comfortable, she always wanted to change it. To her it was plain and uninspired. Laughingly, she considered the possibility that she had had a dreary incarnation in early America.

This kind of analysis is subjective, and we realize that no firm conclusions can be drawn from the kind of sofa you have in your living room. But perhaps we can use our feelings about our material surroundings as another thread in weaving a past-life theory. In the next section, we'll go on to pick up some additional threads by examining your reactions toward different parts of the world.

Session 5
A Trip Around the World

In an earlier session we touched on the idea that our strong reactions to places, cultures, and historical periods can tell us something about our past. You may already have noticed that you have strong feelings about certain countries, cultures, or times in history. These reactions can be positive or negative, depending on whether your particular past-life experience left you with a good or a bad taste in your mouth, so to speak.

You're now going to have a chance to get in touch with some of these feelings, both those that you are aware of and some that you may not have thought quite so much about.

We're going to be taking an imaginary trip around the world, sampling your reactions and noting your impressions and opinions about various places and the people in them.

You may be thinking, "But I don't know enough about some parts of the world to have any impressions," or, "My impressions will be too biased by books I've read, countries I've visited, movies I've seen, and history I've studied." Don't let this concern you. Remember that past-life recall is largely a matter of getting acquainted with your perceptions, your view, or your memory of a past reality. These perceptions may be pieced together from things you've seen or heard during this lifetime. They may be distorted, or even inaccurate, objectively speaking. But the real question remains: Why have I come up with this particular collection of impressions about a given country? Why are my impressions so different from someone else's? As you examine your own individual reactions to a country, you may begin to understand the reasons why your impressions are so uniquely your own.

Please read the instructions for the first three exercises carefully and follow them exactly. Quite a bit of reflection will be needed for you to obtain the most benefit from these exercises. It is suggested that you take them at an unhurried pace and cover only one or two of the countries named per sitting. It is very important that you complete Exercise A for all countries named before going on to Exercises B and C.

Exercise A

For this exercise, you are asked to list as many impressions as you can for each country or region listed below. Just free-associate and jot down *anything* that comes to mind when you think of that part of the world. It is likely that you will find you have more to write for some areas than for others. For some, you may actually have very few comments to note. That's perfectly okay. You might try to picture each place in your mind, or see it on a globe, or just reflect on what images the name of that particular location brings to your mind. Be sure to complete this section for each region named before going on to Exercise B.

Start by noting your spontaneous impressions first. Then, if you feel you need more ideas, you might want to consult the following list of memory joggers. It's provided only to help you in case you can't think of what kinds of things to write down. Feel free to use as many of these ideas or as few of them as you'd like:

Terrain. Climate. Plant and animal life. People—their racial and physical characteristics, clothing and other items of personal adornment, social and economic classes, temperament and behavior. Historical periods. Regions and countries. Cities. Work life and products. Art. Architecture, furnishings, and decorations. Music. Religion. Social life, leisure activities, and sports and games. Food.

For each region given below, list any impressions that come to mind which you would use to complete the following statement:

"When I think of <u>(Name of area)</u>, I think of _____."

1. The Mideast
2. Egypt
3. North America
4. Asia Minor
5. Africa
6. Australia
7. Latin America
8. India
9. Greece
10. Italy
11. Tropical islands
12. Europe
13. The British Isles
14. Japan
15. China
16. Russia

Exercise B

Now that you've finished listing your impressions concerning various areas of the world, we're going to start putting these responses together to obtain a picture of your overall perception of each of these places. Answer the questions below, applying them to each of the sixteen regions dealt with in Exercise A. Your responses to this exercise should be based entirely upon the lists of impressions you've recorded in the previous section. Consider all the questions in regard to our first area, the Mideast, then go on and answer them for Egypt, the second region covered, and so on. Complete all portions of this exercise before moving on to Exercise C.

1. Go over your list of impressions for this region. For each response, note whether you consider it positive (pleasant, nice, etc.), negative (unpleasant, ugly, etc.), or neutral. A simple +/-/0 notation might be the easiest way of recording these reactions.
2. a) How many impressions, if any, did you rate as positive?
   b) How many impressions, if any, did you rate as negative?
   c) How many, if any, did you rate as neutral?
   d) What is the total of your answers to the first three parts of this question? This number should equal the total number of impressions you noted for this region when you did Exercise A.
3. Find your Positive Reaction Quotient (PRQ) by dividing your answer to part *a* of question 2 by your answer to part *d* of that question; that is, PRQ = a ÷ d. For example, if you had three positive responses to this region and your total number of impressions regarding it was twelve, your PRQ would be 3 ÷ 12 = 3/12, or 25%.
4. Find your Negative Reaction Quotient (NRQ) by dividing your answer to part *b* of question 2 by your answer to part *d*: NRQ = b ÷ d.

5. Go back over your list of impressions about this region. Based on it, describe the people who live here (appearance, clothing, classes, temperament, etc.).

6. Look at your list again, and this time use it to describe the environment of the area (terrain, climate, vegetation, etc.).

7. What kind of life-style does your list of impressions suggest (occupations, leisure activities, social life, art, religion, etc.)?

8. Did your impressions seem to focus on specific places, cities, or sections within this larger area? If so, note them here.

9. To what time period are most of the impressions you listed applicable? Estimate, if necessary, as "ancient times," "100 years ago," "the 1500s," etc. Note any specific historical references you may have made.

Exercise C

This exercise is designed to summarize, in a form that is easily readable and usable, the impressions and observations you've noted in Exercises A and B. To complete this composite picture, refer directly to the answers you gave in Exercise B for each location listed. When you have answered the questions below for each area, you will have an overview of your "memories" concerning the various parts of the world.

As you work on this composite view, you should begin to see certain areas emerging in a very positive light, and others that perhaps you do not find at all appealing. These two groups are likely to be the regions that are most important to your past-life theories. The areas that remain largely neutral, on the other hand, are probably either places where you haven't had prior incarnations, or ones in which your earlier lifetimes are not exerting a particularly strong influence at present.

Perhaps you will be able to use this section most effectively if you arrange your answers in chart form, with the regions listed across the top of your page and a shortened version of each question down the left side, as is illustrated below:

	Mid-East	Egypt	North America	etc.
1. PRQ				
2. NRQ				
3. Drawn to people?				
4. Be like people?				
5. etc.				
6.				

Here are the questions in complete form:

1. What is your Positive Reaction Quotient?

2. What is your Negative Reaction Quotient?

3. Are you drawn to people like the ones you described in answer 5 (of Exercise B)?

4. Would you like to be like the people in your description?

5. Give your opinion of the environment you described in answer 6.

6. Do you find the life-style you described in answer 7 appealing or not?

7. Note the aspects of life-style you found most appealing or unappealing, as the case may be.

8. Are any places or sections of this region predominant in your impressions (refer to your answers for item 8)? What are these predominant areas?

9. Did you focus on any particular time periods (refer to answer 9)? Which ones?

10. Have you ever traveled to this area? Would you like to?

11. Does your selection of such things as books, movies,

and the museum trips you take reflect an interest in this region?

12. Is any influence from this part of the world shown in your clothing, house, furnishings, etc.?

13. Do you think you may have lived here?

14. If so, identify two personal characteristics of yours which may have come from that lifetime.

The information you have just gathered together in Exercise C now forms a compact picture that will serve as an important source of past-life insights. The time you put into your trip around the world might have been considerable. But as you begin to glean past-life clues from your composite picture, it is quite possible that you will be amazed at how much you are able to learn about yourself through this series of exercises.

Some things, of course, will stand out quickly. You'll notice the parts of the world that hold pleasant associations for you. You'll see the ones that you find unattractive. A simple review of your Positive and Negative Reaction Quotients will tell you this. You may come to understand your reactions more deeply, however, when you look at how you view each country's people, environment, and history.

For example, let's compare two women's reactions to England. One had a high Positive Reaction Quotient; one had a high Negative Reaction Quotient. But the one with the favorable reaction had emphasized impressions of the countryside, manor houses, and gardens, while the woman with the negative reaction had focused on castles and a cold, damp climate. We might imagine that the first person had a pleasant lifetime among the English country gentry, while the second harbored unhappy memories of an experience in a castle.

You may have been surprised to find that you had some strong impressions about areas you'd never before considered, areas you thought you knew nothing about. For example, one person was amazed to note that she had thought about volcanoes, warmth, fruit, dugouts, wooden bowls, a relaxed life, blue water, warm surf, dancing, and innocence in connection with tropical islands—very strong and definite impressions, indeed. Yet if someone had asked her, she'd have said she knew nothing about that part of the world.

You may have noticed that specific cities or regions form the basis of your impressions for some parts of the world, while vast areas went virtually unnoticed by you. For one person Latin America became Peru, as his list of responses showed; most of another man's impressions, on the other hand, dealt with the Mayan culture.

As you described the people in certain countries, did you notice habits and personality traits that are part of your own makeup? One man who described the deep spirituality of the Indian people recognized the similarity between their concern with the soul and his own spiritual search in this lifetime.

Even clichés among your responses may ring true. The thrifty Scottish people remarked by one person tied in to his own frugal nature. Might he view the roots of this trait as having come from Scotland? Maybe so—if his other impressions of Scotland hit home in some way.

Perhaps you saw some patterns as you compared and contrasted your responses to each of the different parts of the world. For example, if you found that you usually liked the environments that you described as warm and dry and disliked those you described as damp and foggy, that can tell you something about two possible past lives—one in a desert climate and another in a damp one. If you found that for most parts of the world you described people in lower-class circumstances, this would be a different kind of clue than descriptions of the rich would be.

The attitudes that came through in such descriptions would be equally important. Someone who perceived the rich from a perspective of resentment and distaste may have been downtrodden in the past. Someone who described them in terms of admiration may have been wealthy or looked up to the wealthy in a previous incarnation.

And so, as you look over your composite view, you may

see items that tie together like individual pieces of a jigsaw puzzle. At first, when you spread a jigsaw puzzle out on a table, all you see are odd-shaped pieces of assorted colors. You start putting your puzzle together by looking for colors that match and shapes that interlock. You begin to fit some of the greens together, for example, and soon see that the pieces are going to form the image of a tree. From there, it's easier to recognize the other pieces of the tree and fit them in.

So it is with your composite view. First you note the impressions that are similar to one another or that seem to connect in some way. These connections may tell you something about your memories of a certain country or its people. You may notice that you are drawn toward distinct historical periods or social classes, while others leave you cold. You may recognize personality traits, interests, and distastes that are part of you today. These insights become the seeds of past-life theories.

However vague or well-developed your theories may be at this point, you can continue filling in your puzzle as we continue gathering clues. And just as you often piece together several portions of a jigsaw puzzle simultaneously, you may find that your composite view suggests more than one past-life theory.

Exercise D

As a final wrap-up for this session, answer the questions below. This exercise is not long, and your answers can be quite brief, but do take some time and examine your responses to the previous exercises carefully in order to complete this section.

1. Go back over the composite view you came up with in Exercise C, looking for patterns of similar or interconnected responses. Note any such patterns you are able to discover.

2. Do these patterns suggest any past-life theories to you? Be as specific as you can in your descriptions of these theories, but don't worry if many of the details are still

missing at this time. More clues will be forthcoming in our later sessions. At certain points you may wish to return to this exercise to incorporate additional information into your theories as it becomes available to you. By all means do so whenever the urge strikes.

3. Are there any further observations you would like to make regarding any of the exercises in this session of the course?

Session 6
Hereditary and Environmental Influences

Let's begin our examination of the role heredity and environment play in our lives by looking at the relationship between these influences and the ones we bring with us from our previous incarnations. Thus far, our work has been based on the assumption that our interests and characteristics are strongly shaped by former lives. How, then, do we account for the effects of heredity and environment?

Modern genetics has shown pretty conclusively that we inherit through our genes not only our physical makeup, but many of our mental and psychological traits as well. If this is true, how can we say that past-life influences, rather than simple genetics, have caused a person to be fat or thin, a mathematician rather than an artist, or whatever the case may be?

We have a similar puzzle with respect to environment. We know that our early childhood experiences, our family setting, and virtually everything going on in the world around us all have an influence on the way we think about and react to life's events. How, then, can we attribute traits of temperament and personality to past-life experiences? Are we denying the role of heredity and environment in making us who we are?

Probably the best answer is, yes and no. Yes, we are denying that heredity and environment are the absolute molding agents in our lives, forces which shape us without regard to our own choice. On the other hand, no—we are not denying that heredity and environment have a very real effect on our lives. But rather than seeing them as factors which determine who we are, perhaps we should view heredity and environment as conditions that we're drawn to in order to meet the results of choices we've made in the past. In other words, heredity and environment interact with this thing we call karma in such a way that each life is a continuation of patterns, good and bad, that we've established in previous lives. Here's how it might work.

First of all, it's important to remember that in the reincarnation theory the essence of who we are is nonphysical. It's the part of us that existed before we were born into the current flesh-body and the part of us that will live on after the body dies. If we imagine, for the sake of illustration, that our nonphysical essence is like a malleable substance— say, a piece of clay—we can begin to see how our choices shape our inner being. With each choice we make, that claylike substance is shaped, forming a record of sorts. A talent developed here, a problem fed there, a happy experience, a painful one—they each leave their mark on our inner beings, shaping them into forms that become our individual identities. And when our nonphysical essence is drawn into physical form, it attracts to itself just the right heredity and environment to fit the inner identity. We might imagine our heredity and environment to be a glove, custom-made to fit the hand.

Or consider it this way: Suppose that claylike essence we spoke of a moment ago is also magnetic. Just as our magnetic lump of clay would draw to itself iron filings that would encase it and give it a hard outer shell, our inner identity encases itself in physical and environmental circumstances.

It's important to remember that patterns which have taken on concrete form in our physical or environmental circumstances usually can't be changed instantaneously; the inner form must be changed before a new outer shell can be constructed to conform to it. For this reason, body traits can be some of our most enduring records of past-life experiences. The physical makeup we come in with is pretty much indicative of some patterns built in prior lives. Because of this, we can learn to read our body's record of what we may have built or experienced in the past.

For example, consider the case of a man born with a partial paralysis of the right arm, making it impossible for him to open his hand completely. This could be part of a pattern built in a past life, one spent as a closefisted miser, unwilling to extend a helping hand to those around him. The man's inability to extend his hand in the present is the logical consequence of the pattern he created. Thus his experience gives him the chance to learn how limiting his previous self-centered values can be.

Another person who received a reading from Edgar Cayce was told that his continual gastrointestinal problems are a direct result of an earlier life, when he had been a glutton.

Of course, not all body clues point to shortcomings or lessons we need to learn. Some are simply records of the past, like the skillful hands of a person who had been an accomplished artist, the sharp hearing of a former Indian, and the physical agility of someone with a previous incarnation as a great athlete. These clues become especially important when it seems that the person was just born with them, rather than having labored in this lifetime to develop such physical traits. One woman who came to Edgar Cayce for a reading made a living modeling her beautiful hands.

Her reading told her that in a former lifetime she had used her hands to help others.

Our bodies can also store memories of past-life traumas that we haven't let go of yet. Birthmarks may be the carryovers—scars, if you will—of injuries incurred during former incarnations. One woman, for instance, carries a bright red birthmark on the back of her neck, and she has a continuing problem with psoriasis on the same spot. When she considers this condition and other clues she has pieced together, she theorizes a possible death by guillotine in the French Revolution.

Sometimes our body clues point to compensation for a past situation. Consider the case of one woman who now has a problem with obesity. This, along with some other past-life clues, suggests to her that she might have struggled with poverty and starvation during a previous lifetime.

There are, as we have seen, many possible ways in which our bodies can reflect experiences from our past. Thus it is important to realize that a single body clue, all by itself, may not instantly suggest a past-life theory. But it can be an important piece in the puzzle.

Exercise A

It's time for you now to take an inventory of your own body clues. As you answer the questions below, some ideas about past lives may occur to you. Be sure to make note of these in response to question 18, which asks for any additional comments you may have regarding the exercise. But if you don't get any hunches as you go along, that's okay too. What's important now is just that you think about and answer the questions. This will give you several useful clues as to your previous incarnations. Time and guidelines for weaving these clues together to form comprehensive past-life theories will be provided later on in the course.

Section One: Physical Strengths

1. Consider your childhood as well as the present time. Did you, or do you, have any special body skills and characteristics that are physical strengths? Examples of this might be strong, broad hands that enable you to play the piano, or finger dexterity that allows you to do precision work, such as model building. List any such physical traits you possess; then indicate which of these you were apparently born with or developed naturally at an early age, as opposed to those you worked consciously to develop.

2. Again considering your childhood as well as the present, are any of your five senses particularly sharp? If so, state which of your senses is special in this way and describe the ways in which this acuteness is demonstrated.

3. Have you ever had any special athletic ability, either now or in the past? List your specific skills, as well as the body strengths necessary for these abilities. For example, you might list cross-country skiing, which would require great stamina and strong legs. Or maybe as a child you were the table-tennis champion of your block; this would show exceptional hand–eye coordination.

Section Two: Physical Weaknesses

4. List any trouble spots in your body where you frequently experience illness or discomfort. Include any chronic health problems (such as a bad back or recurrent sinusitis) as well as areas where illness tends to crop up repeatedly for you (for example, periodic trouble in the stomach or the respiratory system). Indicate any of these problems that you find especially bothersome to your mental outlook.

5. List any of your senses that are especially weak or are nonfunctional.

Section Three: Birthmarks and Features

6. List any birthmarks you may have and state where they're located. If you have feelings about any of these marks, be sure to note them as well.

7. Do you have any specific features that others often

notice or that you are particularly aware of? For example, maybe others frequently comment on your tiny feet. Or maybe you have always been very aware of having a long neck. Note any such features here, as well as whether you consider each one to be an asset or a problem.

Section Four: Your Behavior Regarding Your Body

8. List any habits you have involving the care and/or use of your body that are unlike those of most people you know.

9. List any body habits you make a conscious effort to maintain.

10. Do you have any body habits about which others have complained? What are they?

Section Five: Your Attitudes Toward the Body

11. What physical ability do you wish for or have you striven to acquire?

12. Is there any particular physical injury or weakness you are afraid of having to face?

13. Are there any physical body types that you find generally attractive or repulsive? Explain.

14. What physical characteristics do you look for and admire in others?

15. Have you ever suddenly been attracted to a person? Describe what you consider to be that person's most striking physical characteristics.

16. Have you ever had an unreasonable dislike for anyone? What physical traits of this person do you remember?

17. What physical weakness or handicap do you notice most readily in others? How do you feel about people who have this condition?

Section Six: General Comments

18. Are there any other insights that have occurred to you as a result of this exercise? Include, but don't limit yourself to, any past-life theories suggested to you by this inventory of your body and your feelings toward it.

Just as our physical heredity can reflect past-life influences, the environmental forces that appear to shape our interests, abilities, and temperament can be seen as instruments bringing our soul patterns into action in this three-dimensional world. Our early interests, our fears and distastes, and even our talents and hobbies may on the surface be traced to people who inspired us, educational experiences that whetted an appetite or ability, early traumas that awakened a fear, and so on. But the deeper question remains: Did those environmental influences arise strictly by accident? Or did they come our way in order to awaken certain patterns the soul needed to experience? During this course we're going to work under the hypothesis that there is indeed a reason behind the specific environmental circumstances into which each of us was born. Thus we can look to our interests, fears, and talents to discover clues to past experience.

Sometimes the things that we liked to do when we were children can tell us about our earliest inclinations. Many times these activities are forgotten by the time we're adults. But we're left to wonder: could those very early interests, talents and hobbies be clues to carryovers from our previous incarnations?

One person remembers that when she was a child she loved to design cities and the architecture in them. She'd use paper and cardboard to construct the fronts of stores and houses, and she'd plan the layout of streets. She also enjoyed designing articles of clothing for her dolls and cutting them out of paper. Was this child remembering a past skill in architecture or design? Her tendency actually to cut her creations out of paper, rather than just drawing them, may also tell her something. Possibly it would show a need to be concrete, or maybe a special talent for working with three-dimensional models.

One young man's family informs him that as a toddler he was obsessed with drawing pictures of planes going down. They say that he repeatedly listened to the "1812 Overture" on the record player and that he would cry when the cannons went off. This man's childhood drawings and fascination with the "1812 Overture" may come from a memory of an earlier incarnation in a military setting. Interestingly enough, he has no interest in things military now that he is an adult.

Another person tells of having been the only little girl on the block who played pirate. She had the whole outfit: black eye patch, sword, and T-shirt with broad horizontal stripes. The picnic table was her boat, which she could ride all day. And, of course, there had to be buried treasure; she'd bury something and make elaborate pirate maps, burning them around the edges to give them that charred-parchment look. Possible memories of seafaring adventures could have been influencing this child unconsciously. Or the game could have been the form her childish mind built around some deep-seated interests. In this case, the woman has had a lifelong interest in maps and a good sense of navigation. Although today she uses this interest and ability primarily to get around in an automobile, she may well keep her skill with maps and navigation in mind as one piece of her past-life puzzle.

One woman recalls that she never played house—she played preacher. She'd line up all her dolls and preach to them for hours. Here is a case of a childhood interest that has clearly been carried through to adulthood. Today this woman is a gifted lecturer whose ability to speak on subjects like meditation, dreams, and the setting of spiritual ideals has had an impact on thousands of lives. Did she develop this talent all in the space of her current lifetime? Or does her childhood interest perhaps suggest a past-life carryover?

Exercise B

Quite possibly, as you read these stories about other people's childhood interests, memories from your own childhood began emerging. We're about to take a few moments to allow you to think about those memories.

In this exercise we will be dealing with actual events, rather than fantasy. Therefore the experience you'll be

having here is not, strictly speaking, a reverie. Nevertheless, several of the techniques used in reverie may prove
helpful here. You might wish to review quickly the material
on reverie that was given in the second session of our
course.

Relaxation of both body and mind is extremely important.
Before beginning this mental trip back through the years,
take some time to let yourself grow quiet. You may benefit
from going through the entire relaxation routine presented in
the earlier reverie chapter. At the least, you should get into
a physically comfortable position, close your eyes, take
several slow, deep, natural breaths, and let any tensions slip
away from you.

It might be helpful for you either to make a cassette tape
of the material below to serve as your guide through this
experience, or have a friend slowly read the material to you.
Whatever method you choose, do not interrupt the flow of
your memory in order to write your responses to the
questions that appear in the text. These queries are intended
merely to direct your attention to various details of your
experience so that you will be able to recall them at the
conclusion of the exercise. The questions will be repeated
for you at that point.

And now it's time for you to follow whatever relaxation
technique you feel will be most effective, and then use your
memory to revisit the areas of your childhood described
below.

Let yourself be carried back to an early childhood experience. Visualize with your mind's eye the event as it unfolds
around you. As completely as you can, enter into this
memory, becoming the child that you were when the inci-
dent first occurred.

In your chosen recollection, what are you doing? Whom
are you with? How are you feeling? Stay with this memory
for as long as you like, letting the experience proceed at its
own pace toward its natural conclusion.

Now look back over your other childhood memories.
What games do you remember enjoying? Were there any

that you made up? What did you do on a rainy day in the summer? Were there special toys or belongings you particularly prized?

Did you like to draw? To color? Or to finger-paint? If you did, what kinds of things did you draw?

How about favorite stories? Were there any you begged to hear again and again? Did you like to read stories and books on your own? What kind? Do any stand out in particular?

What about friends? Think about the friendships of your childhood. How were they different from one another? How were they alike? Were there particular activities you enjoyed doing with certain friends?

Continue thinking about your childhood for a few moments, as long as the memories last.

When your memories of early childhood have finished running their course, return to the present and answer these questions about them.

1. In the first childhood scene you revisited in this exercise, what were you doing? Whom were you with? Do you remember how you were feeling?

2. In your other recollections of early childhood, what games do you remember especially enjoying? Were any of them games that you yourself made up?

3. What types of things did you do on rainy days during the summer?

4. Did you have any special toys or belongings that you particularly valued?

5. Did you like to draw, color, or finger-paint? If so, what kind of things did you draw most often?

6. Did you have any favorite stories? Were there any that you liked to hear over and over again? Did you enjoy reading books and stories on your own? What kind? List any that stand out in particular.

7. Think back to your closest childhood friends. In what ways were these friendships alike? How were they different from each other? Were there any specific activities you most enjoyed doing with certain friends?

8. List any circumstances in your early childhood that you consider especially fortunate.

9. Describe any circumstances from your early life that you feel were particularly unfortunate.

10. Did you have any childhood longings that were notably strong or persistent? What were they?

11. Briefly, how would you describe your childhood temperament and personality?

12. Note any additional memories you may have had or comments you would like to make.

Session 7
Analyzing Your Emotional Reactions

Our emotional reactions to conditions in the world around us vary greatly from individual to individual. This suggests the question: Why do different people react so differently to the same thing? Why is one person deathly afraid of heights, for example, while another loves skydiving, and a third is completely indifferent to flying or being in high places? Why is one person a dog-lover, while another has a great fear of or aversion to these animals? A basic assumption of this course is that there is *some* cause behind such individual differences, something in each person's past experiences that makes him tend to respond in the specific way that he does.

Of course, it is possible for these response-shaping experiences to have occurred during the present lifetime. Perhaps our dog-lover spent his early years in a happy home in which the presence of a beloved canine pet was an important element of the caring, supportive family atmosphere. And maybe the person who fears dogs was threatened or attacked by a large member of the species when he was young.

Similar explanations, operating through just a single lifetime, could no doubt be found for a number of the emotional reactions each individual displays.

And yet, valid as these current-lifetime explanations may be in specific instances, they are not the only ones available to us once we have accepted the theory of reincarnation. It is most probable that each of us exhibits certain emotional responses that cannot easily be traced to earlier experiences during this lifetime. Such reactions must have come from somewhere, and we are presented with the likelihood that many of them originated in the events of our previous incarnations. If this is true, our emotional responses, being in many cases the reflection of past-life memories, are among the most important clues we can investigate in our effort to discover what our experiences in former lifetimes might have been.

We are now going to take a close look at some of your emotional reactions to see what they can reveal about your prior incarnations. When we are finished with the following exercises, the clues you gather from your positive and negative responses to various conditions around you will be added to the ones you obtained in our earlier sessions—those discovered through your examination of your home and physical surroundings, your reactions to different areas of the world, your body, and your early childhood experiences. As we shall see in future chapters, each of these types of clues can be a valuable aid in piecing together theories about our past lives.

Exercise A

Certain conditions evoke strong emotional responses in many people. In this exercise, you'll be identifying your own reactions to a number of these stimuli. Start by consulting the rating chart on page 205 which lists possible responses ranging from extreme fear or distaste to great enjoyment. Choose the number from 1 to 5 that best describes your reaction to the condition named, and note any comments you would like to make regarding each entry. Thus for each item your answer will consist of the name of the stimulus or condition, the number rating of your response to it, and any comments you feel are relevant.

Just to give you some ideas, it would be appropriate to put down as a comment any qualifying statement you might have regarding your reaction to each item. For example, one person wrote of feeling great fear in lake or ocean water, but enjoying a swimming pool immensely.

Another type of comment would be suggested if you can think of a possible explanation for any of your reactions related to your earlier experiences in this lifetime. If, for instance, you have a marked fear of being in water and recall that as a young child you almost drowned, this would be worth noting.

On the other hand, if you have no present-lifetime explanation for one of your responses but discover that it seems to fit in with a past-life theory you've been formulating, this too would be worth writing down. As an illustration of this, suppose your answers to earlier exercises have caused you to theorize an incarnation in ancient Israel, and in completing this inventory you notice that at present you feel very comfortable among Jewish people; you might well want to make note of this obvious tie-in.

These possibilities are given only as suggestions, and you shouldn't limit yourself to comments of the types described here. Don't hesitate to make any sort of observation you yourself feel will be helpful.

In filling out this self-analysis survey, consider your childhood reactions to the stimuli listed as well as your current feelings about them. And remember, it's your emotional responses we're looking for, not your intellectual opinions. If, for example, you realize logically that racial prejudice is foolish, and yet you find that you feel very uncomfortable when among members of a certain ethnic group, do make note of this reaction. It came from somewhere, and if you omit it you could be depriving yourself of a piece of information that might prove very useful in your search for self-understanding and knowledge of your former lives.

Here is the scale to be used in rating your emotional reaction to each of the items listed below:
1. This condition or stimulus causes me great fear, distaste, or discomfort.
2. It gives me some anxiety or discomfort.
3. I have a neutral response to it.
4. I find it rather pleasant or comfortable.
5. I greatly enjoy it or feel totally comfortable with it.

And here is the list of stimuli to which you should note your responses, along with any relevant comments:
1. Being in water.
2. Being in high places.
3. Being in enclosed places.
4. Being in wide-open spaces.
5. Being alone outdoors.
6. Being abandoned.
7. Crowds.
8. Solitude.
9. Loud noises.
10. Silence.
11. Books and reading.
12. Wearing heavy clothing.
13. Wearing high collars.
14. Wearing hats.
15. People of certain nationalities or ethnic groups (specify).
16. People with certain foreign or regional accents (specify).
17. People of certain religions (specify).
18. People with certain physical traits (specify).
19. People of certain age groups (specify).
20. People of certain political orientations (specify).
21. People of certain professions (specify).
22. Authority figures.
23. People of the same sex as you.
24. People of the opposite sex.

25. People who are early.
26. People who are late.
27. Mice.
28. Birds.
29. Snakes.
30. Other animals (specify).
31. Sunlight.
32. Darkness.
33. Heat.
34. Cold.
35. Humid climates.
36. Arid climates.
37. Wind.
38. Lightning.
39. Fire.
40. Death.
41. Hunger.
42. Pregnancy and childbirth.
43. Traveling at high speed.
44. Flying.
45. Bridges.
46. Tunnels.
47. Stairs.
48. Guns.

Exercise B

Now we're going to examine some of your emotional reactions that you consider positive. In answering the questions below, use your own definition of what constitutes a positive emotional response. It can be one that you find especially enjoyable, uplifting, or pleasant in any way that you feel is noteworthy. As with the previous inventory, your comments regarding each item are very important, and it will be most helpful if they are included in each specific answer rather than all together at the end of the survey. The same types of remarks suggested for Exercise A would also be quite suitable to most of the items in this section. Once again, consider your childhood reactions as well as your current ones, and concentrate on your emotions rather than your intellectual opinions.

1. The items listed in Exercise A are ones that are frequently mentioned when people are asked to name things that they respond to, either positively or negatively. No doubt there are other stimuli that evoke a strong positive emotional reaction in you. List here any such items which were not included in the preceding survey, along with any relevant comments you'd like to make regarding each item.

2. Are there any special sensory impressions or reactions that you intensely enjoy? Describe them.

3. Do you get strong feelings of excitement or enjoyment from any particular group games or activities? List the activities and describe your feelings toward them.

4. Is there any particular physical activity that you find especially exciting and stimulating—that is, which creates on thought or participation strong emotional enjoyment?

5. Is there any type of physical activity you enjoy reading about? Name one or two books involving it.

6. Have any other books caused you a powerful positive emotional reaction? What were these books about?

7. Do motion pictures dealing with any particular physical activities appeal to you? Name one or more such movies.

8. Do you remember seeing any other motion pictures about which you had strong positive feelings? What were the subjects of these movies?

9. Have you had any outstanding positive emotional experience in relation to music? Describe the type of music, the feelings it brought forth, and the circumstances under which this response took place.

10. Has any other stimulus or event in your life caused an exceptionally powerful positive emotional reaction in you? Describe any such occurrences, and indicate what you feel was the essential quality of each of these events that made you respond so strongly.

Exercise C

Like the things that cause positive reactions in us, those which bring out strong fears and dislikes can be clues to memories we are carrying from our past lives. In these cases, of course, the remembrances are likely to be of unpleasant experiences. Psychologists and psychiatrists certainly work with this principle within the time frame of one lifetime when they delve into recollections from early childhood in order to understand adjustment problems that have arisen in an adult. Working with the reincarnation hypothesis, we can see how memories from even earlier in our experience might be making themselves known through our aversions and the things we especially fear or dislike.

The questions below will guide you through an investigation of your negative emotional reactions and the insights they can help you develop regarding your remote past. Be sure to include any relevant comments; you can refer back to Exercise A if you need a quick refresher on the types of remarks that are likely to be most helpful. As with the foregoing sections, think about your reactions from both your earlier years and the present, and focus on those experiences which are or have been strongly emotional ones for you.

1. The inventory in Exercise A lists some things that often come up when people name their major fears and distastes. Are there any stimuli not covered there that cause a strong negative reaction in you? List any such items and include any clarifying remarks concerning each one.

2. Have you ever responded with strong fear or aversion to any books or stories you've read? Name the books, and describe the feelings they brought out and any insights you have regarding them.

3. Have any motion pictures ever caused a powerful negative reaction in you? Name the movies and describe the emotions you felt.

4. Has any music ever brought about a significant nega-

tive reaction in you? Describe any such listening experiences.

5. What circumstances in your life do you complain about most?

6. What faults do you notice most in others?

7. Note an outstanding physical fight you've experienced. Did it bring out any strong negative emotions in you?

8. Is there any specific physical injury or disease you are especially afraid of?

9. Is there any type of circumstance or activity which you deliberately avoid? Describe these conditions and the reason for your aversion to them.

10. Is there any experience or activity you especially fear?

11. Is there any type of person you are afraid of? In this question, "type" can refer to age, sex, race, religion, social class, occupation, or any other grouping of people that you fear.

12. What do you fear most?

13. Is there any other item or circumstance that evokes a powerful negative reaction in you? Describe the stimulus, the emotions it brings out, and any ideas you might have about why you respond in this way.

Session 8
Constructing Past-Life Theories from Present-Life Clues

In an earlier session we saw how we can gather clues about our previous incarnations from our bodies and our early-childhood experiences—or, in other words, from our heredity and the environment into which we were born. The reason these two factors are such valuable sources of past-life information is that they are the result of the choices we have made in our former lifetimes. That is, our past decisions have produced in us a certain degree of soul development and a need for the soul to learn specific lessons, and each individual's heredity and environment are provided in order to make available the opportunity to learn those lessons.

When we stop and think about the idea that hereditary and environmental circumstances are conditions through which we can experience the things our soul needs to learn, the concept becomes mind-boggling. Each and every individual is drawn into the precise situation that best meets the needs of his or her soul development. This suggests an interconnectedness to life so complex that only the mind of our Creator could conceive it. When we look at heredity and environment in the light of reincarnation, we see our genetic links with other people, as well as the experiences we have with them, as part of an orchestrated flow of life—a flow that reflects the soul needs of every human being on the face of the earth at any given moment.

But it's crucial for us to keep in mind that the special appropriateness of our heredity and environment and the interconnectedness of our soul's journey with those of the people around us do not lock us into a predetermined destiny. We are each free to make choices moment by moment—free to use a constructive influence from the past or to neglect it, free to try to overcome a negative influence or not to. These choices will effect change in ourselves and the situations in which we live. Thus they will establish patterns in our lives and help determine the conditions of our future rebirths.

We are now going to practice putting life patterns and past-life theories together. We will be using our understanding of the Laws of Continuation, Consequences, and Compensation to figure out how former incarnations may be related to current life situations. If you feel you need to review these laws, turn back to Session 3 of this course. They are stated in summary form on page 155.

Once again, we will be using actual case histories from

the Edgar Cayce life readings. In the first group of cases, one of the past incarnations of each person will be described, and you are to see if you can guess what circumstances this experience might have produced in the current lifetime. Then we will reverse the process: you will be told something of each subject's present situation, and it will be up to you to try to determine what experiences in the past might have led to these current conditions.

In each of these two sections, all the case histories are presented first, immediately followed by the answers. Do give some careful thought to each case and formulate your own theory before checking the actual answer and going on to the next person's reading.

As you attempt to answer the questions below, you should bear in mind that there is no one correct solution for any of the cases. The exact progression of circumstances from lifetime to lifetime is based on so many individual factors that the possibilities are literally infinite. That's why it will also be important, when you theorize about your own past lives, to realize that you are choosing only one possible scenario out of many.

And now it's time for you to try to describe some current situations that might be produced by the past-life experiences depicted below.

Case 1: In her reading from Edgar Cayce, one woman was told that she had been with the people of Nehemiah in Old Testament days, when the rebuilding of Jerusalem's walls took place. She was too young to take part in the actual building, but she did help later on with the decoration of the walls. Keeping in mind the operation of the Laws of Continuation, Consequences, and Compensation, how might you expect her experience in ancient Israel to influence her today?

Case 2: This woman was told that she had lived a nomadic life as an Indian in what is now the Chicago area. What might we expect in her life today?

Case 3: One man's life reading placed him in early New York City. He had been one of the original settlers and had made significant contributions to the establishment of the city's civil laws. He also had taken part in planning the city's physical layout. What sorts of things might we expect of this man today?

Case 4: Another person was told that he had fought in the Crusades. Apparently he had started out with spiritual ideals, but he soon found that motives of material gain took over when the plundering of those wars began. Can you guess what the twentieth-century results might have been for this man?

Answer 1: As you can see, there are many possibilities. This woman may have picked up on the experience she was too young to have in the Old Testament life and become a builder today. She might have followed through with her past experience and become a decorator. Or maybe she developed a consuming interest in stonework or that period of biblical history. Any of these possibilities, as well as several others, would be a consistent outgrowth of her earlier experience. In point of fact, during her current lifetime this woman showed a flair for decoration, especially in working with cloth, brocade, and drapery.

Answer 2: Here we can see how the same life experience may lead to any of several rather divergent paths, depending on the needs of the individual soul. In her present life this woman might have continued her nomadic life-style and been someone who was always on the move. Or she might have compensated for her former rootlessness by becoming a staid homebody. In actuality, she found quite a balance between these two possibilities. In this life, she was someone who valued her home very highly and did not enjoy travel for travel's sake, but she did take frequent trips for educational purposes.

Answer 3: We could probably imagine this man in a career in government, architecture, or engineering. We might suppose that his early positive experience in New York left him inclined to like that city or even to be drawn to it today. As it turns out, he was a New Yorker in his modern-day lifetime. And though we don't know about his actual career, he did have an inclination toward lines, figures, and architectural drawings.

Answer 4: We can theorize quite a few possibilities for this soul. Maybe his own material success was blocked in consequence of his earlier plundering. Perhaps he was even robbed. On the other hand, maybe he continued to be a materialistic person, needing to relearn the importance of spiritual values. Or he could have gone the opposite way and become a cleric who renounced material gain for the spiritual path.

In the Cayce reading for this man, we are told that he had a very suspicious nature and was inclined to doubt other people's sincerity whenever they disagreed with him in any way. Here we get an interesting insight into the Crusades experience. This person had been influenced by other people to abandon his spiritual motivation and begin plundering instead. To this day, he has continued to be suspicious of others' purposes in his dealings with them. We can imagine that his life reading helped him see that he himself is responsible for his own life and motives.

Like the man described in this case, each of us must come to accept responsibility for our own choices and the situations that result from them. It is in helping us reach this realization that our past-life theories can be of greatest value to us. As we grow in our understanding of the ways in which our experiences during previous incarnations may be influencing circumstances in our lives today, we can become more willing to take responsibility for our choices. We can begin to see that current conditions are the product of our past decisions; we can become aware that through our present choices we are building our own futures; and we can realize that we are free to start making new choices, if need be.

Now let's approach past-life theories from the opposite direction. Still using the case histories from Edgar Cayce's life readings, we will find out a little bit about each person's modern-day life. Try to guess what kinds of past experienccs may have made the person or the life situation the way it is today.

Case 5: One man who received a reading from Cayce was plagued with self-doubts and fears. Where might this have come from?

Case 6: Our next example concerns a woman who in her present life had a great dread of bearing children. What, from another lifetime, might have caused this?

Case 7: This case involves a woman who had a tough problem with obesity. What might you guess about her past?

Case 8: One man who came to Edgar Cayce had great personal charisma. His reading said that in this life he was one of those people who has the power to bring joy or gladness through a nod or a wink and that he would repeatedly find himself in a position where other people were dependent on him for their standing or place in the social world. What sort of past life might have left him with this ability?

Answer 5: This illustrates just how important it is to have several different kinds of past-life clues before piecing together a plausible theory. There are so many kinds of experiences that could cause doubt and fear later on that we're at sea in trying to determine which one is at work in this particular case. We would need to know much more about this man—his tastes, interests, specific fears and dislikes, and so on—in order to make an educated guess about his past experience. In working with this course to uncover your own past lives, you have been obtaining those additional pieces of information from the various exercises. Each bit of information is another clue, another piece in the puzzle.

In the case of the man with doubts and fears, his Cayce reading described a former lifetime in which he had been a critic. He had apparently been ruthless in his criticisms of others, and now he was experiencing the consequences of that life through troubling self-doubts and fears. The solution, he was told, would lie not in denying his critical abilities, but in channeling them along constructive lines. In his current life we might imagine him becoming a trouble-shooter or a movie critic as two possible constructive uses of his critical discernment.

Answer 6: Well, the obvious possible explanation is that in a former lifetime the woman might have died in childbirth. Or maybe she had borne a child out of wedlock, to great censure or even punishment. Perhaps she had some other unhappy experience with children before. As it turns out, the woman was told of an earlier life as a settler in America, where she had witnessed the burning of her house and children. Presumably this tragedy was part of an Indian attack.

Once again, we can see how difficult it would be to arrive at the actual explanation of the woman's fear of childbirth without having any additional information from which to formulate a past-life theory. But, just to illustrate how different clues can be pieced together to form a coherent hypothesis about a previous incarnation, let's try to imagine some of the other things this person might have discovered about herself if she had been taking our course rather than getting her past-life information from Edgar Cayce. In addition to her dread of childbearing, maybe she would have noticed a tendency to fear for the safety of people she loved. Perhaps she would have developed a strong distaste for the Indian culture. And maybe she would have felt afraid whenever she heard the sound of fire sirens in the night. All of this is pure speculation, of course. But it should show you how we can look to our own personalities for important past-life information.

Answer 7: Again, this is a good example of how the same situation in different individuals can have very different past-life causes. Maybe this person had starved to death in another life, and the unconscious memory of starvation has caused her to eat more than she needs; it's even possible that her body remembers such an experience and has developed a tendency to store fat as some form of self-protection. Or maybe in another life she had been someone who could eat to the point of gluttony and yet not gain weight. Her current obesity would then be a delayed reaction to her previous habit pattern. What turned out to be the actual cause of her condition, according to her Cayce reading, was a lifetime in which she had been thin and agile and had laughed at people who were overweight. Now she was getting a chance to feel the shoe on the other foot.

Answer 8: We can speculate that the man must have been in positions of power before, even if we can't get at the specifics of when or where. Often just this amount of information is sufficient to help us work with our past lives. In the case at hand, for example, this would be enough to let the man know that he was being called upon to use his power with love and wisdom. Surely anyone who theorized a past of great power would want to be aware of the pitfalls of power so that he could try to avoid them. This shows how it's often not necessary to know all the particulars of a former lifetime in order to extract a lesson from it.

You're probably curious about the man in question, however, just as you would be about your own past life. In his case, it turns out that he had been a high-ranking Roman who, with the simple gesture of a thumb up or a thumb down, could determine the fate of someone in the arena. It's not clear whether he ever actually gave the thumbs-down sign. If he did not, that would explain why he was given his gift of power all over again, to use constructively. But it might also be true that he was guilty of condemning some people and had already experienced the consequence of that action in some intervening incarnation. If so, his current lifetime could be viewed as an opportunity to see if he'd learned his lesson. He was presented with power once more, in a less crucial area, to determine whether he could use it in a positive way this time around.

So we've now applied the law of cause and effect to several real-life situations. You've practiced tracing the laws in both directions—starting with the past life and figuring out the outcome, and starting with the current life and trying to discover the past. You can see that we are dealing with an inexact science. The possible causes and effects will always be individualized to fit the soul's own choices and circumstances.

In many ways, it will be easier to discover your own previous lives than it has been to figure out those of strangers. This is true because you know so much more about yourself, and also because you will have the advantage of your own intuitions, which we will be encouraging through reveries and the use of dreams and meditation.

In formulating your past-life theories, always keep in mind that the broad patterns, as in the example of the man with great personal power, will be more important than the details. As you work with trying to learn from a broad pattern that you suspect is operating in your own life, the details will come. If any fragments or theories about your previous incarnations occur to you now, or at any time as we proceed, write them down so that you don't forget them. They'll be very valuable to you later. And now we're going to go on and dig out a few details—and maybe some patterns, too—with a reverie on your talents and hobbies.

Session 9
Exploring Your Talents, Hobbies, and Interests

One of the most practical aspects of reincarnation theory has to do with our talents, skills, and interests. In the Edgar Cayce readings, many individuals were told not only that they had learned or acquired abilities and vocational urges in other lives, but that these skills and talents were present and could be used in their current incarnations. This is exciting, because it suggests that each one of us is drawing on the accumulated skills and interests of many lifetimes. That makes us all very talented indeed. But talented though we may be, it can sometimes be hard for us to recognize our abilities. And until we recognize them, our skills may lie dormant, unused.

How, then, do we go about recognizing our talents? Well, it usually helps to start out by getting a clear picture of whatever it is we're looking for. Just what is a talent? The dictionary might define it as a natural ability or endowment that can be cultivated into a refined hobby or occupation. Note that this definition can include not only the skills that we have actively developed and are using in our lives, but also those unexpressed ones which we would be interested in developing if we were to get the chance. This point is important to our study, for influences from our past lives often manifest as urges rather than actual achievements. Therefore, in our examination of our talents we will be considering our latent interests as well as our active abilities.

The word "talent" is often misunderstood. It is frequently associated with people who actually perform in areas like art, music, or drama. We're too quick to assume that if we aren't gifted in these areas, we have no talent. This is neither true nor fair to ourselves. Talent can be expressed in many ways. Just as the contents of a mixed packet of flower seeds emerge and unfold in a wide variety of forms and colors, so do people unfold according to their unique patterns. In searching out our own talents, we need to consider a wide range of interests, abilities, and hobbies. We need to consider the obvious and the less obvious alike. And we should be careful not to rule out any ability or interest just because it doesn't fit our notion of what a talent should be.

Consider the woman who loves to watch birds. She can identify every bird that comes to her feeder. She knows what they like to eat, when they migrate, and what their various calls sound like. Is this a talent? You bet it is—even if she never thought to call it that.

Or how about the man with a great memory for details? That's not exactly tap dancing, but it's a talent, nonetheless. Other mental traits also represent special talents. The ability to work with figures, the knack for solving a murder mystery after the first two chapters of a book, a keen sense of humor—these are all talents, and they spring from each individual's unique past experiences in this lifetime and in others.

And, of course, there are all the traditional talents and hobbies to consider: music, needlework and sewing, pottery, sculpture, artwork of all kinds, fishing, sports, gardening, collecting things, sailing, photography, science fiction writing, composing poetry . . . We could go on listing hobbies for hours and still not run out of examples, and perhaps we would still not have hit your particular hobbies and talents. So it's going to be your job to do some pretty thorough thinking about yourself in order to identify your own abilities and interests.

Now we're going to look at a few questions that might help you in this inventory. It will be most beneficial if you take time to really think about these questions, so be sure you are relaxed. You might want to close your eyes as you consider the answers to them. Or you might want to have paper and pencil handy so that you can write some of your thoughts down. Whichever method you prefer, take a moment here to get yourself relaxed. Then proceed whenever you're ready.

Some of our talents are already developed, and are part of our daily lives. We frequently use such abilities in the activities we choose to participate in during the periods when there are no external demands on our time and energy. And so, a good way to begin your search for this kind of skill is to ask yourself this question: What do I do with my leisure time?

Now remember, don't fall into the trap of thinking that you can consider only recreational activities like stamp collecting. Maybe you like to spend your leisure time visiting with friends. That might indicate a social skill. Or maybe you like nothing better than to relax in your big chair, watching television sports. That's a hobby, and it's just the kind of thing you should try to become aware of now. So think about this question, and consider making a few notes about it for yourself: How do you like to spend your leisure time?

Continuing to focus on your actual life for a moment, let's look at another area in which you are likely to use the active talents you have developed. If you are employed, try to list the skills you need to have in order to do your job well. Don't overlook anything. Run through a typical day's work, and just see how many skills you can come up with. As you do this, you might note to yourself which of these activities you seem to perform better than others. And by the way, if you're a homemaker, that counts as employment. Pause in your reading for a minute while you complete your list of job-related abilities, either in your head or on paper.

Now let's move on to another question, this one a bit more in the realm of wishful thinking: How would you like to spend your leisure time if only you had the time, money, or talent to do whatever you pleased? In answer to this query, you might think of activities that would take a few hours here and there, or you might think of major adventures that would take literally a lifetime to live out. The sky's the limit here—not only in regard to the material resources your fantasy would require, but also concerning the personal skills it might involve. Take a minute to think about this question: What would you like to do with your leisure time, if only you could?

And now consider one final question: What kinds of people do you find most interesting? For example, if you watch a television news-magazine program or read a publication like *People* magazine, do you like stories about business tycoons, or musicians, or mountain climbers? There are probably many types of people that fascinate you. But as you think about it you are likely to find that these people all fall into several broad categories based on the kinds of things they do. Once again, take a moment to think about this now: What kinds of people do you find interesting?

Exercise A

We've spent the last several minutes stirring up some thoughts, getting you ready to see just how many talents and interests you have. Now it's time to use these thoughts to complete an inventory of your talents, interests, and hobbies.

As you will see, there are but two main questions in this exercise. The first asks you to name the talents, interests, and hobbies that are active in your life. In answer to this question, you are to list the things you thought of when you considered your actual leisure activities and the skills you may now have to use in your job.

Items listed in this answer should be current. That is, if you used to oil paint ten years ago but haven't done it since then, don't include oil painting here. On the other hand, if you hunt only in the fall and it happens to be spring as you're making up your list, hunting would qualify as a current hobby.

In the second question you are asked to name your undeveloped talents and interests that are not expressed through current hobbies or leisure activities. Here you would list all those things you would like to do, if only you could. Answers to this question can include things you suspect you would be able to do if you only had time for lessons, money for necessary supplies or equipment, or the opportunity to be in the right setting. Activities you thought of when you were asked to imagine what you'd like to do with your leisure time would be appropriate here. So would those things you find interesting about other people's occupations, unless you have already named them as activities you yourself engage in. You might also list former hobbies and other things you know you can do, but just have not been doing for one reason or another.

Take some time now to inventory your own talents and interests by answering these two questions. Your lists can be as long as you'd like, and you can take as long as you need to complete them. But there is one rule: Make sure you include at least ten items in each answer.

1. What talents, interests, and hobbies are active in your life? Include here the skills you use in your present job, as well as your current leisure activities. Remember, these items should be part of your life *now*, and you should be able to name at least ten of them.

2. What undeveloped talents and interests do you have that are not expressed through your current career, hobbies, or leisure activities? Here you can list the things you would like to do, if only you could; activities you think you'd be able to do if you had the time, material resources, and opportunity to develop your skill; former hobbies and other activities that you know you could do but have not been taking part in for some time; and things that make other people's lives and occupations interesting to you, as long as you have not already listed these pursuits as part of your answer to question 1.

Now that you've completed the inventory of your talents, both expressed and unexpressed, we're going to relate them to your former incarnations in two ways. First, we're going to work with using your present skills as a springboard to past-life memory. And then we're going to look at how you might bring out some of your hidden talents and put them to use this time around.

Exercise B

Your first step in this exercise will be to pick one talent or hobby from your answer to question 1, above—in other words, an ability that is active in your present life. Choose one that's a special favorite for you, something you really enjoy doing or feel you do especially well. Once you've made your selection, we will be using your chosen talent as a central element in the reverie described below.

Before you actually enter into this experience, you might find it helpful to review the introductory material on reverie presented earlier, in Session 2. If you will be enlisting a friend to help guide you through the experience, it's just about time to turn the material over to him now. If you will be using the cassette-tape method, you can start hunting up the equipment. Whatever method you decide upon, do not neglect to prepare yourself by relaxing your mind and body as thoroughly as possible. As you may recall, a text has been provided to guide you through one relaxation routine; it is presented on pages 145–147, in the second session of this course.

Like the relaxation routine referred to above, the reverie material that follows includes suggested durations of pauses at various points in the text. These recommendations, which can be particularly useful if you are making a tape recording of the material or having a friend read it to you, are given so that you will have a chance to visualize the fantasy images more vividly and enter into the experience more fully. Remember that they are not intended to be ironclad and should be altered in any way that will make them more suitable to your individual needs.

One more short reminder might be helpful before you actually begin the reverie itself. Several questions are included in the reverie description below. Do not interrupt the flow of the experience to answer these queries on paper. Merely notice in your mind's eye the details they call for. The relevant questions will be repeated at the conclusion of your venture into your imaginary world, and you will be able to record your responses to them then.

And now call to mind the active talent in your life that you have chosen to focus on. Then take as much time as you need to lay aside your concerns with the mundane world and go through whatever procedures for mental and physical relaxation you feel will be most beneficial to you. And, when you are fully prepared, move on to the material below and lose yourself in this guided experience in imagination.

Think of your talent or hobby now, the one you selected as being especially enjoyable or rewarding for you. Whatever that activity may be, see yourself doing it at this moment in your current life. (10 sec.)

Where are you when you engage in your hobby or
express your talent? In your mind's eye, look around and
become aware of the sights, sounds, and smells that may be
a part of the setting for your particular activity. Pretend it's
a game, to see just how many things you can become aware
of in your surroundings. Allow yourself to become immersed in this world. (30 sec.)

Now focus your attention on what you are doing. Don't
just see yourself involved with your hobby or expressing
your talent; actually imagine yourself doing whatever it is.
Feel your body doing its part, whether your body is active
or still during your chosen activity. (10 sec.)

Let your mental state be like the one you have when
you're involved in this favorite activity. What are your
emotions? What do you think about while you're busy with
your hobby? Take time to imagine detail here. Let yourself
actually go through the steps or process of your hobby
mentally. Feel what it's like. (1 minute)

And now, as you remain totally immersed in your imagined activity, let the setting slip away and let another setting
take its place—any surroundings at all where you can
imagine a similar activity going on. (10 sec.) Let the new
setting just come before your mind's eye. Just notice what it
is. Be aware of yourself in these new surroundings. (10
sec.)

Are you still engaged in your activity? Is it exactly the
same, or has it changed in any way? (10 sec.) Are there
other people around you? If so, what are they like? What do
they look like? (10 sec.) If you're alone, what are your
feelings? Take a few moments to experience the scene
unfolding in front of your mind's eye. (1 min.)

When your reverie experience has reached its natural
conclusion, allow yourself some time for quiet reflection on
it. Then answer the following questions about it.

1. What talent or hobby did you choose to think about in
this exercise?

2. Briefly describe the first setting you pictured when you
imagined yourself engaged in your chosen activity.

3. What changes occurred in your surroundings when you were asked to see a new setting come before your mind's eye?

4. Was your hobby or talent altered in any way when you imagined yourself expressing it in a different setting?

5. How would you characterize your mental state when you engage in your hobby or express your talent?

6. Did any new thoughts or feelings come to mind when your imaginary setting changed?

7. Sometimes the things that we spontaneously imagine can be the very clues we're looking for in trying to reach a better understanding of our past. Give some thought now to the exercise you've just completed, and see if you can arrive at an answer to the following question: Did the image you conjured up when you were asked to see your activity taking place in another setting tell you anything about where your interest originated or where you have used this talent before?

While the specifics of the setting may or may not have been accurate, the nature of the change in setting or the way in which the activity itself changed could be a reflection of how your present-day ability relates to experiences from the past.

8. Are there any other observations you would like to make based upon your reverie experience?

Exercise C

Just like the talents we actively use, our undeveloped or unexpressed abilities and interests can spring from past experience. With these, the challenge is not so much to know where they came from, but to make the most of them now—to allow our hidden assets to become working assets in our lives today. We're going to take a step in that direction now, working at the level where all creation begins: with our thoughts.

Start by referring once again to the inventory you completed in Exercise A. Select one talent or ability from your answer to the second question, in which you were asked to list your interests and abilities not being expressed through your current activities. Choose from this list one item that you'd particularly like to see active in your life today, one that would give you great personal satisfaction or that would make your life easier or better in some way.

When you've made your selection, you're going to take a first, small step toward affirming this ability as part of you. On the opposite page you will find a drawing of a hot-air balloon. This balloon is ready to lift you to new heights of accomplishment and satisfaction. Only one thing is missing, and that's direction.

You'll notice that the balloon bears a great big banner right around the middle. But the banner is blank. It's up to you to symbolically give your balloon direction by writing your undeveloped talent or ability right across the balloon's blank banner. Make it big. Don't be afraid to write your ability in nice, bold letters. Do so now, so that you will be able to ride your balloon in a direction you really want to go.

Now that you've labeled your banner, your balloon is ready to lift off and take you to new horizons within yourself. But for this to happen, you'll need to set aside the balloon on paper for a moment and create another balloon, in consciousness. Once again you will be letting reverie carry you where you might not otherwise think to go. One nice thing about imagination is that it allows you to go wherever you'd like to go and do whatever you'd like to do. You're free to create and experience another reality for a while.

Once again, get as comfortable as you can, and use whatever technique you've found will enable you to become as mentally and physically relaxed as possible. Then picture this scene in your mind's eye:

You're walking across a spacious, wide-open meadow. The day is fine—sunny and mild, with a soft, warm breeze. (5 sec.) Your spirits are light, and a feeling of expectancy and happy anticipation fills you as you cross this beautiful meadow. You know that good things will happen to you on

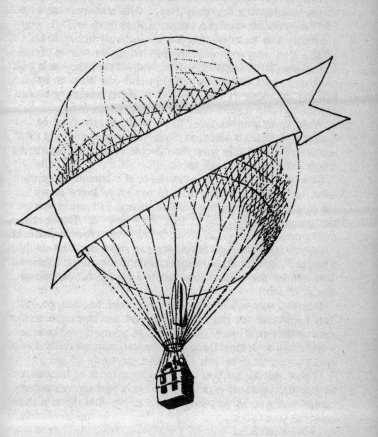

this day, even though you're not sure exactly what they may be. (5 sec.)

You see a beautiful hot-air balloon tethered at the far end of the meadow. Its basket is draped with streamers, and its gaily colored canvas has a banner around it. (5 sec.) As you approach your balloon—for you instinctively know that it's yours—you see your undeveloped talent written in large letters across the banner. As you walk closer, the word on the banner gets clearer and clearer, and you know that this balloon is going to take you to a place where you can experience this special talent or ability. (5 sec.)

Walk up to your balloon. (5 sec.) It's gently swaying in the warm breeze. It seems to invite you to climb aboard and see where it will take you. You decide to do just that. You climb into the basket. (5 sec.)

Slowly the balloon begins to leave the ground. A gentle wind blows through your hair. (5 sec.) You know that you are safe and secure in this balloon, that it will return you to the ground as gently as it has lifted you off. But in the meantime, you are eager to let it take you where it will.

As you travel higher, the air is clean and fresh. The sky is a bright blue, with an occasional white, puffy cloud. (5 sec.) You admire the countryside below as your balloon floats along. (5 sec.)

But in a way you're detached from the scene below you. You know that for the time being you are leaving behind your accustomed way of looking at yourself and at the world. You're letting the old limitations slip away. You're rising above them as you rise above the earth. (5 sec.)

Higher and higher you go, enjoying a sense of buoyancy as you drift upward. A delicious sense of rest and relaxation creeps over you as you drift gently along. And there in the basket of your balloon you sit down, lean back, and completely relax. (10 sec.)

Then you feel a gentle bump, and you realize that the balloon has come to a stop. Curious, you peer over the top of your basket. (5 sec.) And to your amazement you discover that you have landed in just the right place to express your new talent or hobby. Look around. Everything you need is right before you. What do you see? (10 sec.) Are you someplace familiar, or someplace entirely new? Notice as much as you can about the setting you find yourself in. (30 sec.)

Step out into this setting, which has been chosen just for you. You know what to do next. Your talent or hobby comes naturally to you. You begin, tentatively at first, but soon you find yourself thoroughly involved in it. (10 sec.) Take a few moments to imagine yourself engaged in this activity. Become aware of all the sights and sounds that might be a part of it; the other people who may be involved; and most of all, the feelings and thoughts you have as you experience this new expression of your abilities. (1 min.)

Now it's time to get back into the balloon. It's all ready to go. You climb aboard and drift gently and easily back to your real life, the one you left behind when you entered your balloon. You are feeling refreshed and have a sense of contentment as you return. (10 sec.) Continue to feel relaxed as you reflect upon some questions now.

How would your life be changed if you really were able to do the things you lived out in your fantasy? (10 sec.) How would it be changed for the better? (10 sec.) Would there be any drawbacks? (10 sec.) Would people in your life be affected in any way if you were expressing your talent or ability? (10 sec.) How would your daily routine be altered? (10 sec.) Think about these things for a few moments. (30 sec.)

Step back into your everyday life now. You've just covered a lot of territory, and it's time to put together some of the thoughts that may have come at different times during your reverie. To help you with this process, some questions have been provided. The purpose of these questions is to assist you in directing or focusing your thoughts about your hidden talent. They're intended to help you, so please feel free to skip any that you'd rather not answer.

In asking you to concentrate on an undeveloped talent that you might consider making an active part of your life, this exercise can become the stimulus for a significant change in your day-to-day activities. Thus its effect could reach far beyond your work with this course. For this reason, more commentary has been included with the questions below than is the case in most of our exercises. The purpose of these comments is to help you decide whether to make a serious effort in your present life to develop your hidden ability, and to give you a few ideas on some of the steps you can take to accomplish this, should you choose to do so. You might find it helpful to read and consider each item in its entirety—question and commentary—before recording your answer to it.

1. What currently unexpressed talent or interest did you choose to explore in this reverie?

2. In your balloon fantasy, what items appeared that were necessary in order for you to practice your talent or hobby? Did any single item stand out as particularly important?

This question asks you to list the specific items you found in your balloon fantasy that were necessary to the expression of your talent or hobby. These things may have been supplies, equipment, special clothing, instructions—whatever it would take to get you going on your new activity. It's important to become aware of what these items might be, because before you can bring out your hidden talent, you must identify the things you will need in order to begin. You're asked to note any one item that stood out, because that item would probably be an important part of making your fantasy a reality. Acquiring it might be a first step in working toward the development of your new talent or hobby.

3. Consider the setting to which your balloon trip took you. What specific conditions made *that* setting a good one for the unfolding of your hidden talent?

This question is similar to the preceding one. In asking you to examine what was special about the setting for your fantasy hobby, it's really urging you to get very clear about what it would take to make your real environment suitable for your new pursuit. For example, maybe you were writing a great novel in your fantasy. The most important thing about the setting was that the room you worked in was quiet, cozy, and filled with great works of literature. In other words, it put you in the mood to write. Now, if you really wanted to bring out your hidden talent for writing, this would tell you of one small but important step you could take. You could make the effort to create a space—even a very small one, just one corner of one room—that would help put you in the mood for writing.

There is, of course, a certain level of reality-testing that must be done here. You have to decide whether it's realistic to alter your life-style in order to bring out your hidden talent. For example, maybe in your fantasy you were surfing along the Caribbean coastline. It may not be at all practical for you to think of creating that setting in your life. You would have to evaluate whether this particular activity would be important enough to justify making such a drastic change in your whole life-style.

This consideration ties in with question 4. Suppose you decide that you can't make the wholesale changes in your present environment that would be necessary to duplicate the setting of your fantasy. It may nevertheless be possible to incorporate some of the elements of that setting into your life, and this may be enough to allow you to proceed with the development of your hidden ability.

4. Think about the conditions you named above which made your fantasy setting so suitable for the expression of your chosen talent. Can you identify any ways in which some of those same conditions can be developed in your real life?

5. How would your life be improved if you engaged in this hobby regularly? Would there be any drawbacks?

Here you are asked to zero in on how this activity might change your life for the better, and also on what the possible drawbacks might be. If you are in doubt about bringing out your hidden talent, these two questions should help you get a clearer picture of your options. In some cases you may well decide that, pleasant though your fantasy experience may have been, it just would not be realistic to try to actually begin that hobby or express that talent.

This is where the next question comes in. Often it's more important that we get in touch with the underlying quality of an interest or talent than that we actually engage in a specific activity. For example, the underlying quality of the surfing experience could be any one of a number of things. It might be physical agility and balance; these could be developed right at home or at a local health spa. Or maybe adventure was the real essence of the fantasy. In that case, the person might want to try a few more weekend adventures to new places. Whatever your particular talent or hobby may be, try to get at why this activity would be so enjoyable to you, and then look for other ways that you could foster these same positive influences in your life.

6. Are there ways that you could develop some aspect of your talent or interest without making major changes in your current life-style?

7. Make note of two possible past-life experiences or situations that could have led to this present-day interest or hidden talent.

With this question we return to our original focus. Think about your hidden talent, and try to think of at least two past-life situations that could have given you this interest or ability. This item is similar to the exercises we did with other people's case histories, in which you were told about their present-day circumstances and guessed at possible past-life causes. The only difference is that here the case history you are working with is your own.

8. Are there any other comments or observations you would like to make based on your reverie experience with your unexpressed ability? Consider how this talent or interest might prove beneficial in your present lifetime as well as any insights you may have gained into its possible past-life origin.

By the time you've finished answering these questions, you'll probably be ready for a break. This might be a good point to lay the book aside for a while, let all this concentration on your talents and hobbies—both developed and undeveloped—sink in, and see what insights you may come up with over the next day or so.

Session 10
Discovering Past-Life Clues Through Dreams, Meditation, and Your Religious Feelings and Experiences

According to the Edgar Cayce readings, one of the best and most reliable ways to learn about your past lives is from your dreams. Through dreams, you are your own best psychic and your own safest psychic. Why? Because in the dream you receive all the information you need, and you receive it according to your own timing, when you are ready for it and best able to use it.

Dreams come to us for the good we can gain from them. They come to help and guide us, not just to satisfy our idle curiosity. For this reason, if you have a dream that reveals some aspect of a past life, you can be sure that it was received because the particular past life it portrays relates to a situation or problem you're experiencing at the present time. The dream is helping you see your current conditions from the perspective of this prior experience. It shows you the feelings, attitudes, and emotions involved in that experience. This gives you valuable insight not available from any other source, insight that is reliable and immediately applicable for your particular life situation.

You might ask, If this is so important, why don't I have any past-life dreams? The answer is, You probably do. You just aren't noticing the little telling details in the dreams that are so easy to overlook, such as objects in the scenery or background, the type of buildings or architecture present, or the style of clothes people are wearing.

When we recall a dream, we are often so involved in its emotional aspects that we may overlook many of the subtle, seemingly insignificant hints that can reveal something of our previous incarnations. We can think of these bits and pieces of information as many individual film clips in a roll of movie film. By themselves, the individual clips tell very little; but when the film is run together, the complete story unfolds. Just so, past-life fragments noticed in dreams can be pieced together to form a record of what may have been experienced in the past.

But before you can piece these fragments together, you must have a collection of them. This is where a dream journal is so very helpful. If you are not already writing your dreams down in a special notebook reserved just for that purpose, this would be a good time to start. You will find your journal invaluable, not only for the help it can give you in discovering your previous incarnations, but also for the guidance you'll receive in all areas of your present life.

At this point, you might wish to refer back to Chapter 5 in the second section of this book, which contains several ideas and suggestions for keeping a dream journal. Why not begin tonight, by placing the needed materials next to your bed before you retire and giving yourself the suggestion that you will recall your dreams? And remember to record your dreams as soon as you awaken in the morning, while they are still fresh in your mind.

If, on the other hand, you are already keeping a journal of your dreams, you'll find it valuable to go back over your earlier entries to discover what past-life clues are buried there. And as you receive new dreams, be sure to examine each one for material that may have arisen from your former lifetimes. While there are no hard-and-fast rules about what constitutes a past-life clue, the following are some of the hints that *may* indicate information relating to a previous incarnation:

Objects denoting a foreign influence, such as Spanish shawls, French doors, and Chinese vases;

You or others in the dream wearing the dress or costume of another culture or historical period;

You or someone you know appearing in the physical body of a different race or sex than that of your waking life;

You or someone else speaking a foreign language;

A dream setting in another culture or historical period; and

Dream experiences involving guided tours, trips to museums, or researching record books or documents.

Let's take a look now at some examples of the past-life information that others have found in their dreams, and perhaps you'll get better a better idea of what to look for. Remember, though, that your dreams are messages from you to you. They are expressed in your own individual language and symbols. The best indication that a given dream is presenting past-life material is your feeling that it is doing so, regardless of whether or not it conforms to the examples below.

One woman dreamed she was closing French doors in the home. At the time she had this dream she was in the final stages of divorce. She believes that closing the French doors signified a French incarnation with her husband, and that the relationship which had begun during that lifetime was now coming to a close.

The journal of another individual contains an entry describing a dream in which the dreamer was looking out at the backyard, where flowers that had been planted long ago were now in bloom. While looking outside, the dreamer was ironing a Spanish tablecloth. This person feels that something from a Spanish incarnation is at present being ironed out and coming to bloom.

Sometimes we see people we know today clothed in garments from another time. One man reported seeing his friend in a dream, clothed in a Grecian robe. He feels this is an indication of a lifetime together in Greece.

There are times when past-life information comes to us in a dream before the situation it relates to develops in our present life. It's as if our unconscious is preparing us for what lies ahead. For example, a woman dreamed she was putting on clothes that looked like the dark shrouds worn by Moslem women. A short time later her child became very ill, requiring her constant care for many years. Confined to her home and unable to mix with others, she saw a similarity between her present circumstances and the restricted life of Moslem women in earlier times. This dream, along with a theory that she had once been a Moslem woman, enabled her to cope with her situation better by calling upon the strengths that she had developed in her former life.

At other times, relevant past-life information comes in a dream after a particular event or experience has taken place. It's as though we need to work through a situation before we are really ready to see the cause, which we ourselves have set in motion. For example, one man reported he had been involved for over two years in a very difficult relationship with a friend. He felt he had been betrayed in this relationship. This was particularly painful for him because, to his way of thinking, the betrayal was totally undeserved. During these two years, he worked with prayer and meditation to forgive his friend. He eventually had a dream indicating that he had been successful.

Shortly thereafter he had another dream, in which he saw a large open book. As he leafed through the pages, he saw vivid pictures that told the story of their lifetime together in France, where he had betrayed his friend. He realized that all he had gone through in the present time was a replay of that former experience, only in reverse.

Many people report that they have had past-life dreams that are like movies, with scenery, costumes, and drama. One woman reported dreaming she was one of a group of slaves trying to escape. They were being chased by men on horses. Eventually they were caught, and they were dragged to a clearing in a swampy forest. The woman awoke terrified.

As she was recording her dream, she realized that one of the slave hunters was a man that she knows today. She felt the dream explained why she often felt such aversion toward, and even fear of, this person. Recognizing the origin of these feelings, she made an effort to overcome her attitude toward him. An interesting side note to this is that a month or so later a friend also dreamed of seeing her as a slave. This is especially noteworthy, since at that time the friend had not heard of the woman's dream.

Dreams, for some people, can be even more explicit and involved. One dreamer reported a very long dream in which she was being taken on a tour. The tour began at an ancient Egyptian tomb. The tour guide pointed out a mosaic which pictured a blue-eyed Egyptian queen with children playing at her feet. The guide identified the queen as the blue-eyed queen and said she had been a favorite and beloved ruler of her people. The scene shifted, and the dreamer was shown a bronze bas-relief of horses and men at war, which turned into actual fighting as she watched. She was then taken to a large piece of colonial American furniture, which seemed to dwarf her. She had to reach very high to open a drawer on top, where she found a letter. As she looked at it, she knew that the letter was for her and that it symbolized her dream as a message from the past.

Of course, these are only examples of dreams that give hints of past-life involvement. Each one of us is different. You may have your own way of recognizing clues about your former incarnations. And any dream we have will be our own unique way of presenting truth to ourselves. This is why the Cayce readings stressed that the dreamer is the one best qualified to interpret his own dream. The important thing is to know that this information is accessible to us, and we need only to work with our dreams to unlock these memories.

The Edgar Cayce readings very frequently urged people to adopt the practices of prayer and meditation as a means of furthering their spiritual development. Though they were generally recommended to be used in conjunction with each other, prayer and meditation are not the same thing. Prayer can be thought of as an appeal to God to become active in our lives, while in meditation we sit in silent expectation of meeting Him within ourselves. Another way of phrasing this is to say that in prayer we talk to God; in meditation, we listen as the voice of God within communicates with us.

A fuller explanation of what meditation is, how to go about practicing it, and the effects it can have in your life is given in Chapter 6 of this book. Suggestions on meditation procedures are presented there, but the specific techniques you use are not nearly as important as your sincerity of purpose and *regularity* in your practice of meditation. For, like any other skill, meditation must be learned. Its full value is not likely to be experienced after a single session or a few widely scattered ones. If you feel that meditation would be beneficial to you but are not yet engaging in it on a regular basis, now would be a fine time to begin.

Now let's return to the main focus of our course and see how meditation can help us in our search for knowledge of our previous lifetimes.

Many people were specifically told in their Cayce readings to use meditation to learn more about their former incarnations. In fact, this advice came so frequently that we can assume it applies to all of us. How does meditation aid recall of past lives? You may find that meditation enhances spontaneous recall during your normal daily activities. Or maybe as a result of meditation you'll receive more past-life information in your dreams. Sometimes past-life information will even come during the meditation period itself.

For example, one man was told in his Cayce reading that he had been a writer and teacher in ancient Greece. He was encouraged to use meditation not only to recall the experience in more detail, but actually to remember his writings themselves. He was informed that while the original writings had long since been destroyed, the truths they contained would be of great value today.

Another man was told that he had been a teacher during the American Revolution. He was urged to meditate in order to awaken these memories, and then to write about them, especially those relating to the truth of freedom.

Perhaps you too have had certain meditation experiences that you feel might be reminiscent of a previous incarnation.

These experiences can take several forms. Sometimes sounds seem to occur, as in the case of one person who at times in meditation heard the ringing of temple bells. Sometimes images of objects or articles of clothing related to a former lifetime float past the mind's eye during meditation. For instance, one person asked Edgar Cayce about the significance of seeing a copper screen and the Gulf of Mexico while meditating. Cayce told her that they symbolized a past life during which she first helped her people by preserving their truths and teachings and later took these teachings over the Gulf of Mexico to other lands.

When we think of using meditation as a technique for recalling past lives, we might suspect that we would tend to remember incarnations in which we had been in some type of religious setting. This is often the case, for the very process of attuning to our spiritual nature in meditation can evoke past experiences in which our focus was likewise spiritual.

For example, one person reports that during a period of deep meditation she sensed a cathedral and saw herself as a nun at prayer. The experience was further deepened when she felt herself become that person, kneeling in a cloistered section of a large church. But then something even more startling happened. Suddenly, as the nun prayed from a printed prayer card, she had recall of an even earlier period, in which she had also been a nun and was actually writing the prayer she held in her hand. Thus she was experiencing awareness of three incarnations simultaneously: the woman meditating in her room at home, the nun praying in a large cathedral, and an earlier nun, in coarse robes, writing her devotional prayer.

A physician who came to Edgar Cayce for a reading was told that he had had an incarnation in the Holy Land during the rebuilding of the city and temple. He had been part of a group that accompanied Zerubbabel to Jerusalem. The man had belonged to the priestly tribes and had aided in keeping the records. In his modern life, remembrances of the temple service came to him periodically during his meditation times. Cayce told him that these were actual reflections from that lifetime.

Regardless of the form or content of your experiences in meditation, there may be times when they seem completely foreign to you, consisting of faces of unknown people or glimpses of unfamiliar places or objects. At other times they may be hauntingly familiar or vaguely reminiscent of places you've visited or read about. In some instances, these experiences can be distractions from the attunement you're seeking in meditation; but in other cases you will know that they are something more. This points up why consistency in your practice of meditation is so necessary. You need to establish a certain regularity before you can expect meditation to bring you the special insights that will be truly useful to you on your spiritual quest.

Exercise A

The questions below have a dual purpose. They are intended, first of all, to help you derive specific past-life information from the study of your dreams and through regular meditation. And, by giving you an opportunity to record the insights so gained, these questions should also help you recognize the great value of dream study and meditation, not only in your search for knowledge of your previous incarnations, but in many other areas of your life as well.

Quite possibly you may find that at present you have no answer to give for one or more of these items. But don't be discouraged. Remember that both dream study and meditation tend to bear their fruits slowly, with regular and consistent practice over a period of time. Perhaps more than any other exercise in our course, this is an ongoing one—one which you will find yourself returning to again and again, as future experiences in your dreams and meditation provide you with fresh, useful material to record here. Be sure to do so whenever relevant understanding is received via these two avenues. It may take a while for past-life material to come to you through dreams and meditation; but when it does, you will find it among the most complete, vivid, and helpful information available through any means.

1. Describe any dreams you have had that in your opinion contain past-life information. If you have been keeping a dream journal, you might want to go back over your entries to see if there are any relevant details you may have overlooked.

2. Have you ever had any recurrent dreams, ones that were repeated several times during your life? Take a very close look at these for any material that might relate to your previous lifetimes, and make a note of any such details.

3. Describe any experiences you have had during your waking life that you feel indicate a former incarnation. Include in your description the circumstances of each experience, any ideas you may have about what brought it on, and whatever understanding of your past lives you gained from it.

4. In your dreams or waking life, have you had any experiences related to previous incarnations that you feel can be attributed to meditation?

5. Have you received any past-life information during the meditation periods themselves?

6. Have you noticed any connection between your understanding of past lives and the amount of time and effort you've devoted to dream study and meditation? For this question, don't look at just the number of clues to your former lifetimes you've received. "Understanding" here refers more to your ability to adopt a helpful perspective on the past-life clues you do have and make constructive use of them in your present life.

7. Do you have any other comments to make on dream study and/or meditation? Are there any other insights you feel you've gained as a result of your efforts in either or both of these areas? Don't limit yourself to just the field of past-life knowledge. Include here any aspects of your life that you feel have benefited from your work with dreams and meditation.

Exercise B

As many active meditators would affirm, regular meditation can do much to increase the frequency of our religious experiences and enhance their power. But of course it is also possible for nonmeditators to feel at certain times a special closeness to God. For one person, taking part in the formal rituals of a chosen faith might bring a heightened sense of the Creator's love; for another, periods of private prayer could be the bridge; and a third might find an increased awareness of the Infinite during quiet times spent alone outdoors, even though no activity that would commonly be termed "religious" is engaged in. The circumstances under which an individual can feel the touch of the Divine are beyond enumeration, and the variety of words that might be chosen to describe the experience is almost as great.

At this point, we're going to examine your past spiritual experiences—whether or not they were connected with the practice of meditation—along with your attitudes toward the religious life. There are several ways in which this can be helpful. An investigation of the role religion has in your present life might provide a number of important clues to previous incarnations in religious surroundings. It can also yield details that will flesh out your other past-life theories, ones relating to lifetimes in which your main conscious purpose was not necessarily spiritual development. And, by directing your thoughts toward the spiritual, this exercise may actually stimulate greater recall of your past lives. Reincarnation is of the soul, which is thus the storehouse of all our memories of former lifetimes. As we shift our attention away from our bodies and external events and focus it on the soul, we can expect these memories to become more accessible to us.

1. What religious interests do you have at the present? List the practices and areas of religious thought that are most important to you, and indicate the extent to which they influence your day-to-day life.

2. Are there any aspects of formal religious activity that are especially meaningful to you? Are there any you particularly dislike?

3. Do you have any feelings about people who choose a religious calling as their main vocation in life? If you have different responses to clergy of different faiths or in different settings, or if your reaction applies to those of certain religions but not others, please be specific. For example, you might respond in one way to Christian television evangelists, have a totally different feeling about Jewish rabbis, and be largely neutral toward Buddhist monks.

4. Have you ever considered a religious vocation for yourself? What has your reaction been to this idea, or what would it be? Here again, consider your feelings rather than your intellectual opinions.

5. Describe any moving religious experiences you have had in the past.

6. How much time do you spend by yourself? Do you find this time valuable for you? Are there any particular circumstances under which you enjoy being alone? Are such times connected in any way with your religious experiences or feelings?

7. Do you engage in any habitual activities that regularly give you a spiritual uplift?

8. Do you have any other observations regarding your religious feelings and experiences?

Session 11
Identifying Patterns in Your Life

Up to this point you have been gathering pieces, fragments of unconscious memory that emerge through your fantasies, personality, tastes, talents, and aversions. Now it's time to look at another kind of clue: the past-life influences that can be seen when we examine the patterns in your current life.

What is a pattern? It is simply something that happens in your life again and again, even though the particulars may change. For example, one person may find that there is a lifelong pattern of running into trouble with authority figures, from the schoolteachers of childhood to the bosses on adult job assignments. The people change; the settings change; maybe even the specific nature of the problem changes. But the underlying pattern—being unable to get along with authority figures—remains.

For some people, patterns may emerge in their social life. The number of friends we have, the types of people we gravitate to over and over again, the ways that friends have hurt us, and the ways that they have supported us are all possible areas to look at when examining our lives for patterns. One woman became aware that many of the friendships in her life began when she extended a helping hand to someone who needed it. This was a pattern.

Romantic love relationships are usually rich with patterns. Many people find that they run into the same difficulties in each of their relationships, even though the other person, the setting, and the specific circumstances may change.

What use is there in recognizing patterns of this sort? Consider the idea that we each come into this life with certain things to accomplish, strengths to develop and weaknesses to overcome. We might even think in terms of an agenda for each lifetime, set areas in which we need to grow. The agenda is, of course, determined by shortcomings we have displayed and personal development that we have started in previous lives. The only way we'll be able to meet our own agenda is through encountering situations and circumstances that give us the opportunity to work on what we've set out to accomplish. It's reasonable to assume, then, that the repeated situations we encounter in our social and work lives, in our family and romantic relationships, and even in our dealings with money represent patterns that reflect past-life influences.

Exercise

Some patterns in your own life may be very apparent to you, even without a lot of careful thinking. Others may be a little less obvious. The questions in this exercise have been prepared to help you identify the patterns in many areas of your life.

Consider these questions carefully and answer them as thoroughly as you can, but don't feel stuck if you just can't remember the answers to every one. What's important is that you jot down what you *can* think of for each area covered. This is one of the exercises that is likely to require more than one sitting, and you should take as much time as you need to complete it. Feel free to pause and ponder any insights that may occur to you as you think about these items. The last question of each section will provide you with an opportunity to note any such thoughts you may have.

People who have worked with this exercise in the past have found it easiest and most helpful to construct a series of charts to answer the questions, with one chart being used for each area of life examined. As you will see, this makes the patterns in your responses stand out more clearly and be more easily recognizable. The various jobs, life periods, or interpersonal relationships covered would be listed down the left side of each chart, and the columns would be headed by an abbreviated form of each question in that part of the exercise. The final question of each section, which asks for your general insights regarding the patterns in that area of your life, would then be answered at the bottom of each chart, outside its main body. For example, your chart for the first part of this exercise, in which patterns in your work life are investigated, might be set up something like this:

Job held	How job was found	Hard to find?	Length job was held	Enjoyed most	etc.
paperboy					
newspaper copyboy					
library assistant					
school teacher					
etc.					

16. Insights regarding vocational patterns:

Part 1: Patterns in Your Vocation or Work Life

1. List the jobs you have held during your life. If you can, name them in chronological order, starting with your earliest job and ending with your current or most recent one.

For each job you listed in response to this item, answer questions 2–15, below.

2. How did you find this job?
3. Was it hard to find?
4. How long did you hold this job?
5. What have you enjoyed most about this position?
6. What have you disliked most about it?
7. What special talents of yours have proved most useful in this position?
8. Do you have any talents that you feel might have been used in this job but weren't? What are they?
9. In this position how did you get along with your boss?
10. How did you get along with your co-workers?
11. How did you get along with your subordinates?
12. Have any favorable events or circumstances arisen repeatedly during this employment?
13. Have there been any recurrent problems related to this one job?
14. If this is not your current job, why did you leave it?

15. Do you have any other comments related to this one job?

16. Considering your entire employment history, are there any insights you would like to note regarding patterns in your vocational life?

Part 2: Patterns in Your Finances

Consider as many of the following life periods as you have experienced up to your present age: childhood (to approximately age thirteen), high school (approximately ages fourteen to eighteen), college or transition to adulthood (approximately ages eighteen through twenty-two), early adulthood, middle adulthood, later adulthood or retirement. For each period, answer the first ten questions below. Then answer question 11, taking into account your entire life up to now.

1. What was your primary source of income during this period of your life?

2. What was your secondary source of income?

3. Who was the person with primary control of your money?

4. How well did you budget your money during this period?

5. Was your income adequate to meet your needs?

6. Beyond your basic living expenses, what was your major expenditure?

7. If you had any extra money, what did you spend it on?

8. Were there any recurrent favorable events or situations in the financial aspect of your life?

9. Were there any repeated financial problems during this period?

10. Do you have any other remarks regarding your finances during this stage of life?

11. Note any observations that have occurred to you regarding your lifelong financial patterns.

Part 3: Patterns in Your Family Relationships

1. List by name the people who are your closest rela-

tives: mother, father, stepparents, sisters, brothers, spouse, children, and any others to whom you feel especially close.

Answer questions 2–8 as they apply to each of the relatives you have named. Then go on to item 9, a question about your family relationships in general.

2. In a word or two, how would you describe your relationship with this person?

3. Has your relationship with this person always been this way? If not, can you remember when, how, or why it changed?

4. What has been the best thing about your relationship with this person?

5. What has been the most difficult or troubling thing?

6. Have there been any long-term bright spots for you in this relationship?

7. Have there been any recurring problems?

8. Do you have any other comments about your relationship with this person?

9. Have you reached any other understandings regarding patterns in your family relationships?

Part 4: Patterns in Your Social Life

For each of these periods of life, answer questions 1–10 about your social life: preschool, kindergarten through grade six, grades seven and eight, grades nine through twelve, college or your transition to adulthood, early adulthood, middle adulthood, and later adulthood or retirement. Question 11 concerns the social patterns evident throughout your life.

1. Did you have enough friends during these years?

2. How did most of your friendships during this period begin?

3. How many times per week did you socialize with your friends?

4. How many of your friendships would you say were especially close?

5. What were your favorite activities with your friends?

6. What was the most supportive thing you experienced in your friendships or social life?

7. What was your most hurtful or disappointing experience?

8. Were there any repeated favorable events or circumstances in your social life?

9. Were there any recurrent social problems during this phase of your life?

10. Do you have any other remarks about your friendships or social life during this period?

11. Note any insights you've had regarding lifelong patterns in your friendships.

Part 5: Patterns in Your Romantic Relationships

1. Name the people with whom you have had important romantic involvements in your life. Start with the earliest romance you can remember, and work your way through to the current or most recent one.

Questions 2–5 and 10 should be answered in regard to each of these relationships. Items 6–9 apply to any of them that are now over. And the last question, once again, refers to patterns in this area that have persisted throughout your life.

2. How did you meet this person?

3. What first attracted you to him/her?

4. What pleasant events or circumstances recurred in or lasted throughout this relationship?

5. Were there any repeated or lasting areas of difficulty?

6. How long did this relationship endure?

7. What were the major reasons this relationship came to an end?

8. Who ended it?

9. How did you feel when it was over?

10. Do you have any other comments to make about this relationship?

11. Are there any general comments you would like to make concerning the patterns in your romances?

You probably couldn't help but see a few patterns as you answered these questions. But if you're still having a bit of trouble, here's a hint that you may find helpful. If you organized your responses in chart form, as was suggested toward the beginning of the exercise, go back over your charts and read the columns vertically—that is, read each column from top to bottom. Do you notice any places where you gave pretty much the same answer two or three times or more? If so, you have discovered a pattern. Maybe on the questions about your finances, for example, you repeatedly answered that someone else was in control of your money. Or maybe you found that you always budgeted well. Either one would be a pattern and would tell you something about a strength or weakness that is to be worked on during this lifetime.

Once you become aware of patterns, you'll see that these general issues active in your present life will form the backbone of your past-life theories. The other clues you've gathered will become, then, the details you can use to flesh these patterns out. As you do this, the patterns will grow clearer and you'll be able to see how they relate to the many influences you operate under every day of your life. You will be guided through this process in the subsequent sessions of the course.

Session 12:
Past-Life Reverie

By now, you are no stranger to reverie. As you've progressed through the exercises in this course, we've made sure that time for using your imagination and periods of quiet reflection balanced out the time you spent analyzing your life for clues about your previous incarnations. Those times of reflection and fantasy were brief excursions into the reverie state, and they probably gave you a different kind of understanding than you received when you thought logically about the questions in some of the other exercises.

Now it's time to build on the insights you've gathered thus far. How? By putting them aside and letting your imagination flow. That might sound like a contradiction, but actually it makes a lot of sense. Remember that your conscious mind is only part of the picture. With that conscious mind you've been doing a lot of fact finding and insight gathering. But during all of this activity on the conscious level, your unconscious mind has been busy, too.

Keep in mind that the unconscious is where your past-life memories are stored. And as you've gone through each exercise with your conscious mind, your unconscious has been stirred by the memories the exercises have awakened. Like soil that has been tilled, fertilized, and planted, your unconscious mind has been prepared to bring the seeds of a past-life experience to the surface.

You are now going to have an opportunity to relive this experience in your imagination. Doing so will help you reach a greater understanding of one of the life patterns that you find yourself involved in this time around. The pattern you choose to work with can be any one at all, either positive or negative. Developing a theory about how this pattern began during a former lifetime will help you in this life, whether your immediate aim is to make the most of a positive potential or to overcome a troublesome pattern.

Look back now at the charts you filled out during our last session. Take as much time as you need to select a pattern from one of those charts. Any pattern at all will be fine, so long as it is one you'd like to understand better. Once you have chosen your pattern, your conscious work will be done for a while. All you have to do now is sit back, relax, and let your unconscious mind do its job of presenting a past-life scene to you.

Before starting, you might want to make a quick review of the material on reverie set forth in our second session. Here is a summary of a few of the most important points:

1. Relaxation of the body and conscious mind is essen-

tial. The text of a routine to help you achieve this is presented in Session 2 of the course.

2. It is recommended that you either make a tape recording of the reverie material or have a friend read it to you. In this way you can avoid working your conscious mind during the reverie itself.

3. Note the suggested pauses in the text below, but don't feel bound by them if their location or duration fails to meet your individual needs.

4. Don't interrupt the experience to write down your responses to questions asked as part of the reverie. Merely make a mental note of the details these questions direct your attention toward.

Briefly call to mind once again the pattern from your present life that you have chosen as the focus of your reverie experience. Then begin to prepare yourself for a time of quiet relaxation. Get as comfortable as you can, either sitting or lying down. Take as much time as you need to go through whatever relaxation procedure you have found to be most effective. When you have finished this routine, move on into the following experience in the guided use of your imagination.

Let's take a little time to allow you to see just how good you are at using your mind's eye. Start by picturing any room in your home. It doesn't matter which room you choose. It may be the one you're relaxing in right now, or it may be some other room. (5 sec.)

Whatever room you have selected, imagine yourself walking into that room. As you stand there, just inside the doorway of your room, what do you see around you? (10 sec.) How much can you picture about the doors and windows in this room, for example? (5 sec.) What do the walls look like? (5 sec.) How about the furnishings, the decorations, and the knickknacks and other items that were in this room the last time you saw it? (10 sec.) Just pause a moment for a mental survey of everything you can picture about this room. (30 sec.)

And now, imagine yourself leaving this room, leaving your home, and going outside. Actually see yourself going outdoors. (15 sec.) Now, standing there outside your home, get a mental picture of the sights you can see. Start with what you see as you look straight ahead of you, (15 sec.) then slowly turn to look toward the right. (15 sec.) Then look behind you, (15 sec.) and on around to the view on your left side. (15 sec.) What can you see from this spot outside your home? (15 sec.) Good—you're really learning how to use your mind's eye. See how easy it is?

Now let's try something else. You know the satellite photos that we often see on television weather reports—the ones from way above the earth? Imagine that you can see the earth from way up there. Let yourself see the earth as you would see it from way above the clouds. (5 sec.) It's turning like a giant globe below you, and you're far, far above it, watching the earth turn below. Isn't it amazing how different everything looks from up here? All the details are hidden below the clouds, and all you can see is the great big globe turning lazily below you. (10 sec.)

You know that an experience in a different time and place awaits you. You don't know exactly what the experience will be, but you can feel the anticipation building as you approach the swirling globe below you. (5 sec.)

And now imagine yourself drifting gently toward that globe. The clouds are like soft cotton, and you're light as a feather as you slowly drift through them. (5 sec.) You're relaxed, and a sense of peaceful well-being fills you as you drift through the clouds, on down toward that globe slowly turning below. Slowly, gently, noiselessly you continue. (15 sec.)

And then, so gently that you hardly know you've landed, you find yourself standing on firm ground. Look down at your feet. What do you see on them? (5 sec.) And look at the surface your feet stand on. What is it? (5 sec.) Now, slowly examine the rest of your body and your clothing. Let your gaze come slowly upward from your feet. (10 sec.)

What's the first thing you see as you look around your-

self? (5 sec.) Go on and examine your surroundings for a
moment, noticing everything you can about the place where
you now stand. (30 sec.)

And as you stand in the place where you've landed on the
earth, you become aware of the other people who are part of
this different time and place you now find yourself in.
Notice who they are and what they look like. (15 sec.) You
begin to interact with them in the way that comes most
naturally to you in this time and place. (15 sec.)

And then your pattern comes to mind—the one you'd like
to understand better. And as you contemplate this pattern, a
scene begins to unfold which makes the whole thing clearer.
Just as you can dream at night, effortlessly and creatively,
you can allow this experience to unfold effortlessly, like a
dream. You have plenty of time. Go with the experience that
is unfolding before you. (2 min.)

And now the scene before you begins to grow vague.
Slowly, the world you've been experiencing begins to dis-
solve, and you know it's time to return to your present
circumstances. As the scene in your reverie fades, the scene
outside your home begins to come into focus. And once
again, you are standing outside the home where you live
right now. (10 sec.)

But something's different from before. You now have a
new awareness based on your reverie. You understand
yourself just a bit more fully now. And you have a theory
concerning that pattern which has puzzled you. Take a
moment to reflect on this now. (30 sec.)

Exercise

Now, while your reverie is still fresh in your mind, is the
best time to describe on paper the things you saw, did, and
felt. You might want to jot down just a few abbreviated
notes, or you may prefer to write an entire narrative of what
you experienced in your reverie. Either way is fine; just
make sure that whatever you write will be complete enough

to remind you of the important points whenever you go back and refer to your record later.

When you've finished making these notes about your reverie experience, you'll be ready to begin the wrapping-up process, in which you'll be using all the clues you've gathered thus far to construct your past-life theories. For best results, it might be a good idea to let a day or so go by before proceeding on to the next section.

Session 13
Forming Your Own Past-Life Theories

We've now come to the point where it's time to put your own past-life theories together. You've spent a considerable amount of time gathering clues, looking at yourself and your life from nearly every angle imaginable. If nothing else, you should know yourself better right now than you've ever known yourself before. Any past-life theory you come up with will really be just a way of understanding your new self-knowledge.

This is a vital point. The most important thing about any past-life theory is its helpfulness to you. It's nice to be able to know our ideas about our former incarnations are true, and it's fun to look for verification of them. But in the final analysis, a good past-life theory is one that makes sense out of the situations you are involved in at present, because this kind of theory helps you to make the very most of the opportunities that come your way during your current lifetime.

For example, one young woman came up with the idea that she had had a previous incarnation as a Mormon during the 1700s. She felt that at that time she had been moving westward across the United States in a covered wagon in order to find religious freedom. She was excited about this theory, which seemed to ring true for her. The only problem was that when she did a little basic research, she discovered that there were no Mormons in the 1700s. Joseph Smith didn't found the religion until 1830.

Was this woman's past-life theory a failure, then? No, definitely not. You see, even though the details may not have been accurate, this hypothesis told the woman a lot about herself. In the covered-wagon trip into the American wilderness, she could recognize the pattern of a pioneering spirit. The theme of religious freedom showed her just how important it was for her to be able to formulate her own beliefs, and it helped her deal with her tendency to overreact when she thought her freedom of religion was being violated. And regardless of whether this woman actually had been a Mormon in the 1700s, or at any other time, her theory certainly suggests that she might study the Mormon faith to see what it may hold for her. It might also have encouraged the young woman, who had spent all her life on the East Coast, to take that vacation out west that she'd always wanted to try. Who knows what experiences might have unfolded for her?

As this case illustrates, it's important for you too to realize that the real value of your past-life theories will lie in the insights they give you into how to use your present life. Nonetheless, most of us do want to feel reasonably sure that we're on the right track once we've formulated an idea of our past incarnations. We want to feel we know who and where we've been. And that's where all your careful detective work thus far comes in. By taking the time to make such a thorough survey of the person you are today, and by encouraging your subconscious mind to flow freely, you've gathered everything you need to develop the most accurate and helpful past-life theory possible.

Exercise A

By now you may already have some ideas—either vague feelings or well-defined concepts—about your former in- carnations. On the other hand, you may still be pretty much in the dark when it comes to your past lifetimes. In either case, we're now going to try to arrive at some past-life theories that are as clear as we can make them.

The first step is for you to take some time to review carefully all your responses to the exercises you've complet- ed up to this point. Read over the answers you've given to the various questions and the notes you've made concerning the different exercises. And as you refresh your memory of each exercise, take special note of the things that stand out, the things that surprised you, and the things that seem to be especially important.

The questions below ask you to write down the highlights of the exercises you've been through thus far. Be sure that you consult your original answers in order to complete this review. Something that might not have seemed memorable when you wrote it down during an early exercise may take on great significance in the light of something you came up with toward the end of the course. That's why it's important for you now to step back and view all the various exercises as a whole. Answering these questions slowly and carefully, gathering together the most meaningful of your responses throughout the course, will enable you to achieve the broad-range perspective we're trying to establish here. Take as much time as you need to complete this exercise before going on to the next section.

Questions 1–18: For each session or part of one listed below, note the elements from among your original re- sponses that you feel are most significant. Be sure to consider your general remarks and special insights regarding each session, as well as your answers to the specific questions. In question 19 you will be asked to identify connections among the answers you give for these eighteen items.

1. Awakening memories (Session 1).
2. Wardrobe fantasy (Session 2).
3. You and your surroundings (Session 4).
4. A trip around the world (Session 5).
5. Body clues (Session 6, Exercise A).
6. Childhood interests (Session 6, Exercise B).
7. Positive emotional reactions (Session 7, Exercises A and B).
8. Fears and dislikes (Session 7, Exercises A and C).
9. Talents, hobbies, and interests (Session 9).
10. Information from your dreams (Session 10, Exercise A).
11. Experiences in meditation (Session 10, Exercise A).
12. Your religious feelings and experiences (Session 10, Exercise B).
13. Patterns in your work life (Session 11).
14. Patterns in your finances (Session 11).
15. Patterns in your family relationships (Session 11).
16. Patterns in your social life (Session 11).
17. Patterns in your romantic relationships (Session 11).
18. Past-life reverie (Session 12).

Now that you have completed your review of the exercises you've been through thus far, you're ready to begin piecing this information together. If you remember our analogy of the jigsaw puzzle, this is the stage where you look for pieces that match or interlock. For example, if the costume you found yourself wearing in the wardrobe fantasy happens to be the native dress of a country you particularly liked in your trip around the world, these would be interlocking pieces for your puzzle. Or imagine that you discovered a distinct preference for the Oriental influences in your furnishings; and maybe one of the body clues you noticed was your extremely small feet; and just suppose that you also had a pattern of usually bending to other people's wishes. We might easily speculate that these clues, when seen together, suggest a past experience as an Oriental woman.

The possible tie-ins among clues are as complex as you

are, so it's important that you go over your answers to the first eighteen items of this exercise several times, looking for pieces that fit together. It's possible that not every piece will fall into place at this point. It's also likely that you will discover several groupings of clues, and some clues may well fit into more than one grouping. This is natural, because the same influences are likely to show up in more than one past life.

For example, one woman with a love of Mexican culture found one set of clues pointing toward a peasant lifetime and another suggesting a lifetime of affluence. It's just possible that she had two previous incarnations in Mexico, one as a poor person and one in which she was well-to-do. On the other hand, the two sets of clues might be pointing to a conflict of values that arose within one single lifetime in Mexico. Over time, and in the light of further information that might come to this woman, she will be able to clarify her Mexican past-life theory.

The important thing is that in reviewing and grouping your clues together you get food for thought concerning your former lifetimes. The ideas you conceive while looking for groups of interconnected clues will become the kernels around which your past-life theories can grow and take on practical meaning for you. With this in mind, please give ample thought to the concluding item of this exercise:

19. Search through your answers to questions 1–18 and note any groupings of clues that seem to fit together.

Exercise B

At this point, you have taken your clues as far as you can. You've gathered the significant ones together to form a summary of your work in this course, and you've looked for similarities and interlocking pieces. Now you are ready to begin weaving these clues into a theory about your past lives.

Your first step in doing this is to consider all the information you've gathered so far and select one positive trait, talent, inclination, or pattern that you'd like to work with. It can be something that immediately catches your eye, or perhaps you'll choose a clue that's more obscure, but still intriguing to you. You're free to select any aspect of yourself that came up in any session, just as long as it's a positive one.

Next, try to imagine how this trait might have originated during an earlier lifetime. Ponder as many different possibilities as you can come up with. This is a time for thinking, reasoning, and some creative storytelling on your part. Take a few minutes to make up a past-life scenario that would explain, account for, or even embellish your clue. If the piece of information you're working with is one that falls into a grouping with others, be sure to consider those other clues as sources of insight.

Regardless of how insignificant-seeming the clue you've chosen is, something can be done with it. For example, suppose you notice that when you go out for dinner for a special occasion or to celebrate, you almost always choose a Japanese restaurant. Of course, there are many possible reasons for your choice: maybe you go there because it's the only good restaurant in town, the price is better than at the other places, someone else always makes the decision, or it was your family's favorite spot to eat when you were a child. There are always many factors that go into any decision. But since we're especially interested in detecting reflections of your former incarnations, let's assume that the only reason for your constant choice is that it stems from a past-life influence.

What can you get from a clue like this? First, you would have to suspect that you had a lifetime in Japan. Second, we can assume that it was a pleasant one, for it obviously lends itself to celebration. What kind of life could it have been? Here is where you need to be a good detective and explore many possibilities. One theory would be that you had a comfortable life, perhaps as a merchant or even as a noble, in which most of your needs were supplied. Your taste for the many varieties of Japanese food could be a form of bodily remembering of that good life. Of course, as a good detective, you can also see another, completely different, scenario. Perhaps you had been a poor laborer in Japan, never having enough to eat, and in the present lifetime you've carried over the longing for the food of that culture to appease that hunger from your distant past.

As you construct your own narrative, remember that this is just an exercise in storytelling. Enjoy this use of your creative imagination, and spend as much time in it as you would like. Embroider your story with any details that come to mind, weaving in other clues from your course summary that might logically fit in. Don't restrict yourself to what you know or to the literal facts or recorded history of your story's setting. Simply write what comes into your mind, regardless of how far-out it seems. Giving yourself this type of freedom often brings surprising results.

Answer the first two questions below now, and then go on to item 3 and write your past-life story.

1. What is the positive past-life clue you've selected to work with?
2. List any other clues that seem to fit together with this one. You may wish to refer to question 19 of the previous exercise.
3. Write a past-life scene that would explain this influence in your life today. Be sure to answer such questions as: What happened? Where and when did it happen? Why? Who were the people involved? This is your chance to imagine any details you wish. Weave in as many interlocking clues as possible, and let your imagination do the rest for you.

For the second part of this exercise, you'll be answering some additional questions about your story. But before you actually begin to do so, let's take a minute to discuss the questions you'll be answering.

The first one asks you to explain or list the ways in which you feel this influence is being expressed in other areas of your life. Using our earlier example, which supposed you had a taste for Japanese food, this could be as simple as noting that you also prefer fine silk or have an Oriental pattern on your favorite dishes.

If it is a talent that you've chosen, you might answer by telling how this skill is now being used. Again, it need not be anything major. Someone who feels he has a talent for dancing might find himself particularly enjoying a night out dancing, or choosing to watch movies or television programs in which the emphasis is on dancing. This person might find himself trying a few steps when the radio is playing and he's alone in the house. Of course, if the influence you've selected is a major one, it might predominate even more in your life.

The next question is similar. You are asked to list any experiences in your present life that are similar to elements of your past-life theory, regardless of whether these events are directly related to your chosen clue. As a hypothetical example of this, let's assume that a woman made up a story involving poverty in a French orphanage to explain her extreme patience with children. If this person also discovered a great ability to make do with very little in her current lifetime, she might note the possible connection between her past-life story and this trait as well.

Question 6 asks you to think of ways that you could use inclinations, talents, or abilities from your past-life theory to enhance your life today. Again, your answer can be as involved as you care to make it, or as simple. Using our example of someone who liked to celebrate with Japanese food, such a person might enjoy taking a class in Japanese cooking or using Japanese items as accents in the dining area. He or she might want to read stories about Japan to see if there are any other aspects of the Japanese life-style that are just as appealing. After a time spent investigating the Japanese culture, a trip might be taken to certain areas of the world to explore further involvement.

With the help of these pointers, you should now be ready to answer the three questions below.

4. List areas of your life in which your chosen influence is being expressed today.

5. As you were making up your past-life story, did you notice any similarities to things that have happened to you in this lifetime? They may be unrelated to your initial clue, and they need not be central parts of your story.

6. In what ways can you use the inclinations shown in your past-life story to make your life today better, more enjoyable, or more productive?

This exercise is one that you might want to do several times over, of course choosing a different past-life clue to work with for each repetition. The same is true of the complementary exercise that follows.

Exercise C

In the last exercise we explored the possible past-life explanations of an influence that seems to have a positive effect in your life. Here we will deal with those influences that are not so positive.

Once again the first step will be for you to go back over the notes you made during the initial exercise of this session, in which you summarized the major clues and insights you've gathered throughout the course. This time, select from your summary one troubling circumstance in your present life—any relationship, pattern, or fear that you consider to be a problem. Again, this can be as important an influence as you like. You might decide to tackle something that has been a problem for many years. Or, since this is your first effort at this type of exercise, you may prefer to work with something that is comparatively insignificant. The influence you choose to focus on may be a physical weakness, a recurring pattern that troubles you in a certain relationship, or simply a vague dislike for a certain section of the country. You are free to select whatever negative aspect of your life you please.

When you've completed your review of your notes and made your selection, you will be using your best storytelling skills to create a possible past-life scenario that would account for this present-day influence. Once again, give yourself the liberty to contemplate any possibility. Sometimes the wilder the realms our imagination is allowed to explore, the better, for in such fashion we can be free to really express ourselves, and often our real self comes through. Remember to consider any of the other clues that you may have grouped with the one you've just selected to work on.

Complete the first part of this exercise now by answering the three questions that follow.

1. What negative past life clue have you selected to work with?

2. List any other clues that you have grouped with this one. These related clues need not be negative.

3. Write a past-life scene that would account for this influence in your present life. In your story, describe such things as what happened, where and when it happened, why it happened, and who was involved. Include as many details as you can imagine, no matter how wild they may seem, and remember to consider the interlocking clues that you have grouped with the one you've chosen to concentrate on.

The second part of this exercise consists of the three items below. Before starting to write your answers to these questions, however, you might find it helpful to read through the commentary that follows each one.

4. List any ways in which you are now making choices that reinforce or perpetuate this undesirable influence today.

In identifying the decisions you make that keep this troubling influence alive, consider any situations in which this aspect of your life is brought out. As an example, let's suppose that you have a dislike of large crowds. To explain your aversion, perhaps in your story you imagined a past life in which you had been frightened and out of control in a mob scene. You might note, as a behavior pattern that reinforces this influence, that in your present life you shun the bustle of shopping malls, preferring less crowded shops.

5. What alternative choices would help you grow past this?

This question takes our exploration one step farther. Sticking with our example involving the fear of crowds, you might choose to start attending some type of sporting event, where crowds may be a little more controlled. You could still allow yourself to avoid the peak crowds at the beginning and the end of the game by arriving and leaving early. You might envision yourself, still later, enjoying a visit to a major tourist attraction and not being bothered by the crowds of sightseers.

6. Write a scene in which you picture yourself doing something that would allow you to change in a way that would help you overcome this unfavorable influence.

This concluding item is not a question as much as it is a chance for you to develop your own healing scenario, or plan, for altering these influences. In order to make this change, you may have to forgive someone else, or you may have to forgive yourself. Usually it involves both. Sometimes these things take a long time to overcome and require much hard work. In other instances they yield easily. There are times when we need to allow the wounds to heal before we can begin to take positive steps. At other times direct action can be taken quickly.

A word of caution is in order for cases in which we are dealing with difficulties in our relations with others. It is most important for us to bear in mind that these unfavorable influences are our very own; they result from *our* memories affecting our own lives. This can be quite hard to remember when our problems relate to another person. We must be very sure to realize that we need to work on changing ourselves, not someone else.

Although involved in the situation today, the other person is most likely to have a completely different set of memories affecting him. Our influences and memories are not his. Therefore, the only person we can strive to improve is ourselves—our feelings, our emotions, and our reactions to the memories and influences from our former incarnations. Overcoming unpleasant past-life memories is most definitely an inside job. It is very dangerous, inappropriate, ineffective, and destructive to expect someone else to respond positively when we try to use our own past-life memories to change him in a way that suits our wishes today.

Working with oneself to overcome negative past-life influences provides as great an opportunity for success as building on positive influences does. Such tools as prayer, meditation, and the setting of ideals can be very helpful. You may want to use them over longer periods of time than the duration of this course. You will find their consistent application to be of great benefit in your effort to overcome unfavorable influences from previous incarnations.

Regardless of how long it takes or the method you choose, be assured that this endeavor can be one of the most important you undertake during this lifetime. Allow yourself plenty of time, and be patient with yourself. Most of all, encourage yourself and give yourself the credit you deserve for being willing to change.

Session 14
Your Future Life

This, the concluding session of our program, will help you look forward to your next lifetime—the one you are building now. This is not just a chance to see into your future; it is also, and more importantly, an opportunity to take some steps to determine what that future will be like. By looking ahead we can get an idea of where we're going. If we're content with the course we're on, we can continue along the same path. Or, if we feel it is necessary, we can start making decisions that will set us off in a new direction.

Just as our present life is influenced by our past, our future is being shaped by the way we are living today. The impressions we carry out with us at the end of this lifetime will be the past-life memories of our next incarnation. We have, always, the freedom to direct our thoughts and actions in a way that will produce helpful imprints, rather than scars, upon our soul. Thus we can build toward a better future and a happier tomorrow.

One more time now—relax, get comfortable, and take a few deep breaths. Make whatever preparations are necessary for you to follow this reverie in the way you feel is best—whether this involves enlisting a friend's help, taping the text of the experience, or whatever. Go through whichever procedure you have found most effective in putting your physical body and conscious mind at rest. Lay aside the tensions of your mind and body, so that as you enter the reverie state you will be relaxed, peaceful, ready to let your thoughts flow. And when your future-life story has run its course and you emerge from your experience of it, you will find yourself awakening to your present life with a new and hopeful vision of yourself and your potential.

Imagine that you are standing in your favorite room of your home. (5 sec.) You feel comfortable here. You feel good about yourself. You have the pleasant feeling that, to the best of your abilities now, you are doing what you need to do this lifetime. (5 sec.)

As you look around the room, you're surprised to see a door that you've never seen before. (5 sec.) You're curious to see where this doorway leads. You are totally confident as you walk over and slowly open the door. (10 sec.)

As the door slowly opens, you realize that this is the doorway to your future. At first, there's a soft, radiant light on the other side of the door—a beckoning light. (5 sec.) As you move into the light, you realize that just beyond it is your next lifetime.

Your step quickens as you move toward this new lifetime. (10 sec.) You begin to see glimpses of people who will be important to you in your next life, and places that will be part of your experience. (10 sec.)

As you continue to move into what is unfolding in front

of you, you begin to understand what your next life will be. As the scene develops, you will see people that you knew before, forming new relationships with you. Some will be very similar to roles they now have; some will be very different. And you will discover new reasons why these people are among those who are important to you. (10 sec.)

Allow yourself all the time you need to experience this new life. Gather all the details that you can find. Look not only at the people and places that appear in your future-life scenario, but also, and especially, at your feelings about yourself in this new life.

Let your future life unfold as long as it will. Stay with it as long as you can.

Exercise

When the story of your future life has reached its conclusion, record your answers to the following questions about it. The purpose here is to help you gain a clearer perspective of the experience you've just had and to enable you to make the most constructive use of it in your life today.

1. As briefly or in as much detail as you like, describe your experience of your future life.

2. List the positive influences from the present that you have imagined will have a role in shaping your future.

3. Are there any steps you can take now to accentuate these influences, so that they will be as strong in your next lifetime as you would like them to be?

4. Did you note any negative influences that seemed to be affecting the future you envisioned for yourself?

5. Can you think of any choices you can start making in your present life that would diminish or eliminate the effect of these influences upon your future? Don't limit yourself just to things you can avoid doing. Try to come up with one or more positive alternatives to actions you feel might be building unpleasant patterns for tomorrow. "I will try to stop needlessly criticizing my spouse" is a fair first step,

but "I will pay my spouse at least three compliments a day" is likely to prove even more helpful.

6. Do you have any other comments or observations to make about your future-life reverie?

Conclusion

Now that you have reached the conclusion of our program, it is most important for you to realize that the greatest benefit from this course will come in the weeks and months ahead. As time goes by, you will become more and more aware of the past-life influences in your present life, and more and more adept at using this growing self-knowledge in a positive manner.

There are many ways in which you can encourage and enhance your recall of former lifetimes. The most important of these is through application. The reason application is so vital is that understanding is given us to be used and made a part of our lives. Information about the strengths we've developed in our previous incarnations provides a picture of the abilities we can emphasize in order to build a more creative and fulfilling life now; knowledge of our past weaknesses shows areas in which we can change the types of choices we make so that these flaws can be overcome.

You will find that as you begin to do something with the past-life influences you know about, no matter how insignificant they may seem, you'll discover more about yourself. Your former lifetimes will start to unfold for you, not only in bits and pieces of memories and dreams, but in more complete ways that will enable you to identify clearly the various incarnations that are at work in your life today.

270

As you proceed, you'll be amazed to find your life being touched by people, situations, and events that fit in with your past-life theories and thus help verify what you've discovered. There is every chance that these encounters will enrich your present life, for your understanding of your own past will allow you to meet the circumstances constructively and relate to the people lovingly. And as your insights into your former incarnations continue to produce positive results in your current one, you will be receiving additional confirmation that they are valid.

There are, of course, other ways in which you can verify your hypotheses about your past experiences. Objective research can help as you go about exploring and confirming the aspects of your past-life theories that you find most intriguing. Your research can be as involved as actually checking historical records or as casual as looking for things that seem familiar, whether they turn up in your actual physical surroundings, in pictures and magazines you happen to catch sight of, or in the movies and television programs you view.

You might also want to check the validity of certain past-life theories by talking them over with a trusted friend. Describe your hypothetical incarnations to this person, and ask whether he or she has observed any patterns or associations in your life that might support, contradict, or add to your ideas.

As you seek confirmation of your past-life theories from these external sources, bear in mind that the most important verification by far lies in the helpfulness of this material in your current life. Sit down by yourself periodically and evaluate whether working with these past influences has added help or hope to your existence today. This is the best way to keep from wandering too far afield, from becoming so caught up in your supposed past experiences that you are unable to live fruitfully in the present.

In your search for a more complete picture of your past, you may find yourself coming back again and again to the exercises and reveries in this course. As you begin to see new patterns emerge, you may want to set aside certain times to review your previous work with the various exercises. You might even want to repeat some of them in their entirety, coming up with new sets of responses that can either add to past-life theories you've already started formulating or suggest other previous incarnations you haven't yet begun to suspect. A birthday, anniversary, or New Year's holiday is a good time for this kind of update.

There really is no limit to the amount of help that is available to you through this course. Each time you return to its pages, you'll have a chance to obtain a deeper understanding of yourself and your life in the present and an expanded view of the horizons open to you for the future. Regardless of where you go from here, remember to treat yourself with the love and respect you deserve.

Good luck on your new adventure.

Further Reading

The life and work of Edgar Cayce:

Millard, Joseph. *Edgar Cayce: Mystery Man of Miracles*. Greenwich, CT: Fawcett, 1956.

Stearn, Jess. *Edgar Cayce: The Sleeping Prophet*. Garden City, NY: Doubleday, 1967.

Sugrue, Thomas. *There Is a River: The Story of Edgar Cayce*. New York: Holt, Rinehart and Winston, 1942.

The philosophy of the Edgar Cayce readings:

Face to Face: 12 Edgar Cayce Readings Interpreted for Today. Virginia Beach, VA: A.R.E. Press, 1987.

Puryear, Herbert B. *The Edgar Cayce Primer*. New York: Bantam, 1982.

Reincarnation and karma:

Cerminara, Gina. *Many Mansions*. New York: William Sloan Associates, Inc., 1950.

Langley, Noel. *Edgar Cayce on Reincarnation*. New York: Warner, 1967.

Van Auken, John. *Born Again and Again*. Virginia Beach, VA: Inner Vision, 1984.

Van Auken, John. *Past Lives and Present Relationships*. Virginia Beach, VA: Inner Vision, 1985.

Woodward, Mary Ann. *Edgar Cayce's Story of Karma*. New York: Coward-McCann, 1971.

Woodward, Mary Ann. *Scars of the Soul*. Columbus, OH: Brindabella Books, 1985.

Developing psychic ability:

Cayce, Hugh Lynn. *Venture Inward*. New York: Harper & Row, 1964.

Patterson, Doris T. and Violet M. Shelley. *Be Your Own Psychic*. Virginia Beach, VA: Edgar Cayce Foundation, 1975.

Thurston, Mark A. *Understand and Develop Your ESP.* Virginia Beach, VA: A.R.E. Press, 1977.

Dreams:

Bro, Harmon H. *Dreams in the Life of Prayer*. New York: Harper & Row, 1970.

Bro, Harmon H. *Edgar Cayce on Dreams*. New York: Warner, 1968.

Sechrist, Elsie. *Dreams Your Magic Mirror*. New York: Warner, 1968

Meditation:

Puryear, Herbert B. and Mark A. Thurston. *Meditation and the Mind of Man*. Virginia Beach, VA: A.R.E. Press, 1975.

Sechrist, Elsie. *Meditation - Gateway to Light*. Virginia Beach, VA: A.R.E. Press, 1964.

THE A.R.E. TODAY

The Association for Research and Enlightenment, Inc., is a non-profit, open membership organization committed to spiritual growth, holistic healing, psychical research and its spiritual dimensions; and more specifically, to making practical use of the psychic readings of the late Edgar Cayce. Through nationwide programs, publications and study groups, A.R.E. offers all those interested, practical information and approaches for individual study and application to better understand and relate to themselves, to other people and to the universe. A.R.E. membership and outreach is concentrated in the United States with growing involvement throughout the world.

The headquarters at Virginia Beach, Virginia, includes a library/conference center, administrative offices and publishing facilities, and are served by a beachfront motel. The library is one of the largest metaphysical, parapsychological libraries in the country. A.R.E. operates a bookstore, which also offers mail-order service and carries approximately 1,000 titles on nearly every subject related to spiritual growth, world religions, parapsychology and transpersonal psychology. A.R.E. serves its members through nationwide lecture programs, publications, a Braille library, a camp and an extensive Study Group Program.

The A.R.E. facilities, located at 67th Street and Atlantic Avenue, are open year-round. Visitors are always welcome and may write A.R.E., P.O. Box 595, Virginia Beach, VA 23451, for more information about the Association.

For all UK general inquiries, newsletter and study group information, contact: Edgar Cayce Centre, PO Box 8, Stanley, Co Durham, DH9 7XQ.

Of further interest . . .

EDGAR CAYCE ON
REINCARNATION

The truth about people who have lived
more than once — and what it means for you

NOEL LANGLEY
Edited by HUGH LYNN CAYCE

Edgar Cayce On Reincarnation explores the many startling facets of the concept of man having more than one life. Here are the mysterious accounts of people who have lived before — and remarkable evidence of a unifying force that pervades the universe. Provocative and revealing, Edgar Cayce shows how you can expand your spiritual and mental boundaries and how modern man may achieve immortality.

The late Edgar Cayce's groundbreaking psychic perception in the areas of healing, dreams, ESP, nutrition, health, religion — and reincarnation — have made him the most respected clairvoyant of our time. *Edgar Cayce On Reincarnation* was edited by Hugh Lynn Cayce, Mr Cayce's son and former director of the Association for Research and Enlightenment, an organization dedicated to the practical employment of his father's psychic findings.

EDGAR CAYCE ON DREAMS

**True-life examples of dream interpretation
— and how to make it work for you**

DR HARMON H BRO
Edited by HUGH LYNN CAYCE

Edgar Cayce On Dreams reveals Cayce's revolutionary psychic perceptions on what dreams mean and how to interpret them. 'In dreams, people experience for themselves every important kind of psychic phenomenon, and every level of helpful psychological and religious counsel,' he said. In this fascinating book, astonishing case histories demonstrate how you can bring conscious insight to dreaming that will awaken new possibilities in your life.

The late Edgar Cayce's psychic achievements in healing, ESP, nutrition, health, reincarnation, religion — and dreams — have made him the most respected clairvoyant of our time. Dr Harmon Bro, author of *Edgar Cayce On Dreams,* is the only trained social scientist to have studied Edgar Cayce in person. Editor Hugh Lynn Cayce was Mr Cayce's son and former director of the Association for Research and Enlightenment, an organization dedicated to the practical employment of his father's psychic findings.

EDGAR CAYCE ON SECRETS OF THE UNIVERSE

— and how to use them in your life

LIN COCHRAN
Edited by CHARLES THOMAS CAYCE

Edgar Cayce on Secrets of the Universe reveals vastly important mysteries that, once solved, could radically alter our lives. In this extraordinary work Lin Cochran, a veteran Cayce student, delves into the underlying principles that govern who we really are and how our decisions, our work, and our futures are shaped by forces we cannot always perceive. From improving relationships to shedding fears, this book reveals the channels between your consciousness and the laws of the universe you inhabit, and illustrates Edgar Cayce's dynamic insights into our great hidden potential.

The late Edgar Cayce's groundbreaking psychic perception in the areas of healing, dreams, ESP, nutrition, reincarnation, religion — and self-fulfilment — have made him the most respected clairvoyant of our time. *Edgar Cayce on Secrets of the Universe* was edited by Charles Thomas Cayce, Mr Cayce's grandson and current president of the Association for Research and Enlightenment, an organization dedicated to the practical employment of his grandfather's psychic findings.

EDGAR CAYCE ON MYSTERIES OF THE MIND

The unlimited scope of human consciousness

HENRY REED
Edited by CHARLES THOMAS CAYCE

Edgar Cayce on Mysteries of the Mind examines a force more powerful than the atomic bomb — the human mind. Each one of us uses only a small fraction of its creative energy, but Edgar Cayce revealed that through self-teaching and awareness we can extend the frontiers of our mind's potential. From visualisation to altered states, premonitions to increased will-power, Henry Reed — research psychologist and a noted authority on Edgar Cayce — shows how to discover and use the untapped power that resides within us all.

The late Edgar Cayce's groundbreaking psychic perception in the areas of healing, dreams, ESP, nutrition, reincarnation, religion — and the human mind and soul — have made him the most respected clairvoyant of our time. *Edgar Cayce on Mysteries of the Mind* was edited by Charles Thomas Cayce, Mr Cayce's grandson and current president of the Association for Research and Enlightenment, an organization dedicated to the practical employment of his grandfather's psychic findings.

EDGAR CAYCE:
A SEER OUT OF SEASON

The life of Edgar Cayce

HARMON HARTZELL BRO, Ph.D.

Edgar Cayce: A Seer Out of Season is a fascinating biographical memoir, written by a leading scholar and longtime disciple of Edgar Cayce, which sheds new light on the most gifted psychic of our time. Drawing on hundreds of interviews with relatives, associates, disciples, even sceptics, this definitive work is the first to view the whole of Cayce's life, taking into account his journals, dreams and lectures, case studies of those whose lives were miraculously altered by his ministrations, his riveting descriptions of what he called his reincarnated lives, and the four areas of his contribution to contemporary life and thought: ESP, holistic health, reincarnation and disciplined spiritual growth.

In this landmark book, Edgar Cayce, 'the Father of the New Age', emerges not merely as a medium or a mystic, but as a modern-day seer, albeit a lonely one, isolated by his burdensome gifts and by the awe he inspired in others. Yet in a world that now possesses the terrifying ability to destroy itself, Cayce's timeless ideals of faith, healing, and peace may have finally found their season.